STAR WARS®
X-WING
ROGUE SQUADRON
MASQUERADE

STAR WARS
X-WING ROGUE SQUADRON
MASQUERADE

Michael A. Stackpole
story

Drew Johnson and **Gary Hall**
pencils

Gary Martin
inks

Dave Nestelle
colors

Vickie Williams
lettering

Terese Nielsen
cover art

SEP 6 — 2000

DARK HORSE COMICS

Mike Richardson
publisher

Peet Janes
series editor

Chris Warner
collection editor

Jeremy Perkins
collection designer

Mark Cox
art director

Special thanks to Allan Kausch and
Lucy Autrey Wilson at Lucas Licensing.

This book collects issues twenty-eight through
thirty-one of the Dark Horse comic-book series
Star Wars: X-Wing Rogue Squadron.

Published by
Dark Horse Comics, Inc.
10956 SE Main Street
Milwaukie, OR 97222
www.darkhorse.com

To find a comics shop in your area,
call the Comic Shop Locator
Service at 1-888-266-4226

First edition: June 2000
ISBN: 1-56971-487-8

1 3 5 7 9 10 8 6 4 2

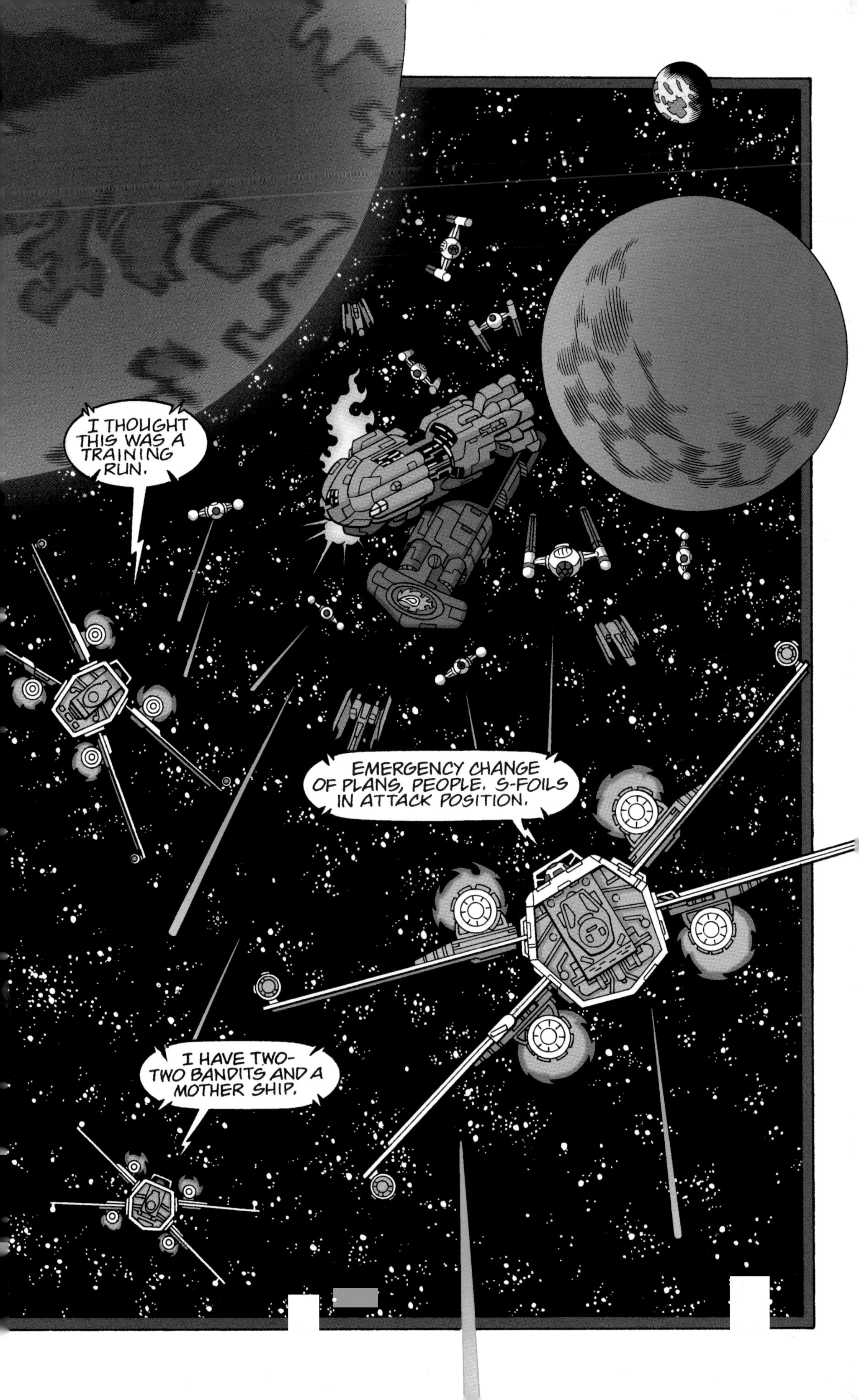
I THOUGHT THIS WAS A TRAINING RUN.
EMERGENCY CHANGE OF PLANS, PEOPLE. S-FOILS IN ATTACK POSITION.
I HAVE TWO-TWO BANDITS AND A MOTHER SHIP.

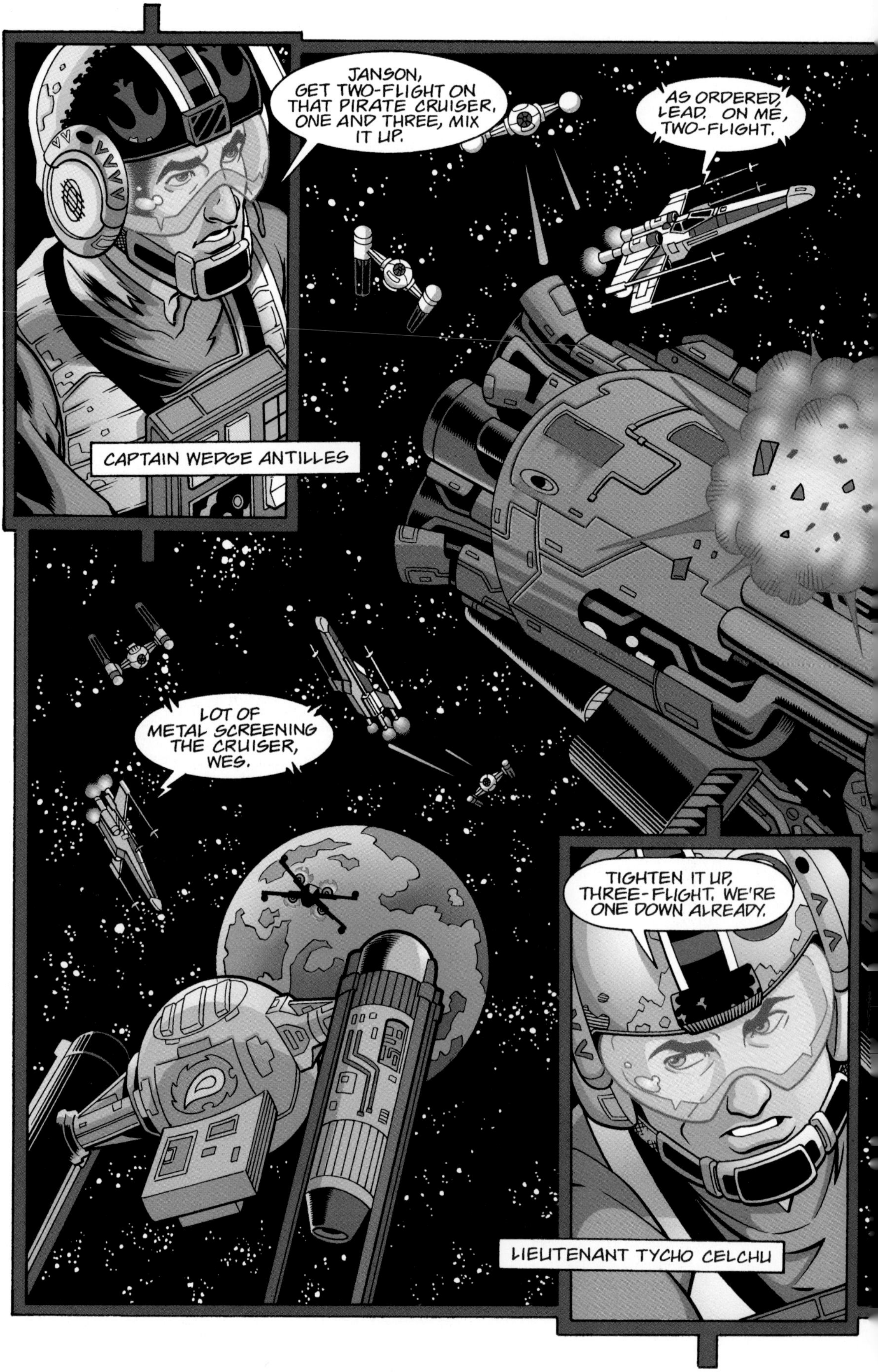
JANSON, GET TWO-FLIGHT ON THAT PIRATE CRUISER. ONE AND THREE, MIX IT UP.
CAPTAIN WEDGE ANTILLES
AS ORDERED, LEAD. ON ME, TWO-FLIGHT.
LOT OF METAL SCREENING THE CRUISER, WES.
TIGHTEN IT UP, THREE-FLIGHT. WE'RE ONE DOWN ALREADY.
LIEUTENANT TYCHO CELCHU

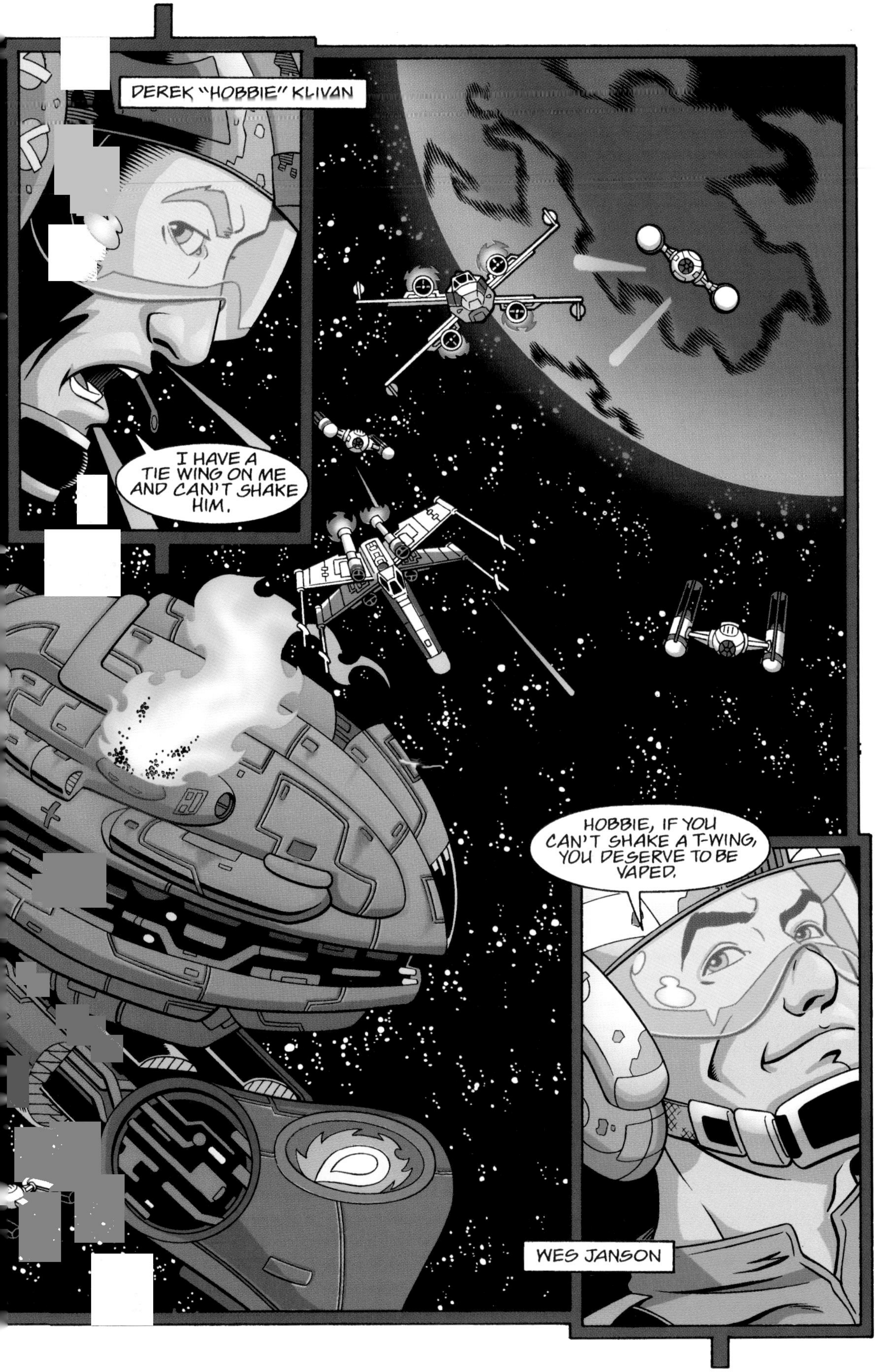
DEREK "HOBBIE" KLIVAN
I HAVE A TIE WING ON ME AND CAN'T SHAKE HIM.
HOBBIE, IF YOU CAN'T SHAKE A T-WING, YOU DESERVE TO BE VAPED.
WES JANSON

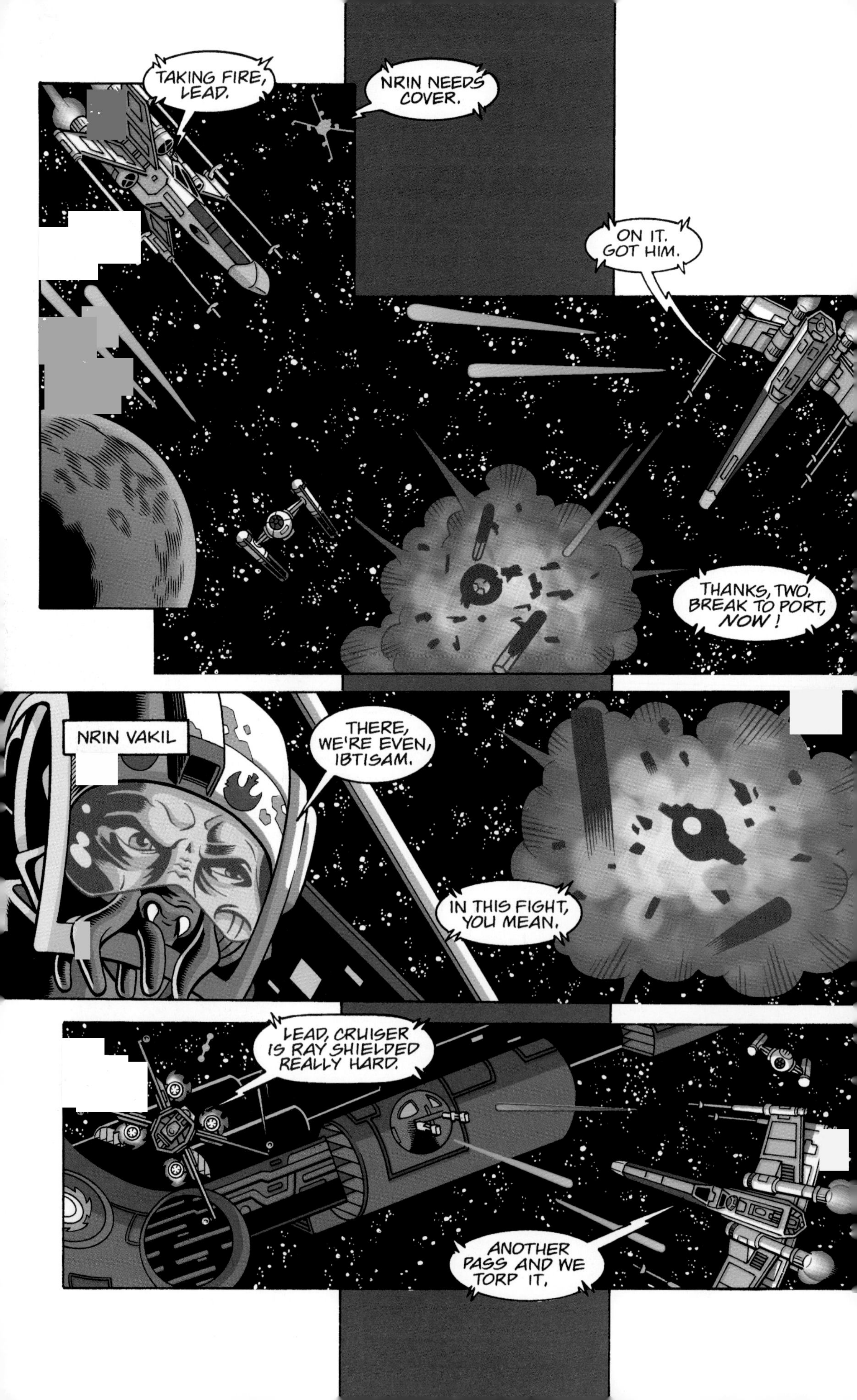
TAKING FIRE, LEAD.
NRIN NEEDS COVER.
ON IT. GOT HIM.
THANKS, TWO. BREAK TO PORT, NOW!
NRIN VAKIL
THERE, WE'RE EVEN, IBTISAM.
IN THIS FIGHT, YOU MEAN.
LEAD, CRUISER IS RAY SHIELDED REALLY HARD.
ANOTHER PASS AND WE TORP IT.

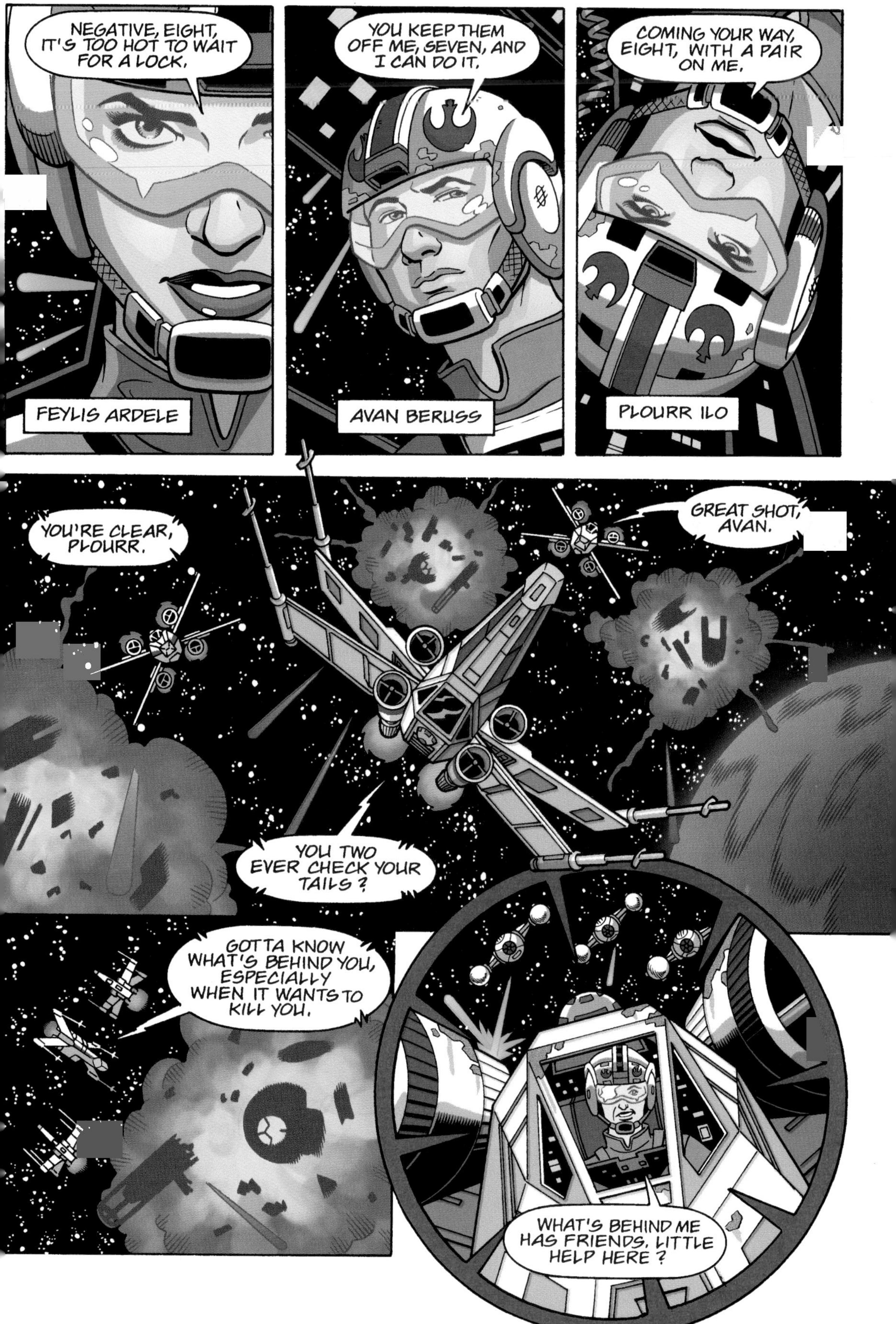
NEGATIVE, EIGHT, IT'S TOO HOT TO WAIT FOR A LOCK.
FEYLIS ARDELE
YOU KEEP THEM OFF ME, SEVEN, AND I CAN DO IT.
AVAN BERUSS
COMING YOUR WAY, EIGHT, WITH A PAIR ON ME.
PLOURR ILO
YOU'RE CLEAR, PLOURR.
GREAT SHOT, AVAN.
YOU TWO EVER CHECK YOUR TAILS?
GOTTA KNOW WHAT'S BEHIND YOU, ESPECIALLY WHEN IT WANTS TO KILL YOU.
WHAT'S BEHIND ME HAS FRIENDS. LITTLE HELP HERE?

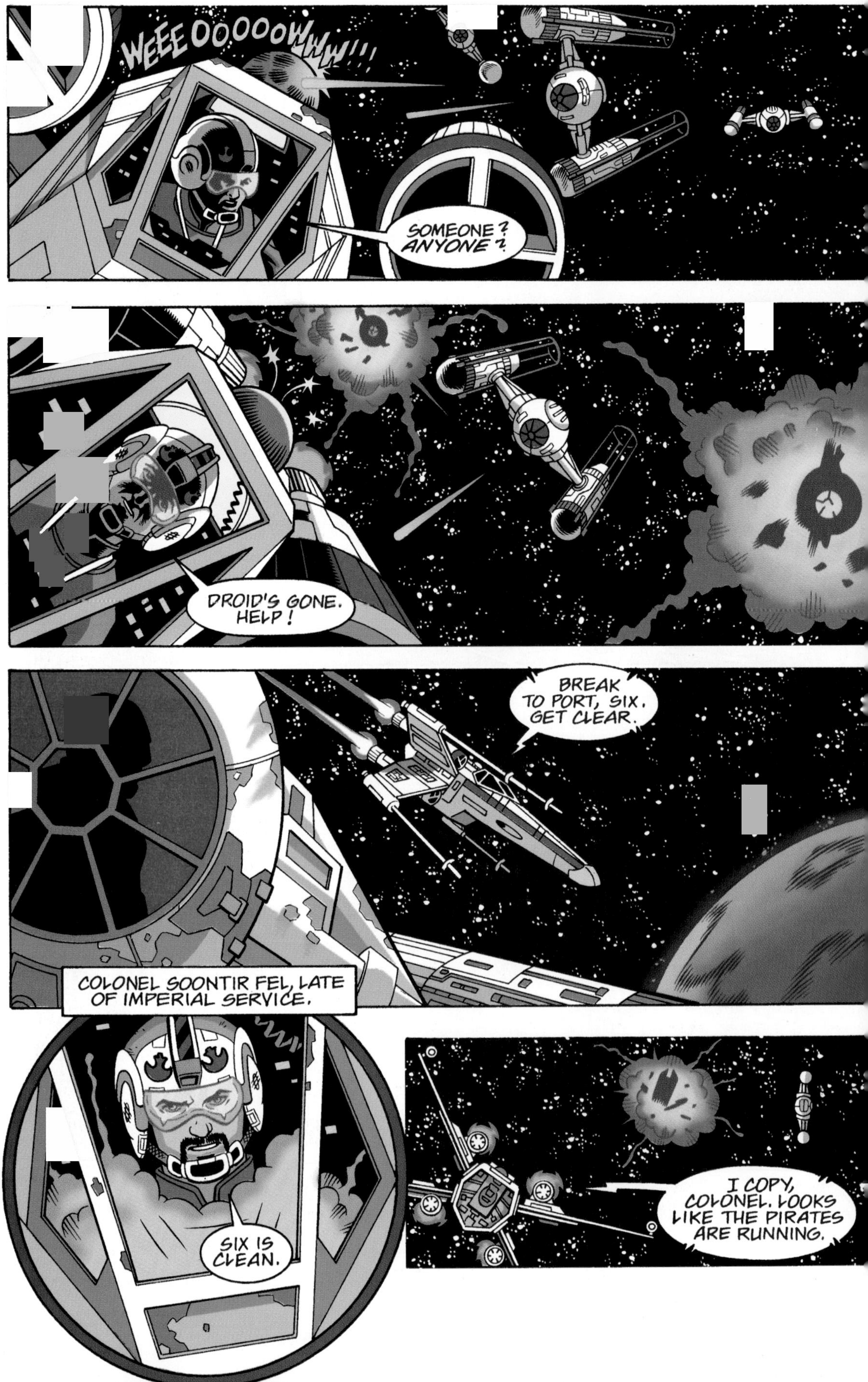
WEEE OOOOOWWW!!!
SOMEONE? ANYONE?
DROID'S GONE. HELP!
BREAK TO PORT, SIX. GET CLEAR.
COLONEL SOONTIR FEL, LATE OF IMPERIAL SERVICE.
SIX IS CLEAN.
I COPY, COLONEL. LOOKS LIKE THE PIRATES ARE RUNNING.

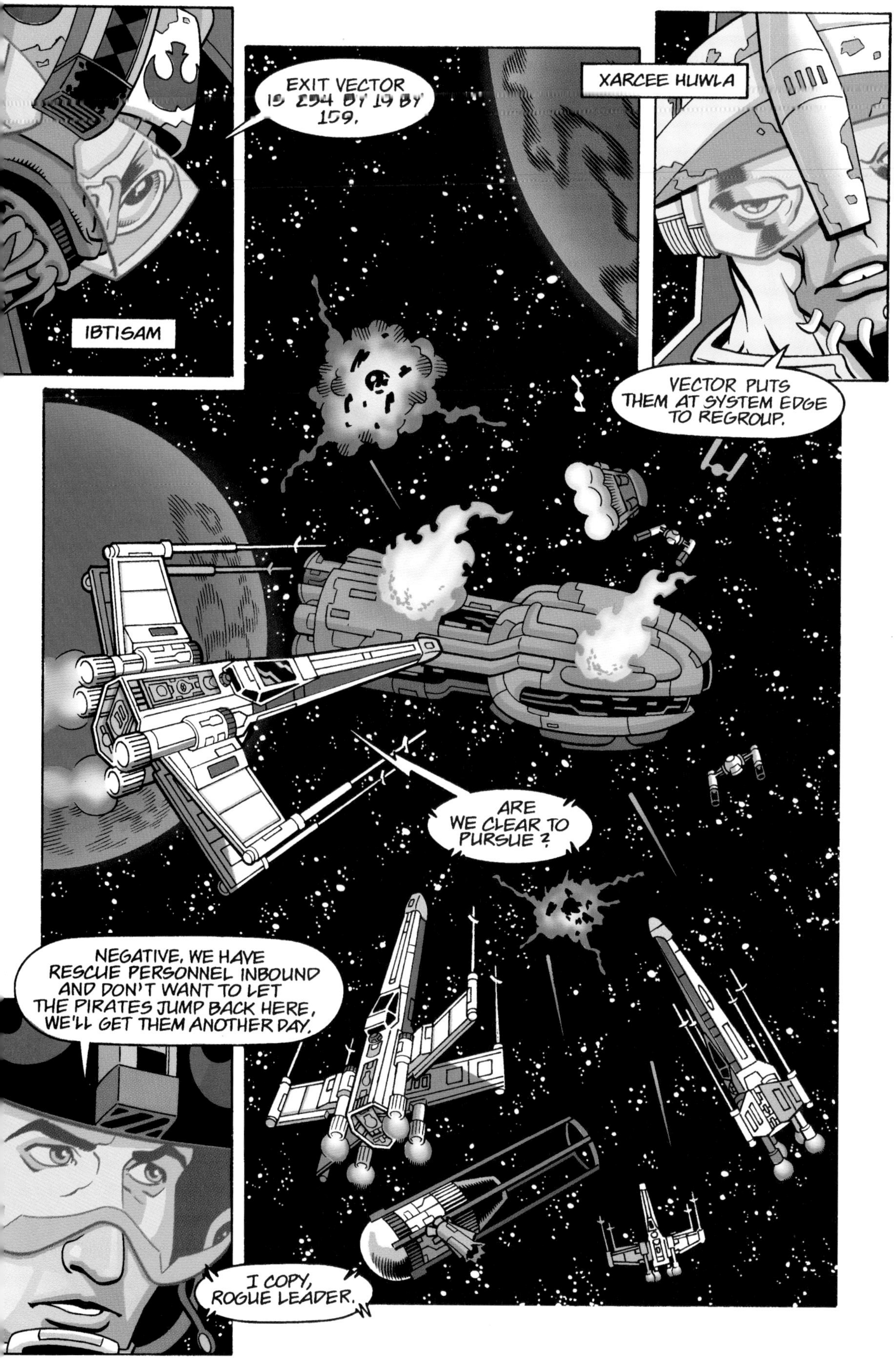
EXIT VECTOR IS 294 BY 19 BY 159.
IBTISAM
XARCEE HUWLA
VECTOR PUTS THEM AT SYSTEM EDGE TO REGROUP.
ARE WE CLEAR TO PURSUE?
NEGATIVE, WE HAVE RESCUE PERSONNEL INBOUND AND DON'T WANT TO LET THE PIRATES JUMP BACK HERE. WE'LL GET THEM ANOTHER DAY.
I COPY, ROGUE LEADER.

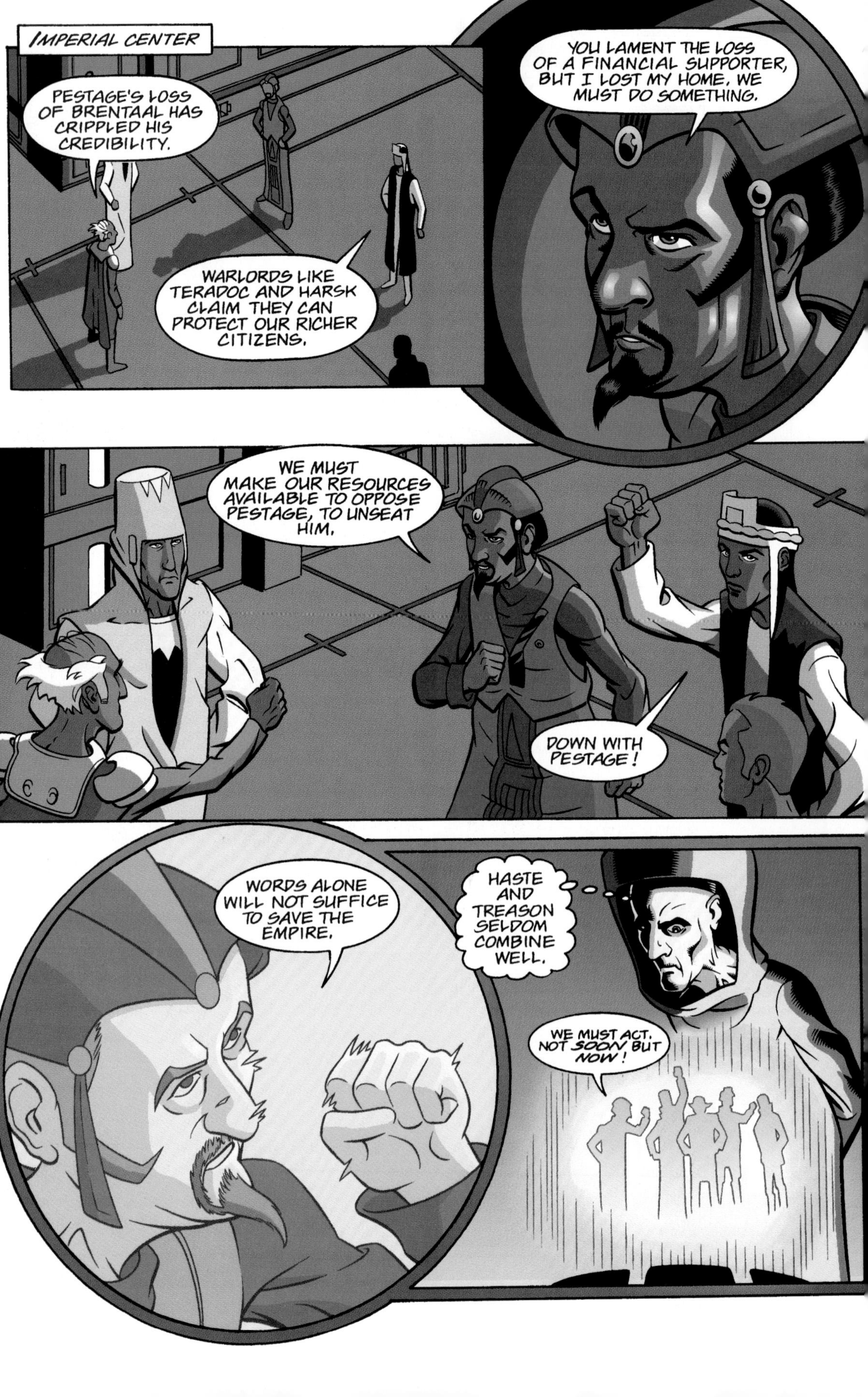
IMPERIAL CENTER
PESTAGE'S LOSS OF BRENTAAL HAS CRIPPLED HIS CREDIBILITY.
WARLORDS LIKE TERADOC AND HARSK CLAIM THEY CAN PROTECT OUR RICHER CITIZENS.
YOU LAMENT THE LOSS OF A FINANCIAL SUPPORTER, BUT I LOST MY HOME. WE MUST DO SOMETHING.
WE MUST MAKE OUR RESOURCES AVAILABLE TO OPPOSE PESTAGE, TO UNSEAT HIM.
DOWN WITH PESTAGE!
WORDS ALONE WILL NOT SUFFICE TO SAVE THE EMPIRE.
HASTE AND TREASON SELDOM COMBINE WELL.
WE MUST ACT. NOT SOON BUT NOW!

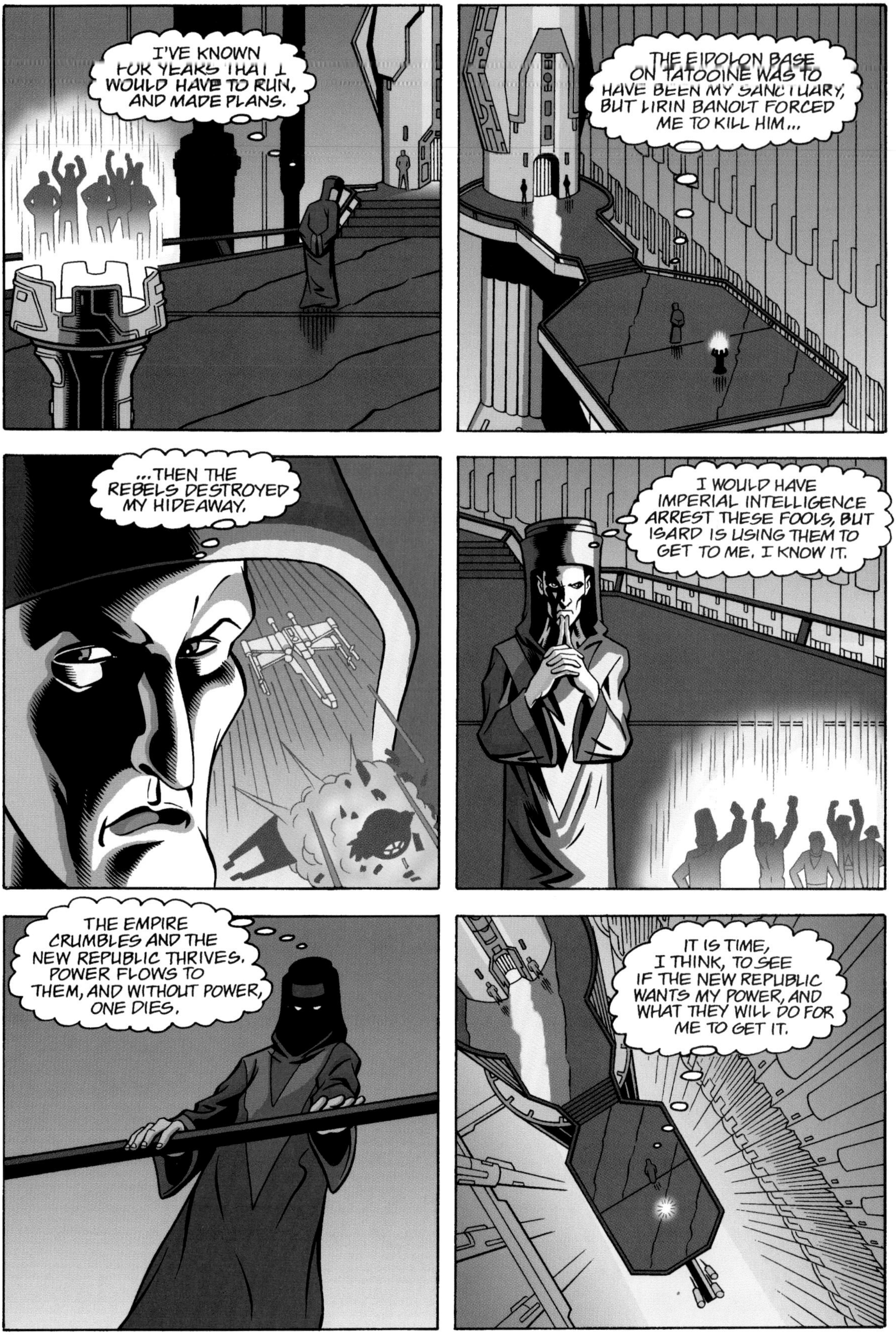
I'VE KNOWN FOR YEARS THAT I WOULD HAVE TO RUN, AND MADE PLANS.
THE EIDOLON BASE ON TATOOINE WAS TO HAVE BEEN MY SANCTUARY, BUT LIRIN BANOLT FORCED ME TO KILL HIM...
...THEN THE REBELS DESTROYED MY HIDEAWAY.
I WOULD HAVE IMPERIAL INTELLIGENCE ARREST THESE FOOLS, BUT ISARD IS USING THEM TO GET TO ME. I KNOW IT.
THE EMPIRE CRUMBLES AND THE NEW REPUBLIC THRIVES. POWER FLOWS TO THEM, AND WITHOUT POWER, ONE DIES.
IT IS TIME, I THINK, TO SEE IF THE NEW REPUBLIC WANTS MY POWER, AND WHAT THEY WILL DO FOR ME TO GET IT.

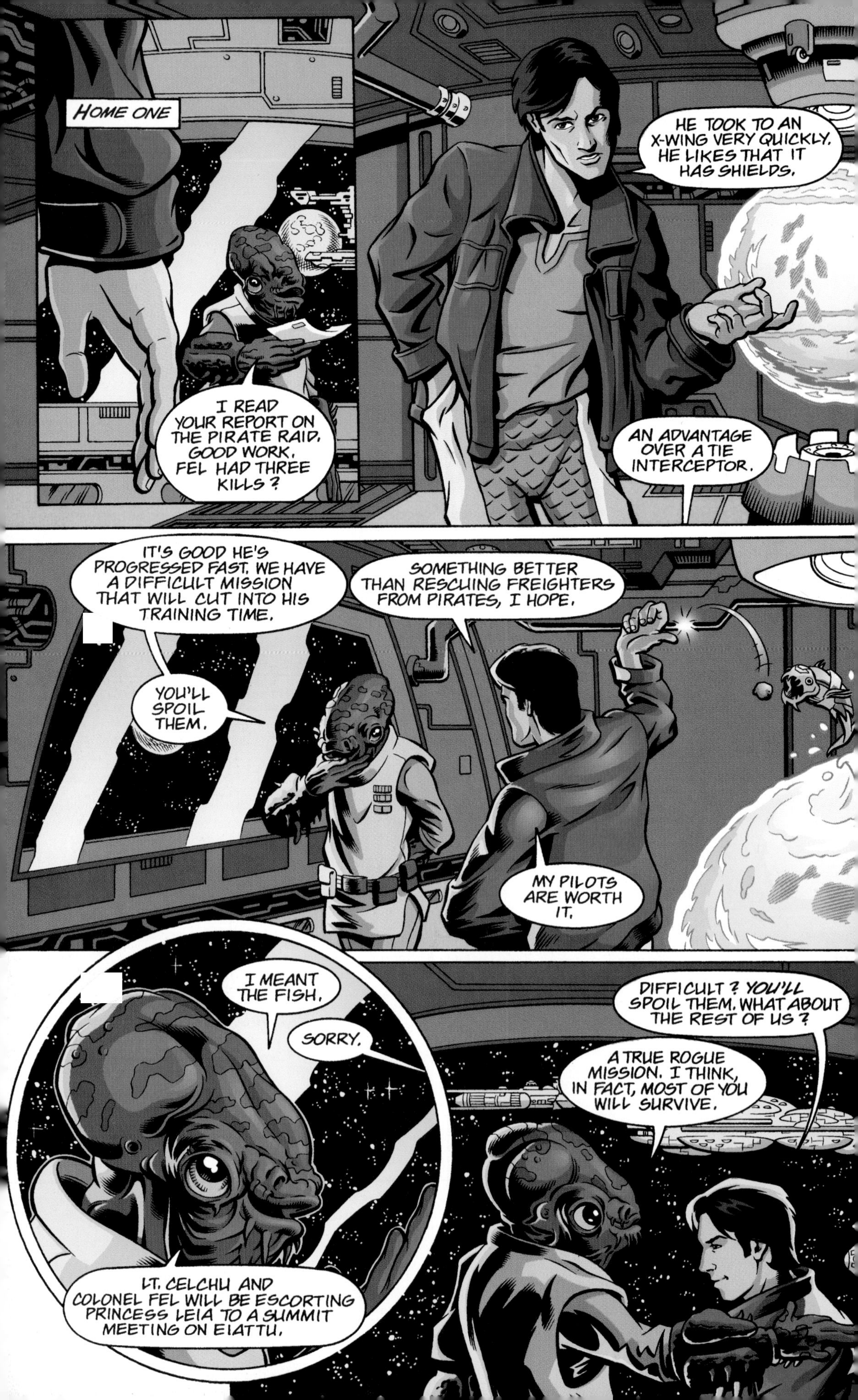
HOME ONE
I READ YOUR REPORT ON THE PIRATE RAID. GOOD WORK. FEL HAD THREE KILLS?
HE TOOK TO AN X-WING VERY QUICKLY. HE LIKES THAT IT HAS SHIELDS.
AN ADVANTAGE OVER A TIE INTERCEPTOR.
IT'S GOOD HE'S PROGRESSED FAST. WE HAVE A DIFFICULT MISSION THAT WILL CUT INTO HIS TRAINING TIME.
SOMETHING BETTER THAN RESCUING FREIGHTERS FROM PIRATES, I HOPE.
YOU'LL SPOIL THEM.
MY PILOTS ARE WORTH IT.
I MEANT THE FISH.
SORRY.
DIFFICULT? YOU'LL SPOIL THEM. WHAT ABOUT THE REST OF US?
A TRUE ROGUE MISSION. I THINK, IN FACT, MOST OF YOU WILL SURVIVE.
LT. CELCHU AND COLONEL FEL WILL BE ESCORTING PRINCESS LEIA TO A SUMMIT MEETING ON EIATTU.

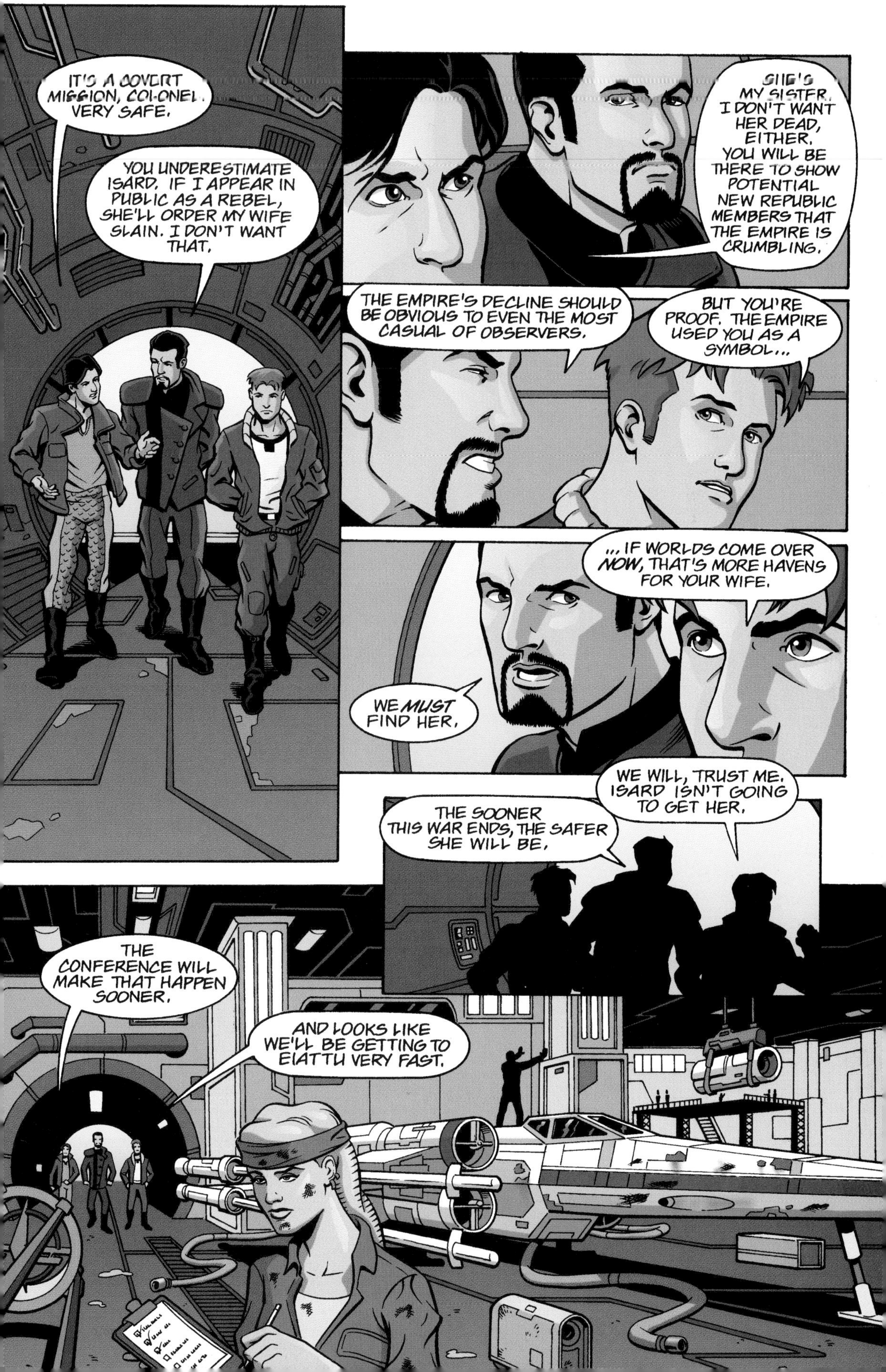
IT'S A COVERT MISSION, COLONEL. VERY SAFE.
YOU UNDERESTIMATE ISARD. IF I APPEAR IN PUBLIC AS A REBEL, SHE'LL ORDER MY WIFE SLAIN. I DON'T WANT THAT.
SHE'S MY SISTER. I DON'T WANT HER DEAD, EITHER. YOU WILL BE THERE TO SHOW POTENTIAL NEW REPUBLIC MEMBERS THAT THE EMPIRE IS CRUMBLING.
THE EMPIRE'S DECLINE SHOULD BE OBVIOUS TO EVEN THE MOST CASUAL OF OBSERVERS.
BUT YOU'RE PROOF. THE EMPIRE USED YOU AS A SYMBOL...
...IF WORLDS COME OVER NOW, THAT'S MORE HAVENS FOR YOUR WIFE.
WE MUST FIND HER.
WE WILL, TRUST ME. ISARD ISN'T GOING TO GET HER.
THE SOONER THIS WAR ENDS, THE SAFER SHE WILL BE.
THE CONFERENCE WILL MAKE THAT HAPPEN SOONER.
AND LOOKS LIKE WE'LL BE GETTING TO EIATTU VERY FAST.

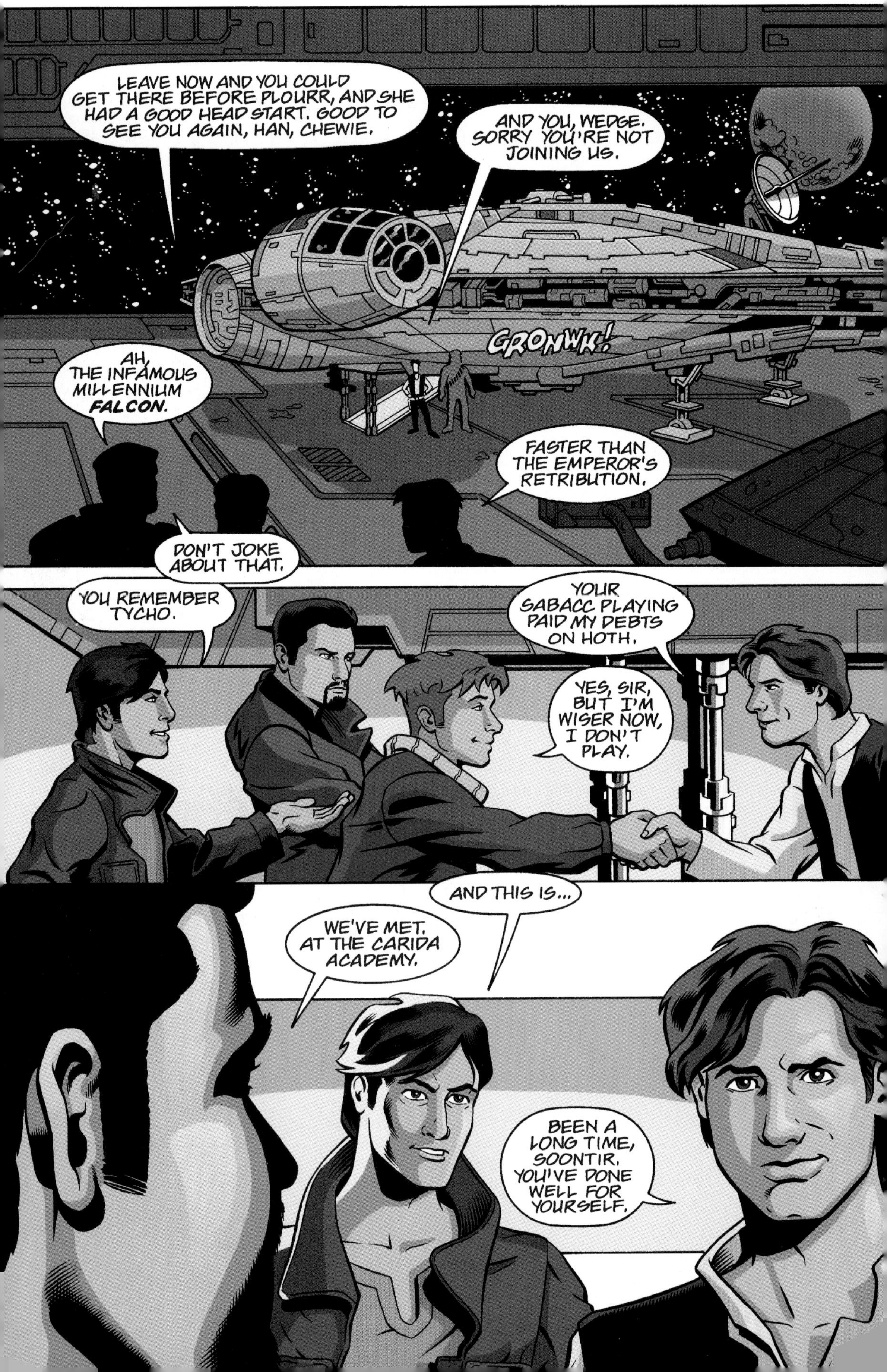
LEAVE NOW AND YOU COULD GET THERE BEFORE PLOURR, AND SHE HAD A GOOD HEAD START. GOOD TO SEE YOU AGAIN, HAN, CHEWIE.
AND YOU, WEDGE. SORRY YOU'RE NOT JOINING US.
GRONWK!
AH, THE INFAMOUS MILLENNIUM FALCON.
FASTER THAN THE EMPEROR'S RETRIBUTION.
DON'T JOKE ABOUT THAT.
YOU REMEMBER TYCHO.
YOUR SABACC PLAYING PAID MY DEBTS ON HOTH.
YES, SIR, BUT I'M WISER NOW, I DON'T PLAY.
AND THIS IS...
WE'VE MET. AT THE CARIDA ACADEMY.
BEEN A LONG TIME, SOONTIR. YOU'VE DONE WELL FOR YOURSELF.

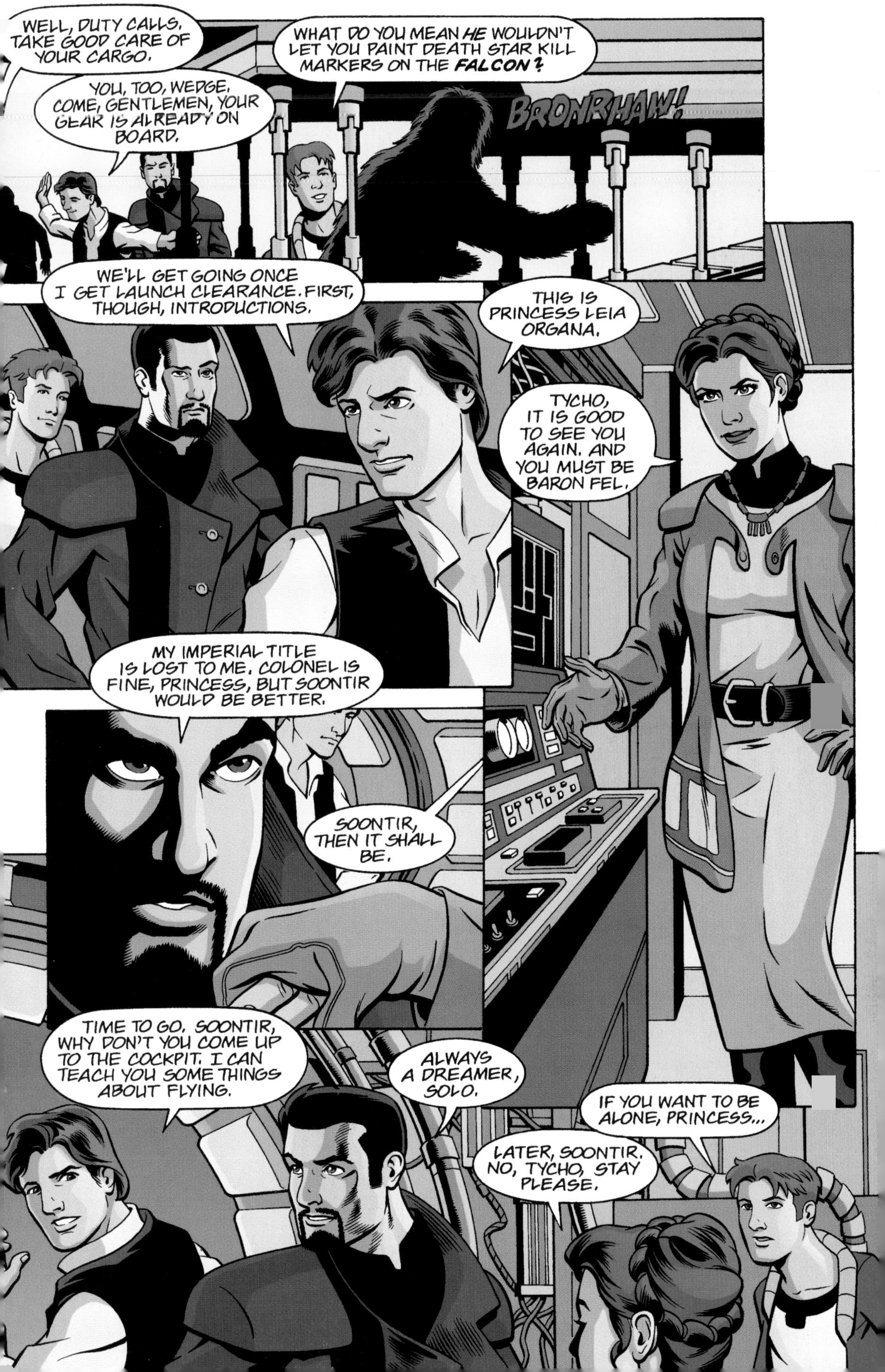
WELL, DUTY CALLS. TAKE GOOD CARE OF YOUR CARGO.
YOU, TOO, WEDGE. COME, GENTLEMEN, YOUR GEAR IS ALREADY ON BOARD.
WHAT DO YOU MEAN HE WOULDN'T LET YOU PAINT DEATH STAR KILL MARKERS ON THE FALCON?
BRONRHAW!
WE'LL GET GOING ONCE I GET LAUNCH CLEARANCE. FIRST, THOUGH, INTRODUCTIONS.
THIS IS PRINCESS LEIA ORGANA.
TYCHO, IT IS GOOD TO SEE YOU AGAIN. AND YOU MUST BE BARON FEL.
MY IMPERIAL TITLE IS LOST TO ME. COLONEL IS FINE, PRINCESS, BUT SOONTIR WOULD BE BETTER.
SOONTIR, THEN IT SHALL BE.
TIME TO GO, SOONTIR. WHY DON'T YOU COME UP TO THE COCKPIT. I CAN TEACH YOU SOME THINGS ABOUT FLYING.
ALWAYS A DREAMER, SOLO.
IF YOU WANT TO BE ALONE, PRINCESS...
LATER, SOONTIR. NO, TYCHO, STAY PLEASE.

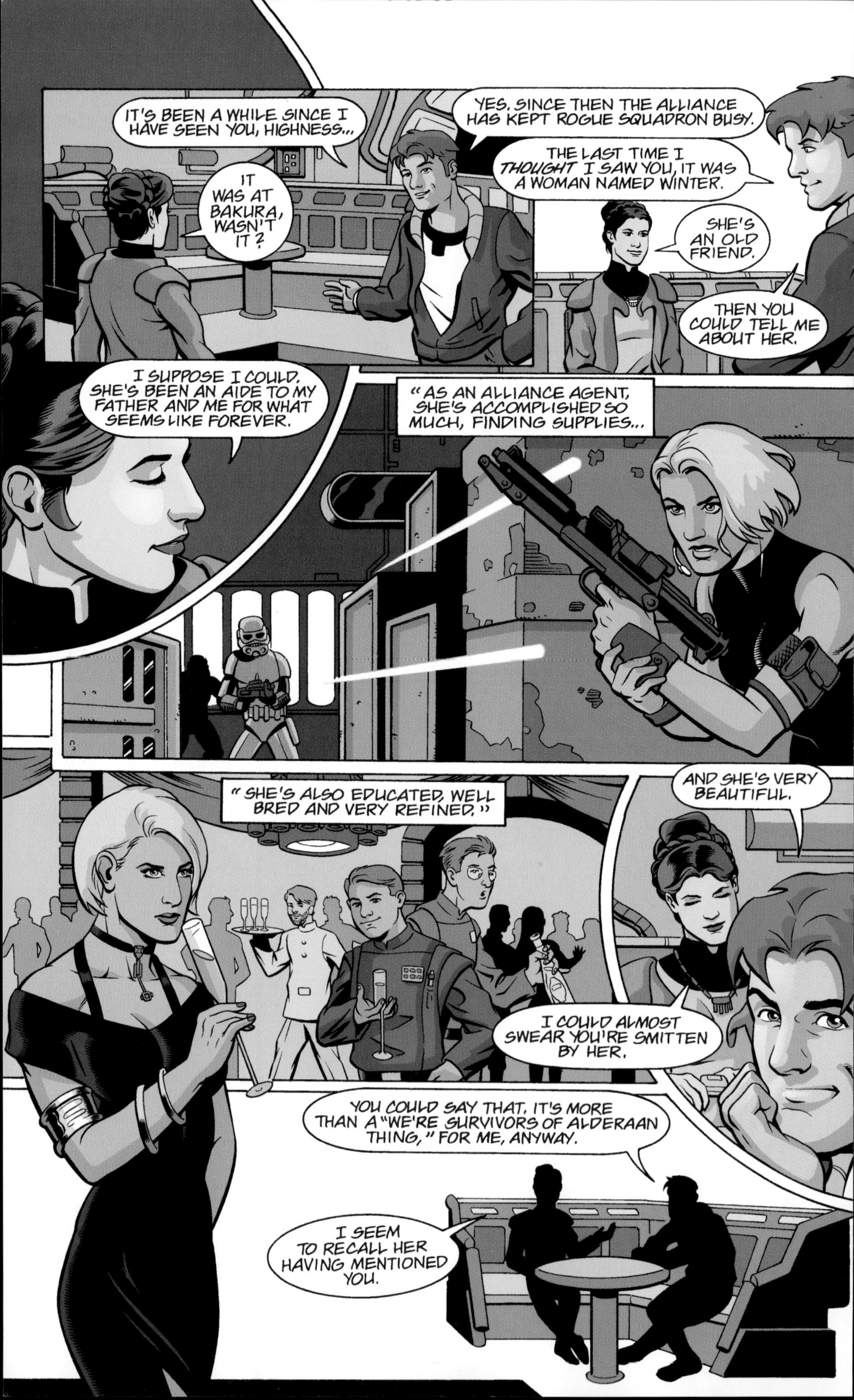
IT'S BEEN A WHILE SINCE I HAVE SEEN YOU, HIGHNESS...
IT WAS AT BAKURA, WASN'T IT?
YES. SINCE THEN THE ALLIANCE HAS KEPT ROGUE SQUADRON BUSY.
THE LAST TIME I *THOUGHT* I SAW YOU, IT WAS A WOMAN NAMED WINTER.
SHE'S AN OLD FRIEND.
THEN YOU COULD TELL ME ABOUT HER.
I SUPPOSE I COULD. SHE'S BEEN AN AIDE TO MY FATHER AND ME FOR WHAT SEEMS LIKE FOREVER.
"AS AN ALLIANCE AGENT, SHE'S ACCOMPLISHED SO MUCH, FINDING SUPPLIES...
"SHE'S ALSO EDUCATED, WELL BRED AND VERY REFINED."
AND SHE'S VERY BEAUTIFUL.
I COULD ALMOST SWEAR YOU'RE SMITTEN BY HER.
YOU COULD SAY THAT. IT'S MORE THAN A "WE'RE SURVIVORS OF ALDERAAN THING," FOR ME, ANYWAY.
I SEEM TO RECALL HER HAVING MENTIONED YOU.

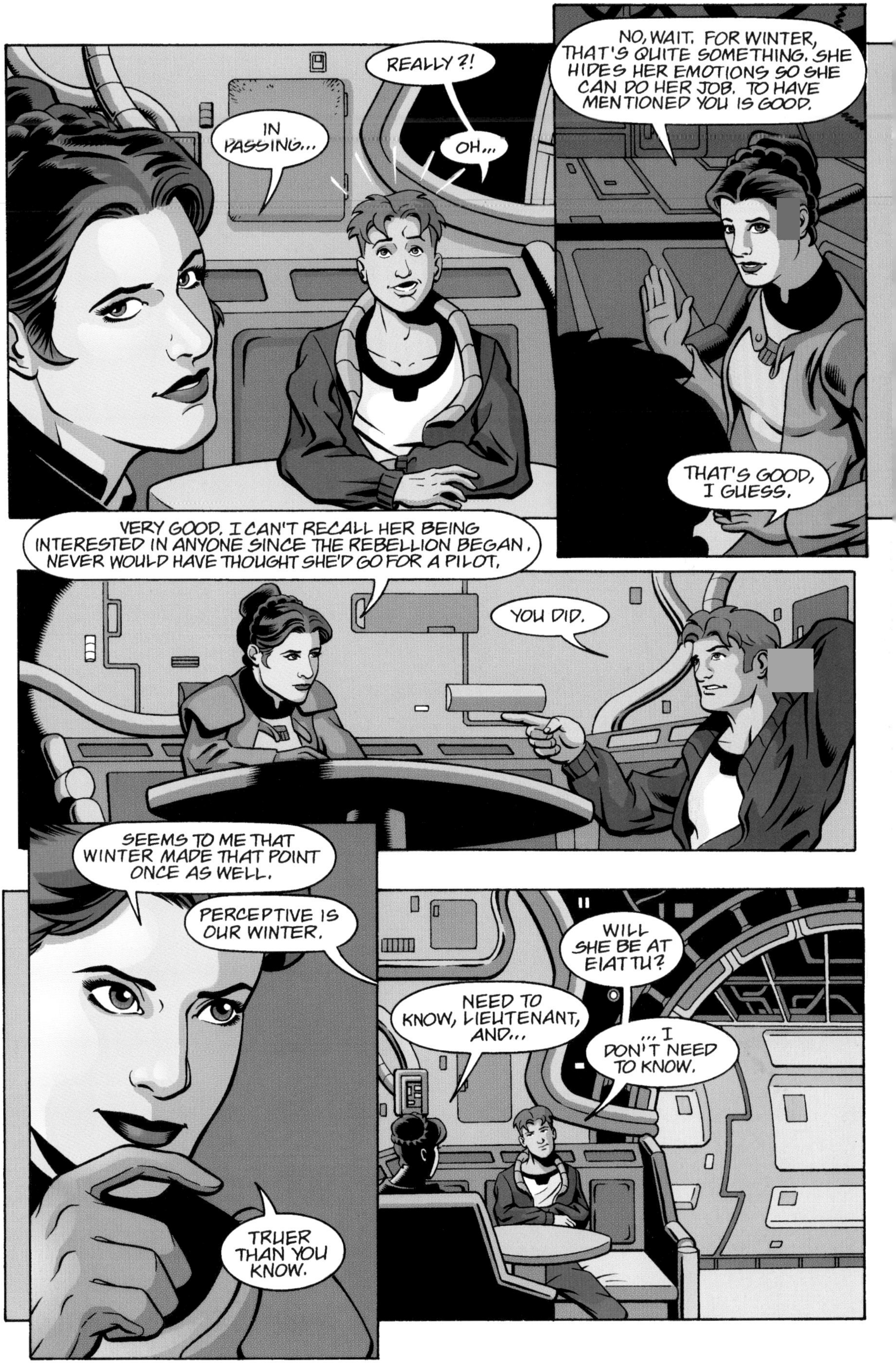
IN PASSING...
REALLY?!
OH...
NO, WAIT. FOR WINTER, THAT'S QUITE SOMETHING. SHE HIDES HER EMOTIONS SO SHE CAN DO HER JOB. TO HAVE MENTIONED YOU IS GOOD.
THAT'S GOOD, I GUESS.
VERY GOOD. I CAN'T RECALL HER BEING INTERESTED IN ANYONE SINCE THE REBELLION BEGAN. NEVER WOULD HAVE THOUGHT SHE'D GO FOR A PILOT.
YOU DID.
SEEMS TO ME THAT WINTER MADE THAT POINT ONCE AS WELL.
PERCEPTIVE IS OUR WINTER.
TRUER THAN YOU KNOW.
WILL SHE BE AT EIATTU?
NEED TO KNOW, LIEUTENANT, AND...
...I DON'T NEED TO KNOW.

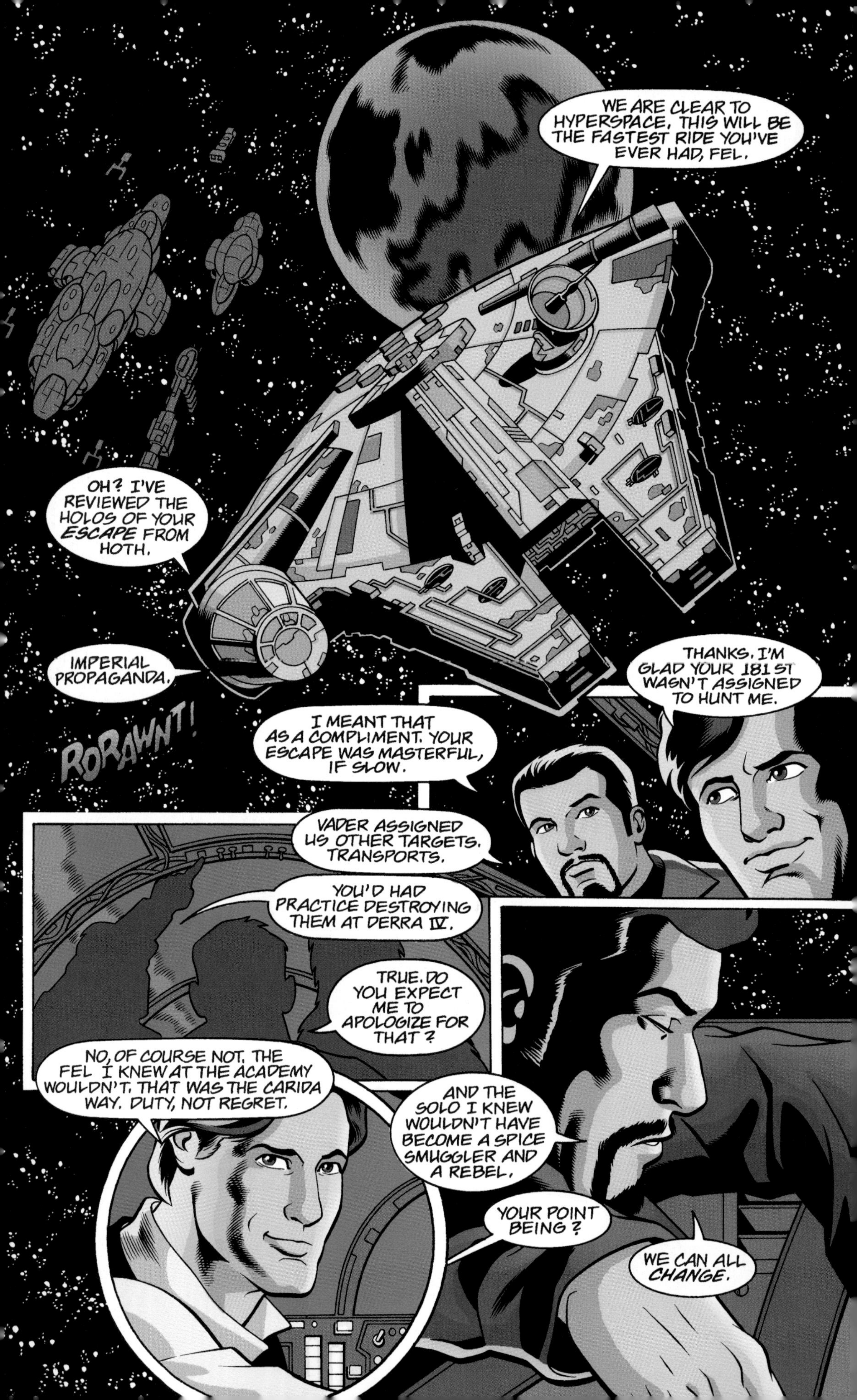
WE ARE CLEAR TO HYPERSPACE, THIS WILL BE THE FASTEST RIDE YOU'VE EVER HAD, FEL.
OH? I'VE REVIEWED THE HOLOS OF YOUR *ESCAPE* FROM HOTH.
IMPERIAL PROPAGANDA.
RORAWNT!
THANKS. I'M GLAD YOUR 181 ST WASN'T ASSIGNED TO HUNT ME.
I MEANT THAT AS A COMPLIMENT. YOUR ESCAPE WAS MASTERFUL, IF SLOW.
VADER ASSIGNED US OTHER TARGETS. TRANSPORTS.
YOU'D HAD PRACTICE DESTROYING THEM AT DERRA IV.
TRUE. DO YOU EXPECT ME TO APOLOGIZE FOR THAT?
NO, OF COURSE NOT. THE FEL I KNEW AT THE ACADEMY WOULDN'T. THAT WAS THE CARIDA WAY. DUTY, NOT REGRET.
AND THE SOLO I KNEW WOULDN'T HAVE BECOME A SPICE SMUGGLER AND A REBEL.
YOUR POINT BEING?
WE CAN ALL *CHANGE*.

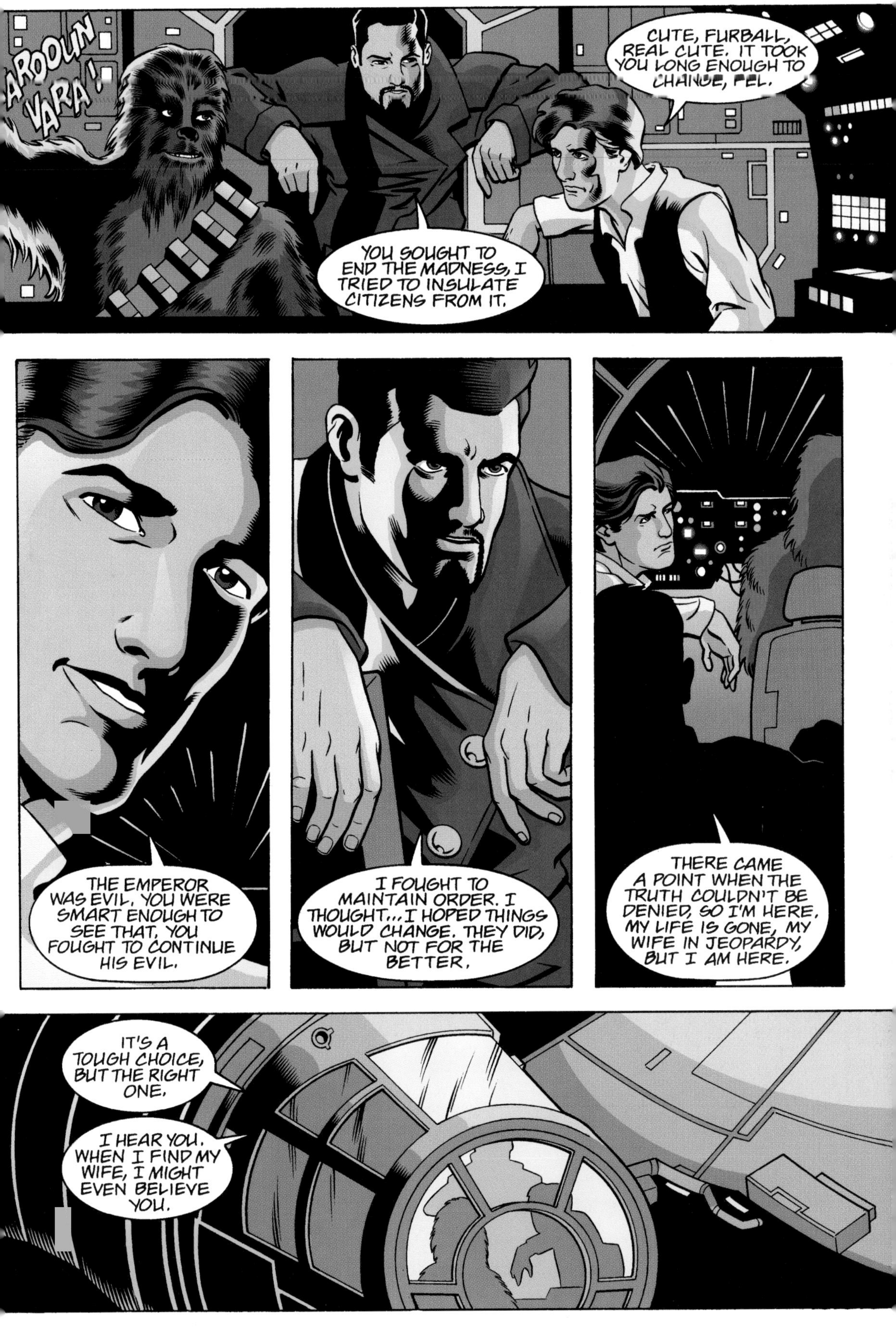
AROOUN VARA!
CUTE, FURBALL, REAL CUTE. IT TOOK YOU LONG ENOUGH TO CHANGE, FEL.
YOU SOUGHT TO END THE MADNESS, I TRIED TO INSULATE CITIZENS FROM IT.
THE EMPEROR WAS EVIL. YOU WERE SMART ENOUGH TO SEE THAT. YOU FOUGHT TO CONTINUE HIS EVIL.
I FOUGHT TO MAINTAIN ORDER. I THOUGHT... I HOPED THINGS WOULD CHANGE. THEY DID, BUT NOT FOR THE BETTER.
THERE CAME A POINT WHEN THE TRUTH COULDN'T BE DENIED, SO I'M HERE. MY LIFE IS GONE, MY WIFE IN JEOPARDY, BUT I AM HERE.
IT'S A TOUGH CHOICE, BUT THE RIGHT ONE.
I HEAR YOU. WHEN I FIND MY WIFE, I MIGHT EVEN BELIEVE YOU.

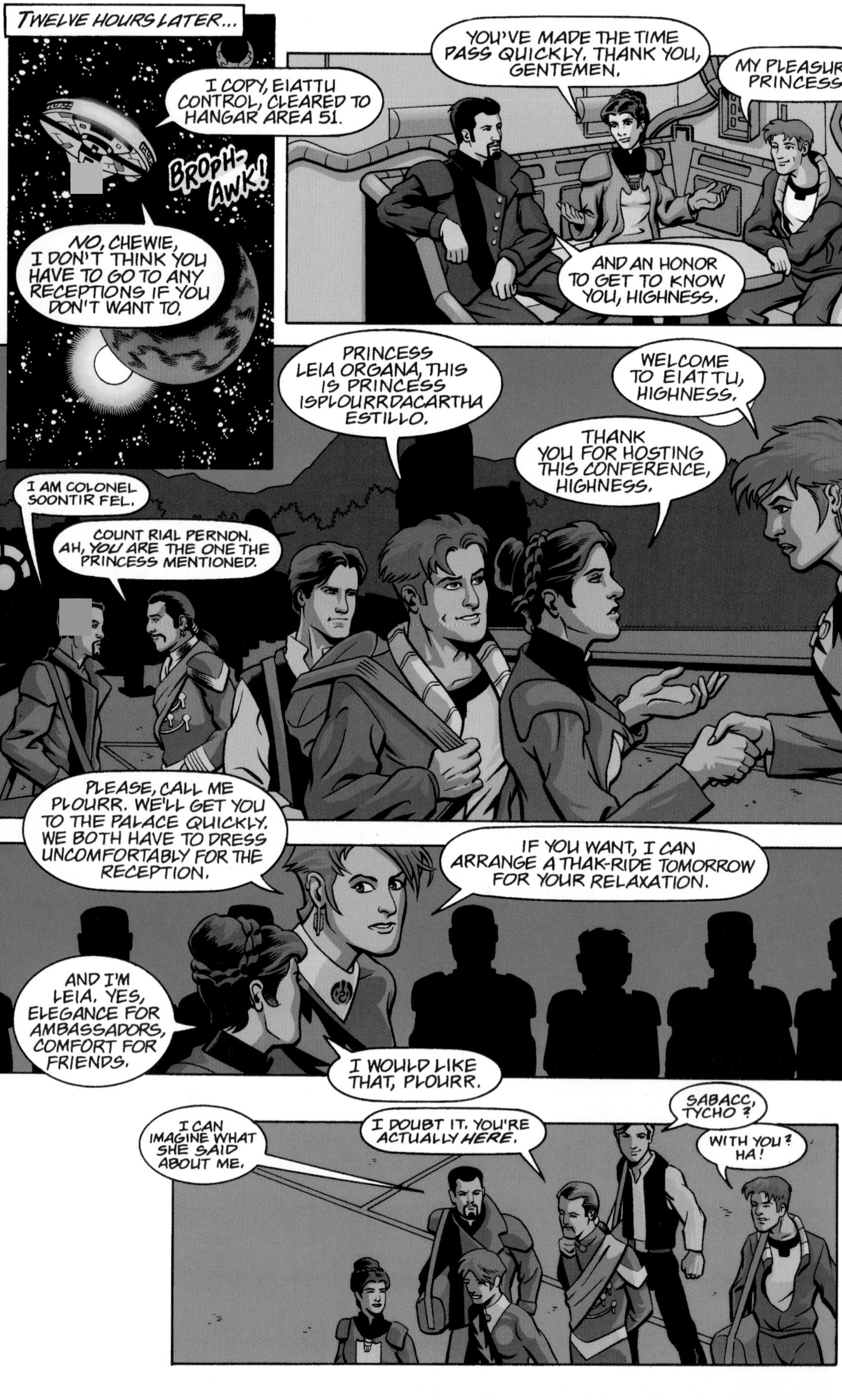
TWELVE HOURS LATER...
I COPY, EIATTU CONTROL, CLEARED TO HANGAR AREA 51.
BROPH-AWK!
NO, CHEWIE, I DON'T THINK YOU HAVE TO GO TO ANY RECEPTIONS IF YOU DON'T WANT TO.
YOU'VE MADE THE TIME PASS QUICKLY. THANK YOU, GENTEMEN.
MY PLEASURE, PRINCESS.
AND AN HONOR TO GET TO KNOW YOU, HIGHNESS.
PRINCESS LEIA ORGANA, THIS IS PRINCESS ISPLOURRDACARTHA ESTILLO.
WELCOME TO EIATTU, HIGHNESS.
THANK YOU FOR HOSTING THIS CONFERENCE, HIGHNESS.
I AM COLONEL SOONTIR FEL.
COUNT RIAL PERNON. AH, YOU ARE THE ONE THE PRINCESS MENTIONED.
PLEASE, CALL ME PLOURR. WE'LL GET YOU TO THE PALACE QUICKLY. WE BOTH HAVE TO DRESS UNCOMFORTABLY FOR THE RECEPTION.
IF YOU WANT, I CAN ARRANGE A THAK-RIDE TOMORROW FOR YOUR RELAXATION.
AND I'M LEIA. YES, ELEGANCE FOR AMBASSADORS, COMFORT FOR FRIENDS.
I WOULD LIKE THAT, PLOURR.
I CAN IMAGINE WHAT SHE SAID ABOUT ME.
I DOUBT IT. YOU'RE ACTUALLY HERE.
SABACC, TYCHO?
WITH YOU? HA!

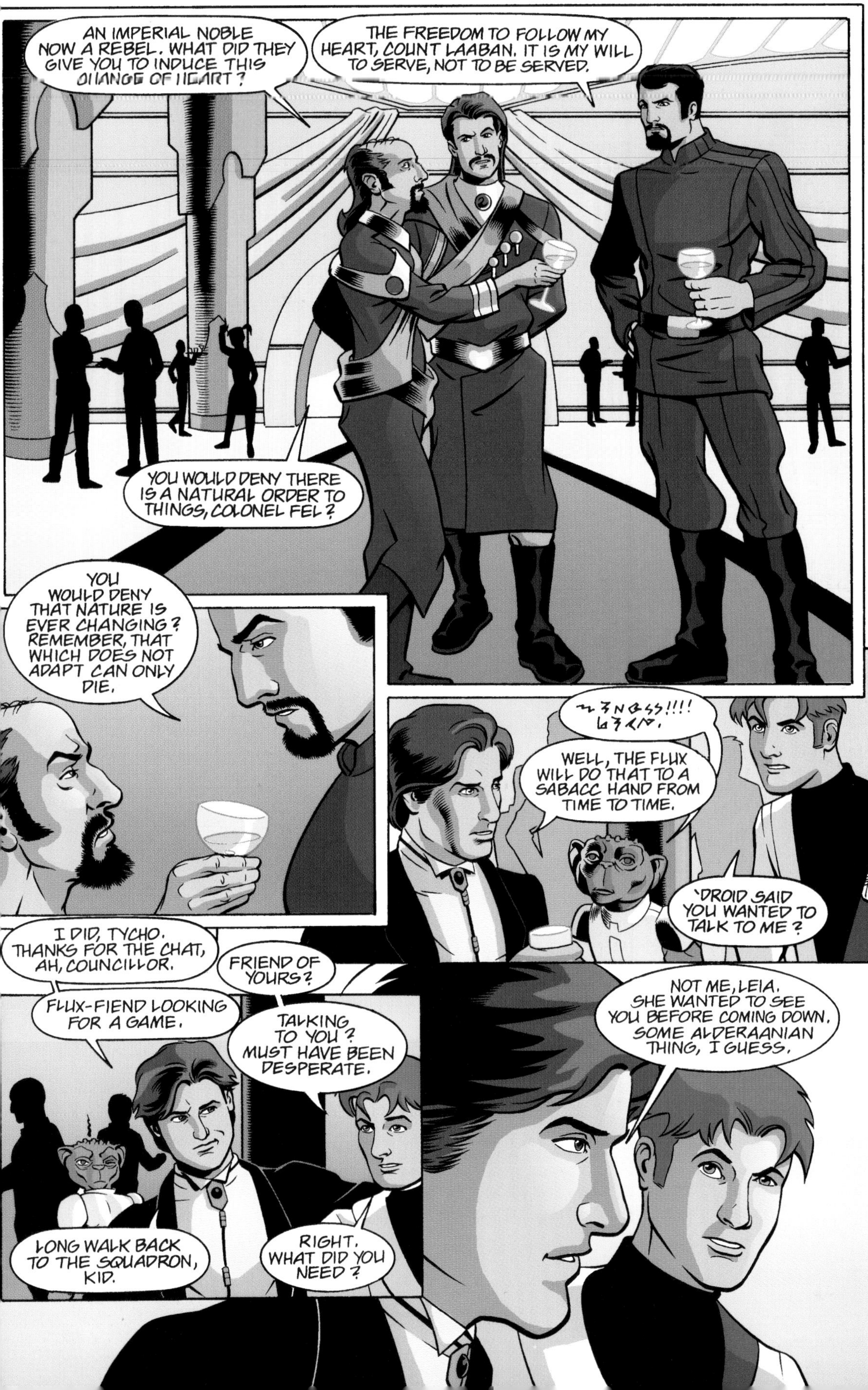
AN IMPERIAL NOBLE NOW A REBEL. WHAT DID THEY GIVE YOU TO INDUCE THIS CHANGE OF HEART?
THE FREEDOM TO FOLLOW MY HEART, COUNT LAABAN. IT IS MY WILL TO SERVE, NOT TO BE SERVED.
YOU WOULD DENY THERE IS A NATURAL ORDER TO THINGS, COLONEL FEL?
YOU WOULD DENY THAT NATURE IS EVER CHANGING? REMEMBER, THAT WHICH DOES NOT ADAPT CAN ONLY DIE.
WELL, THE FLUX WILL DO THAT TO A SABACC HAND FROM TIME TO TIME.
'DROID SAID YOU WANTED TO TALK TO ME?
I DID, TYCHO. THANKS FOR THE CHAT, AH, COUNCILLOR.
FRIEND OF YOURS?
FLUX-FIEND LOOKING FOR A GAME.
TALKING TO YOU? MUST HAVE BEEN DESPERATE.
LONG WALK BACK TO THE SQUADRON, KID.
RIGHT. WHAT DID YOU NEED?
NOT ME, LEIA. SHE WANTED TO SEE YOU BEFORE COMING DOWN. SOME ALDERAANIAN THING, I GUESS.

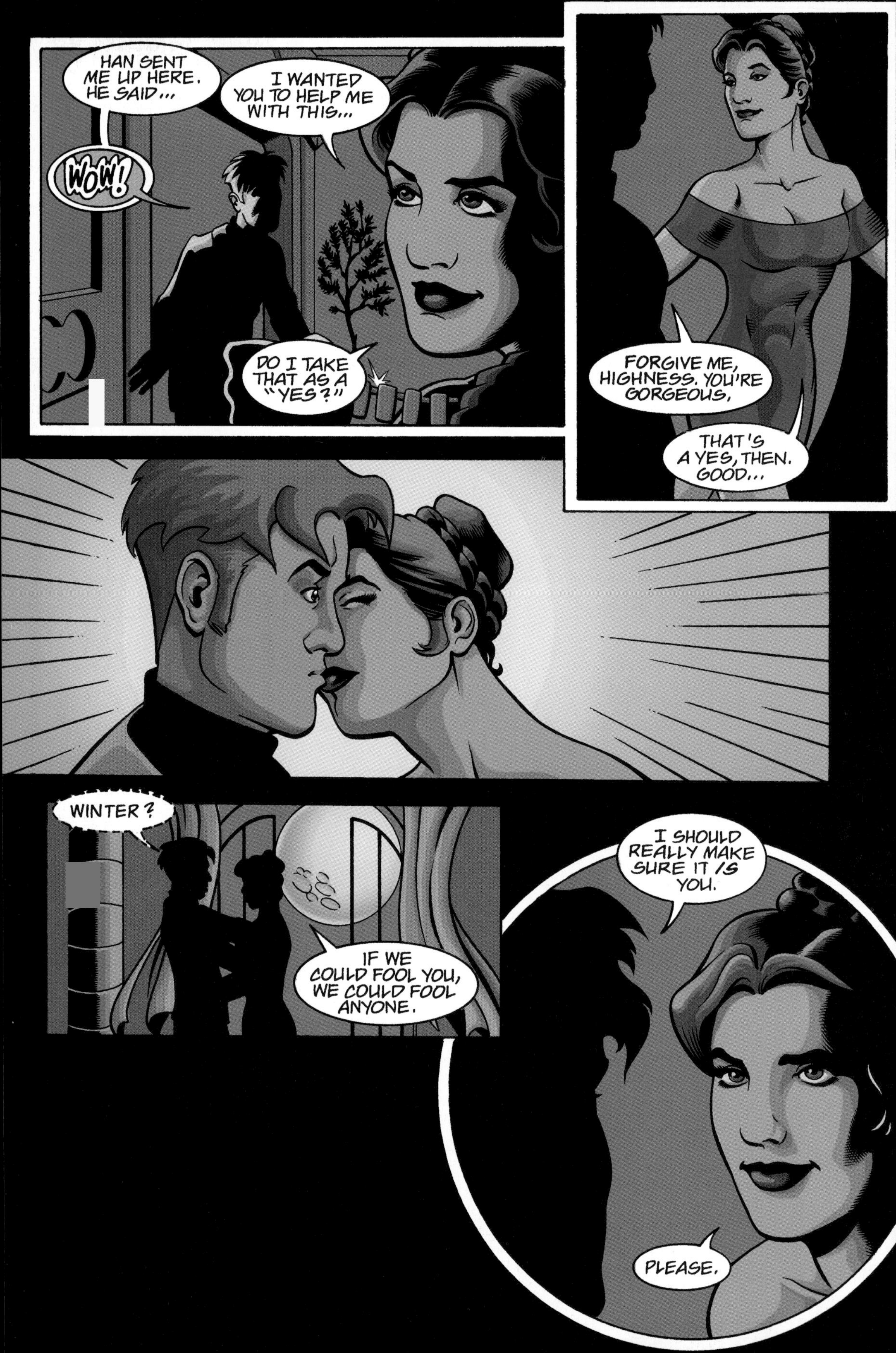
HAN SENT ME UP HERE. HE SAID...
WOW!
I WANTED YOU TO HELP ME WITH THIS...
DO I TAKE THAT AS A "YES?"
FORGIVE ME, HIGHNESS. YOU'RE GORGEOUS.
THAT'S A YES, THEN. GOOD...
WINTER?
IF WE COULD FOOL YOU, WE COULD FOOL ANYONE.
I SHOULD REALLY MAKE SURE IT IS YOU.
PLEASE.

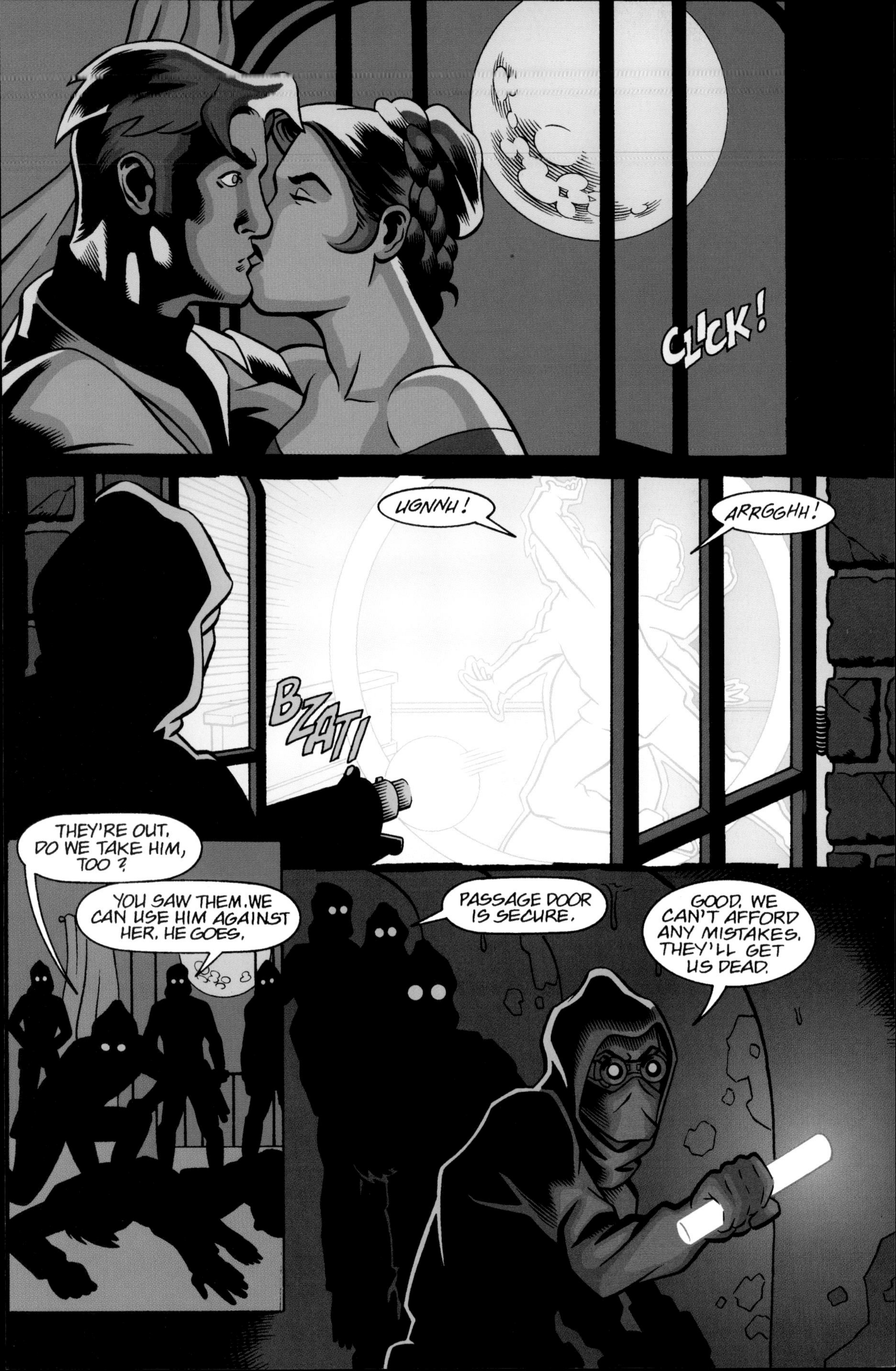
CLICK!
UGNNH!
ARRGGHH!
BZAT!
THEY'RE OUT, DO WE TAKE HIM, TOO ?
YOU SAW THEM. WE CAN USE HIM AGAINST HER. HE GOES.
PASSAGE DOOR IS SECURE.
GOOD. WE CAN'T AFFORD ANY MISTAKES. THEY'LL GET US DEAD.

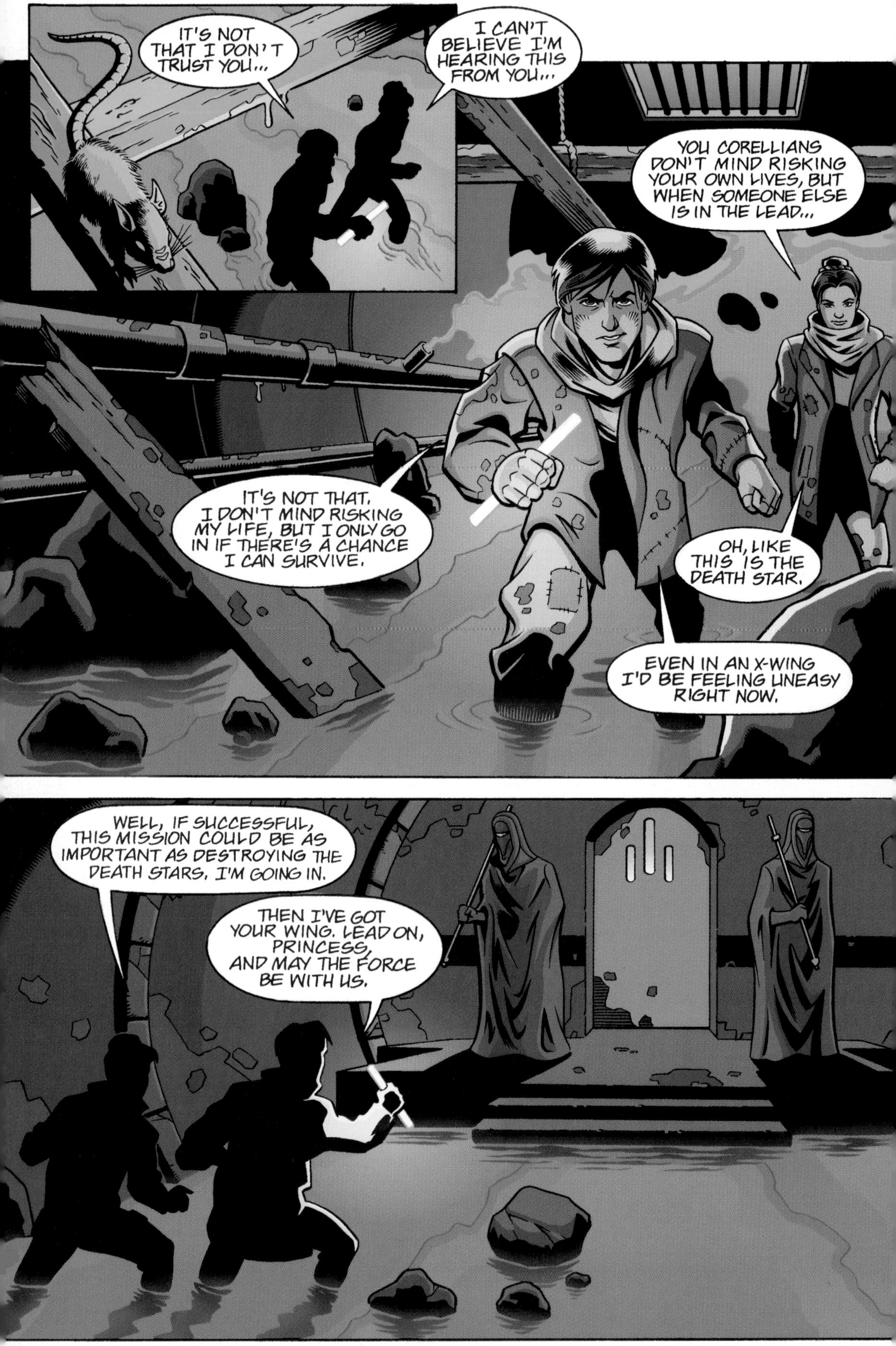
IT'S NOT THAT I DON'T TRUST YOU...
I CAN'T BELIEVE I'M HEARING THIS FROM YOU...
YOU CORELLIANS DON'T MIND RISKING YOUR OWN LIVES, BUT WHEN SOMEONE ELSE IS IN THE LEAD...
IT'S NOT THAT. I DON'T MIND RISKING MY LIFE, BUT I ONLY GO IN IF THERE'S A CHANCE I CAN SURVIVE.
OH, LIKE THIS IS THE DEATH STAR.
EVEN IN AN X-WING I'D BE FEELING UNEASY RIGHT NOW.
WELL, IF SUCCESSFUL, THIS MISSION COULD BE AS IMPORTANT AS DESTROYING THE DEATH STARS. I'M GOING IN.
THEN I'VE GOT YOUR WING. LEAD ON, PRINCESS, AND MAY THE FORCE BE WITH US.

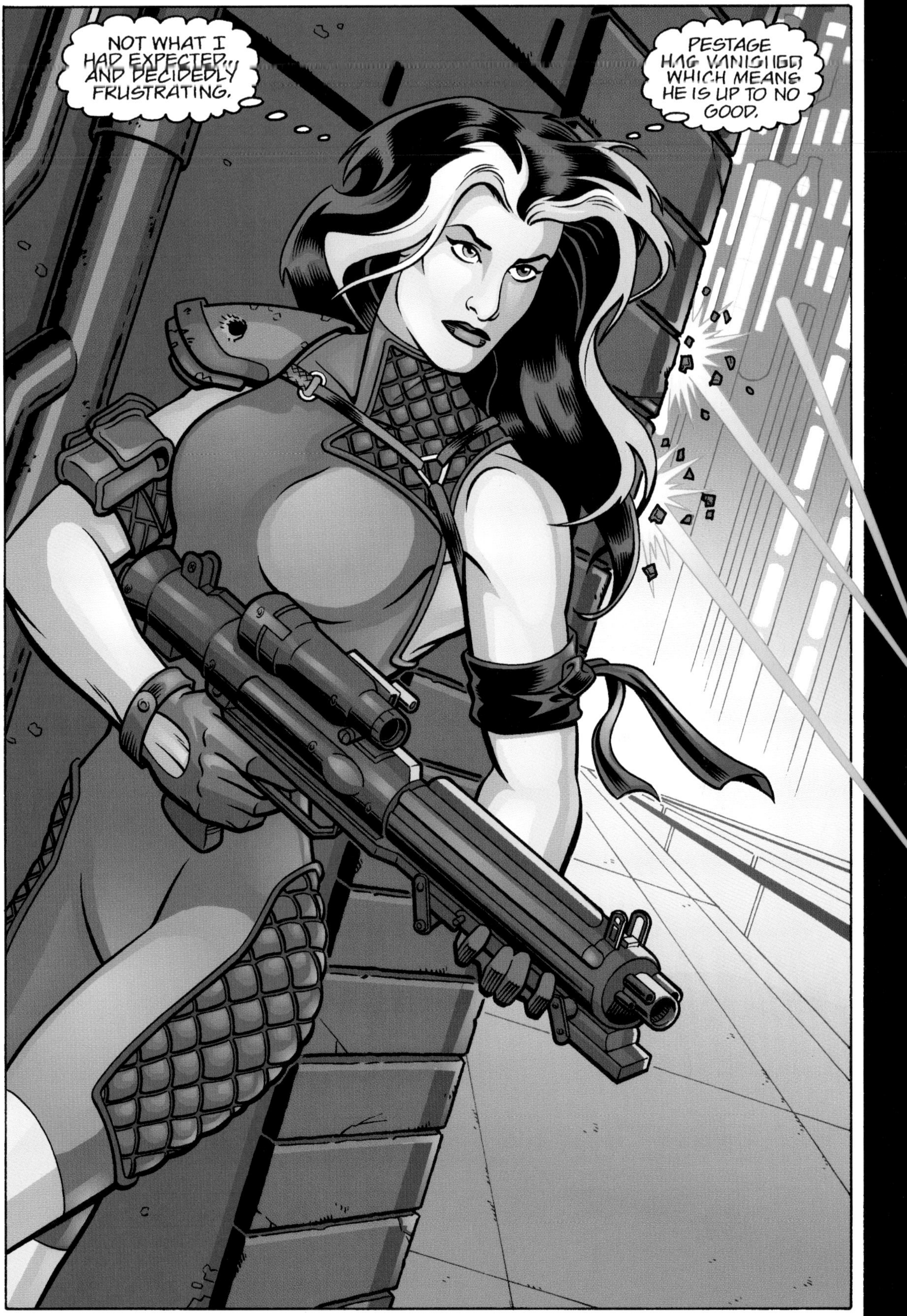
NOT WHAT I HAD EXPECTED... AND DECIDEDLY FRUSTRATING.
PESTAGE HAS VANISHED WHICH MEANS HE IS UP TO NO GOOD.

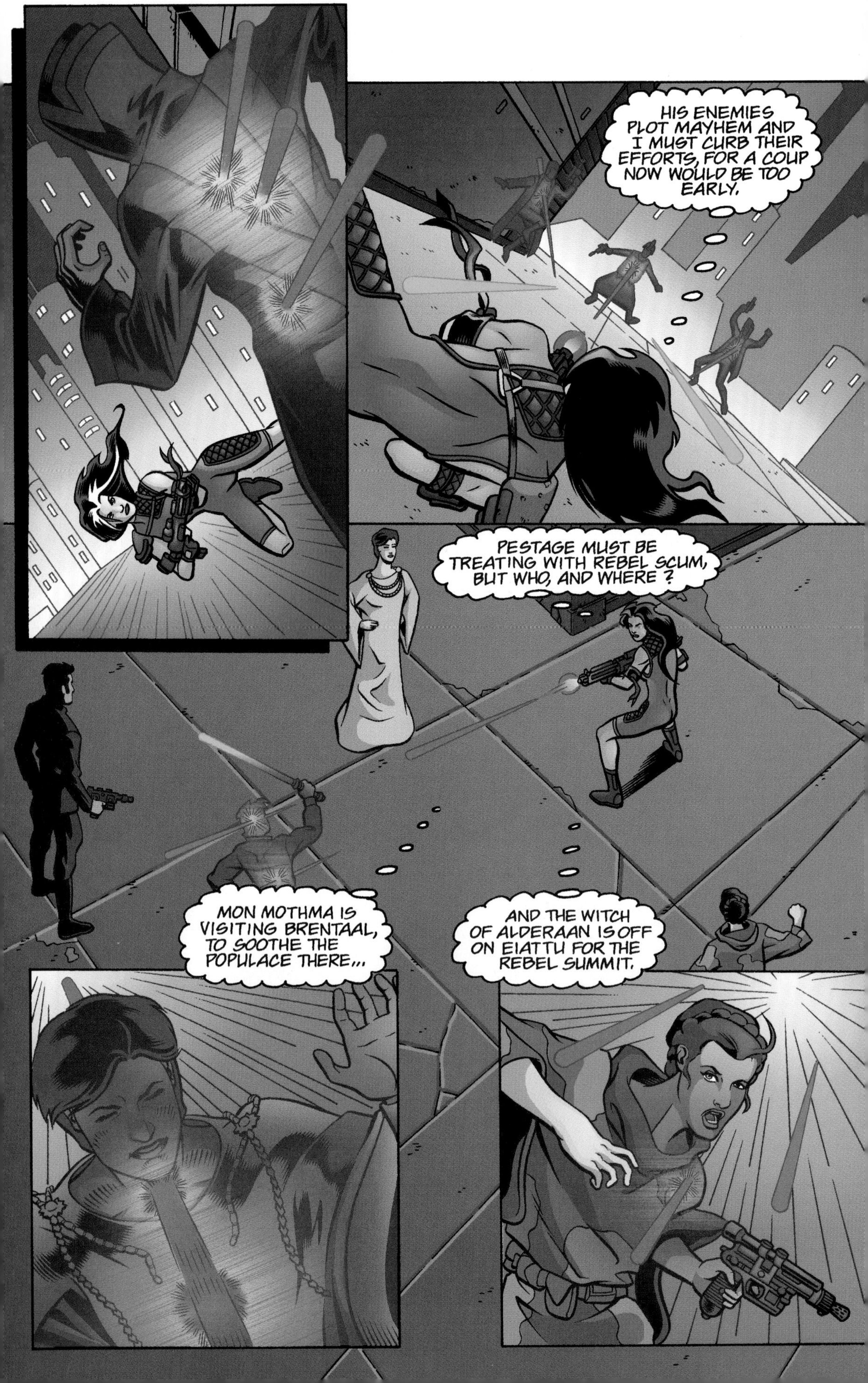
HIS ENEMIES PLOT MAYHEM AND I MUST CURB THEIR EFFORTS, FOR A COUP NOW WOULD BE TOO EARLY.
PESTAGE MUST BE TREATING WITH REBEL SCUM, BUT WHO, AND WHERE ?
MON MOTHMA IS VISITING BRENTAAL, TO SOOTHE THE POPULACE THERE...
AND THE WITCH OF ALDERAAN IS OFF ON EIATTU FOR THE REBEL SUMMIT.

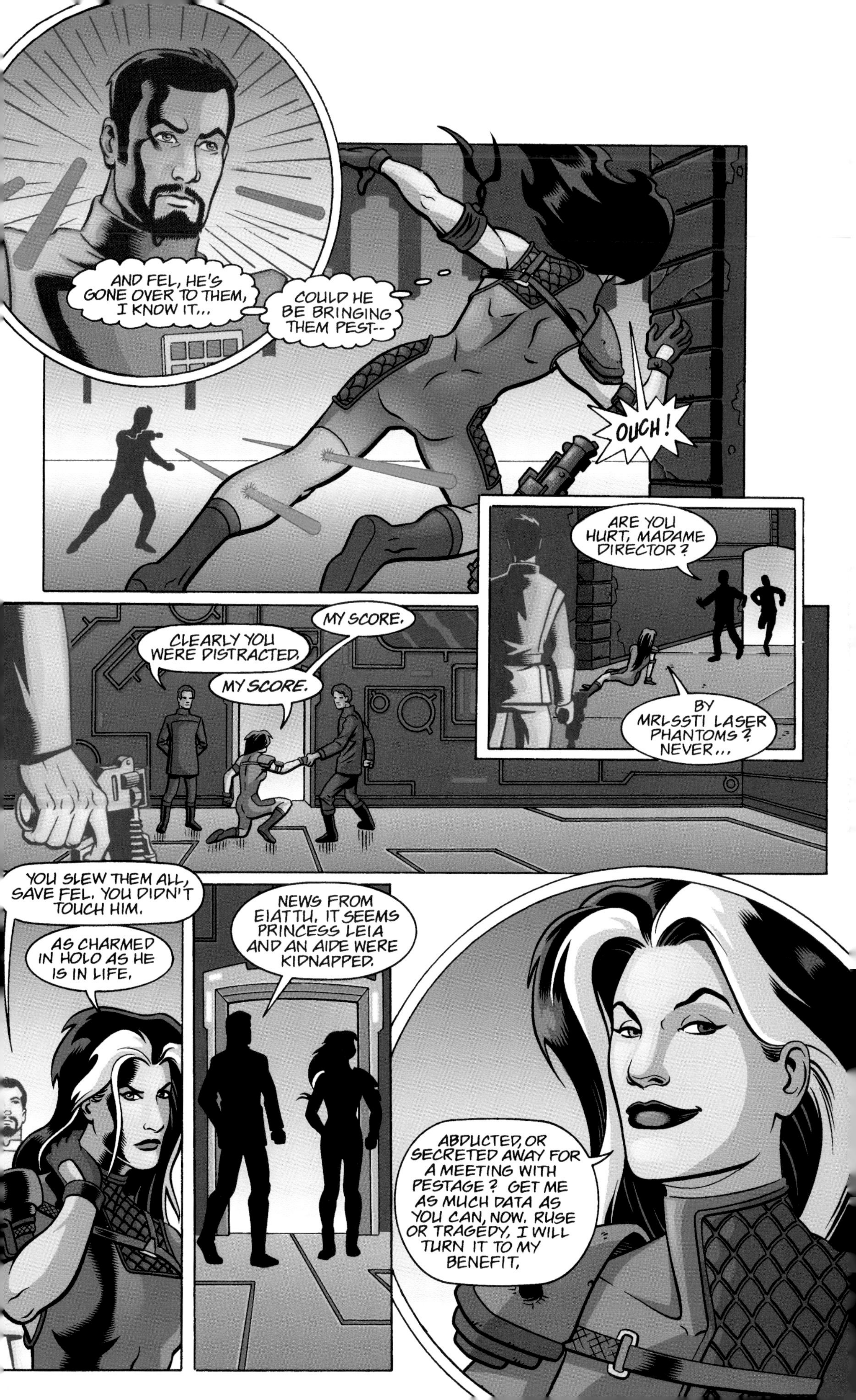

AND FEL, HE'S GONE OVER TO THEM, I KNOW IT...
COULD HE BE BRINGING THEM PEST--
OUCH!
ARE YOU HURT, MADAME DIRECTOR?
BY MRLSSTI LASER PHANTOMS? NEVER...
CLEARLY YOU WERE DISTRACTED.
MY SCORE.
MY SCORE.
YOU SLEW THEM ALL, SAVE FEL. YOU DIDN'T TOUCH HIM.
AS CHARMED IN HOLO AS HE IS IN LIFE.
NEWS FROM EIATTU. IT SEEMS PRINCESS LEIA AND AN AIDE WERE KIDNAPPED.
ABDUCTED, OR SECRETED AWAY FOR A MEETING WITH PESTAGE? GET ME AS MUCH DATA AS YOU CAN, NOW. RUSE OR TRAGEDY, I WILL TURN IT TO MY BENEFIT.

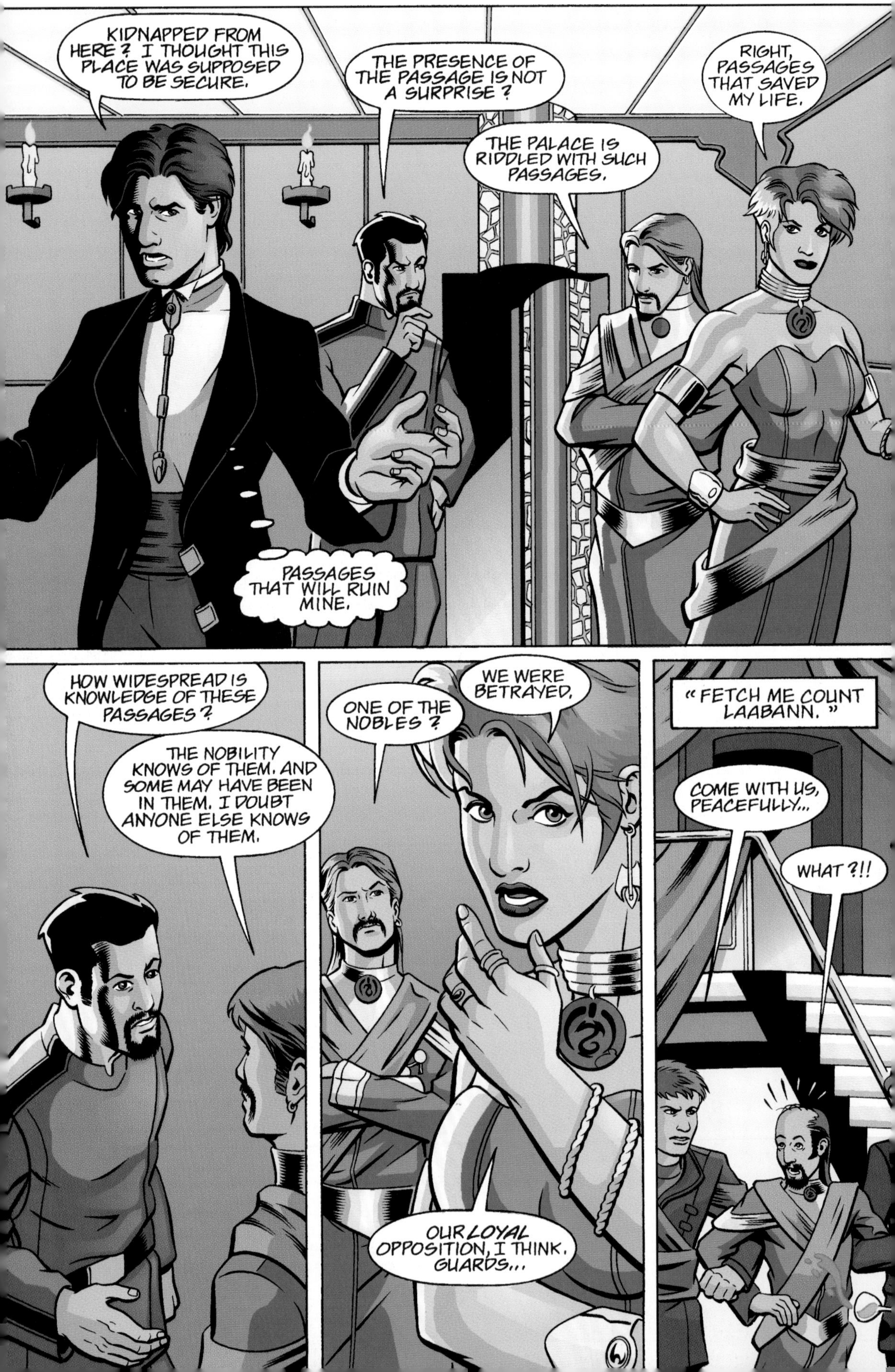
KIDNAPPED FROM HERE? I THOUGHT THIS PLACE WAS SUPPOSED TO BE SECURE.
THE PRESENCE OF THE PASSAGE IS NOT A SURPRISE?
THE PALACE IS RIDDLED WITH SUCH PASSAGES.
RIGHT, PASSAGES THAT SAVED MY LIFE.
PASSAGES THAT WILL RUIN MINE.
HOW WIDESPREAD IS KNOWLEDGE OF THESE PASSAGES?
THE NOBILITY KNOWS OF THEM, AND SOME MAY HAVE BEEN IN THEM. I DOUBT ANYONE ELSE KNOWS OF THEM.
WE WERE BETRAYED.
ONE OF THE NOBLES?
OUR LOYAL OPPOSITION, I THINK. GUARDS...
"FETCH ME COUNT LAABANN."
COME WITH US, PEACEFULLY...
WHAT?!!

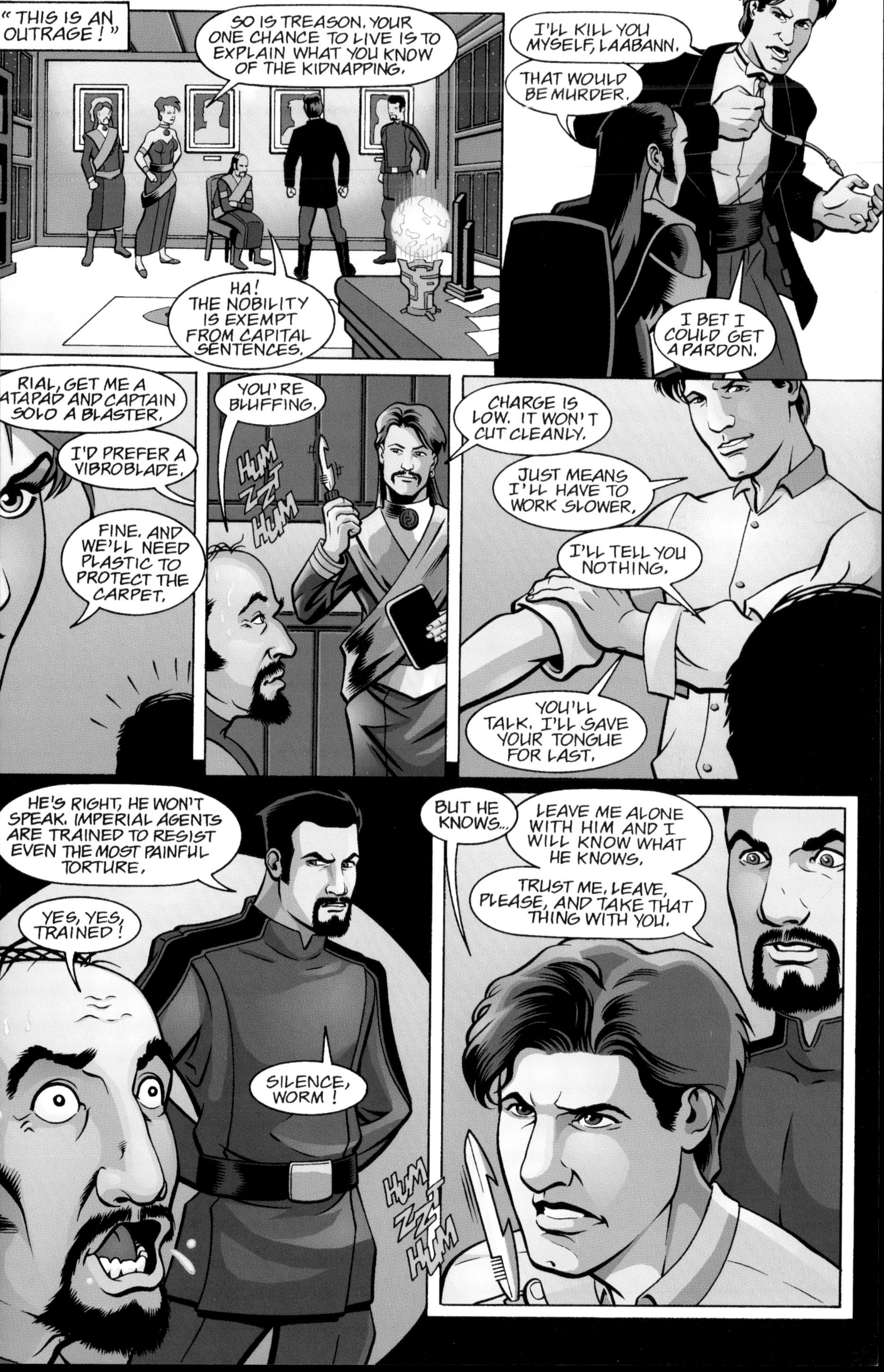
"THIS IS AN OUTRAGE!"
SO IS TREASON. YOUR ONE CHANCE TO LIVE IS TO EXPLAIN WHAT YOU KNOW OF THE KIDNAPPING.
HA! THE NOBILITY IS EXEMPT FROM CAPITAL SENTENCES.
I'LL KILL YOU MYSELF, LAABANN.
THAT WOULD BE MURDER.
I BET I COULD GET A PARDON.
RIAL, GET ME A ATAPAD AND CAPTAIN SOLO A BLASTER.
I'D PREFER A VIBROBLADE.
FINE. AND WE'LL NEED PLASTIC TO PROTECT THE CARPET.
YOU'RE BLUFFING.
HUM ZZT HUM
CHARGE IS LOW. IT WON'T CUT CLEANLY.
JUST MEANS I'LL HAVE TO WORK SLOWER.
I'LL TELL YOU NOTHING.
YOU'LL TALK. I'LL SAVE YOUR TONGUE FOR LAST.
HE'S RIGHT, HE WON'T SPEAK. IMPERIAL AGENTS ARE TRAINED TO RESIST EVEN THE MOST PAINFUL TORTURE.
YES, YES, TRAINED!
SILENCE, WORM!
BUT HE KNOWS...
LEAVE ME ALONE WITH HIM AND I WILL KNOW WHAT HE KNOWS.
TRUST ME, LEAVE, PLEASE, AND TAKE THAT THING WITH YOU.
HUM ZZT HUM

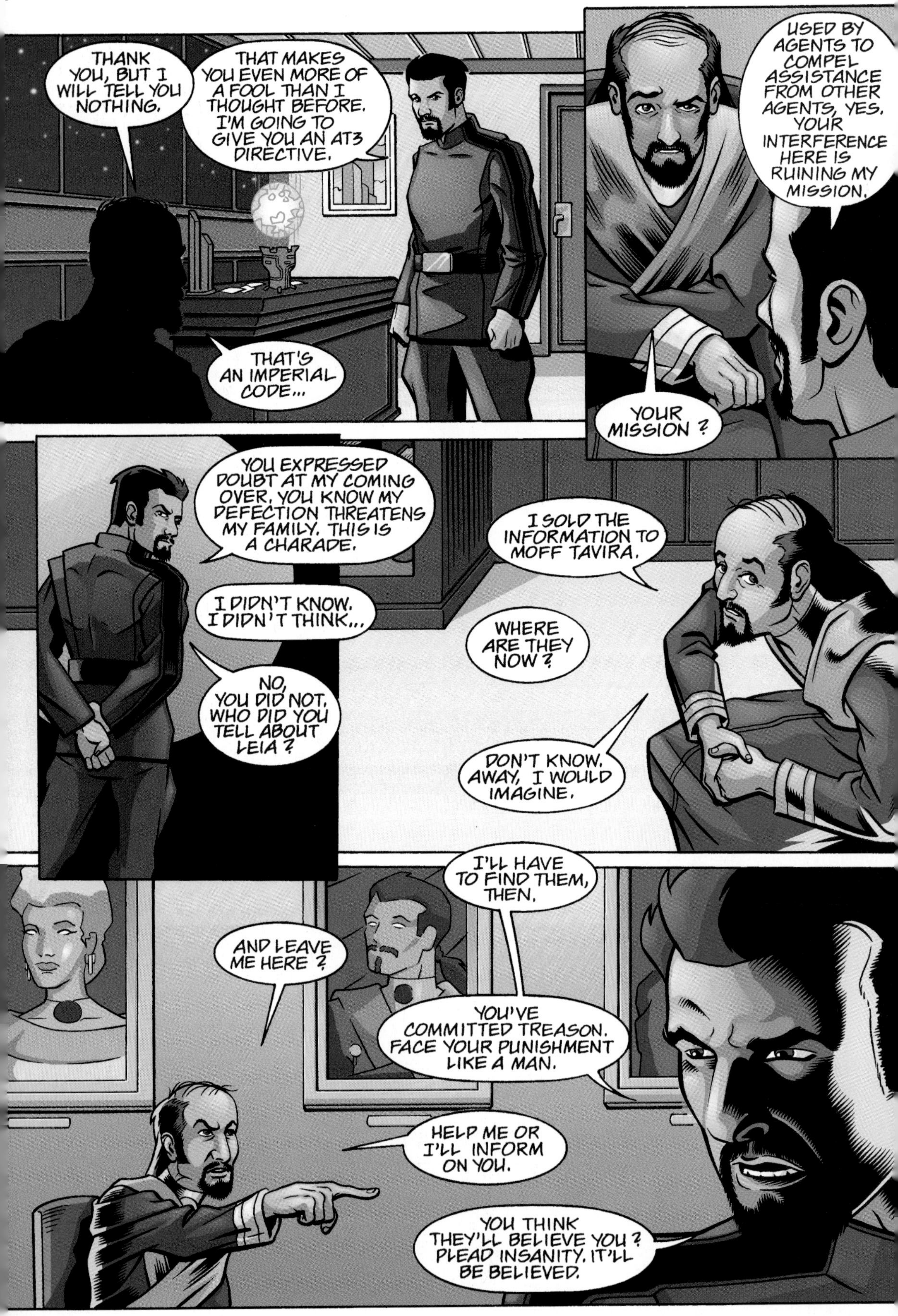
THANK YOU, BUT I WILL TELL YOU NOTHING.
THAT MAKES YOU EVEN MORE OF A FOOL THAN I THOUGHT BEFORE. I'M GOING TO GIVE YOU AN AT3 DIRECTIVE.
THAT'S AN IMPERIAL CODE...
USED BY AGENTS TO COMPEL ASSISTANCE FROM OTHER AGENTS, YES. YOUR INTERFERENCE HERE IS RUINING MY MISSION.
YOUR MISSION ?
YOU EXPRESSED DOUBT AT MY COMING OVER. YOU KNOW MY DEFECTION THREATENS MY FAMILY. THIS IS A CHARADE.
I DIDN'T KNOW. I DIDN'T THINK...
NO, YOU DID NOT. WHO DID YOU TELL ABOUT LEIA ?
I SOLD THE INFORMATION TO MOFF TAVIRA.
WHERE ARE THEY NOW ?
DON'T KNOW. AWAY, I WOULD IMAGINE.
I'LL HAVE TO FIND THEM, THEN.
AND LEAVE ME HERE ?
YOU'VE COMMITTED TREASON. FACE YOUR PUNISHMENT LIKE A MAN.
HELP ME OR I'LL INFORM ON YOU.
YOU THINK THEY'LL BELIEVE YOU ? PLEAD INSANITY. IT'LL BE BELIEVED.

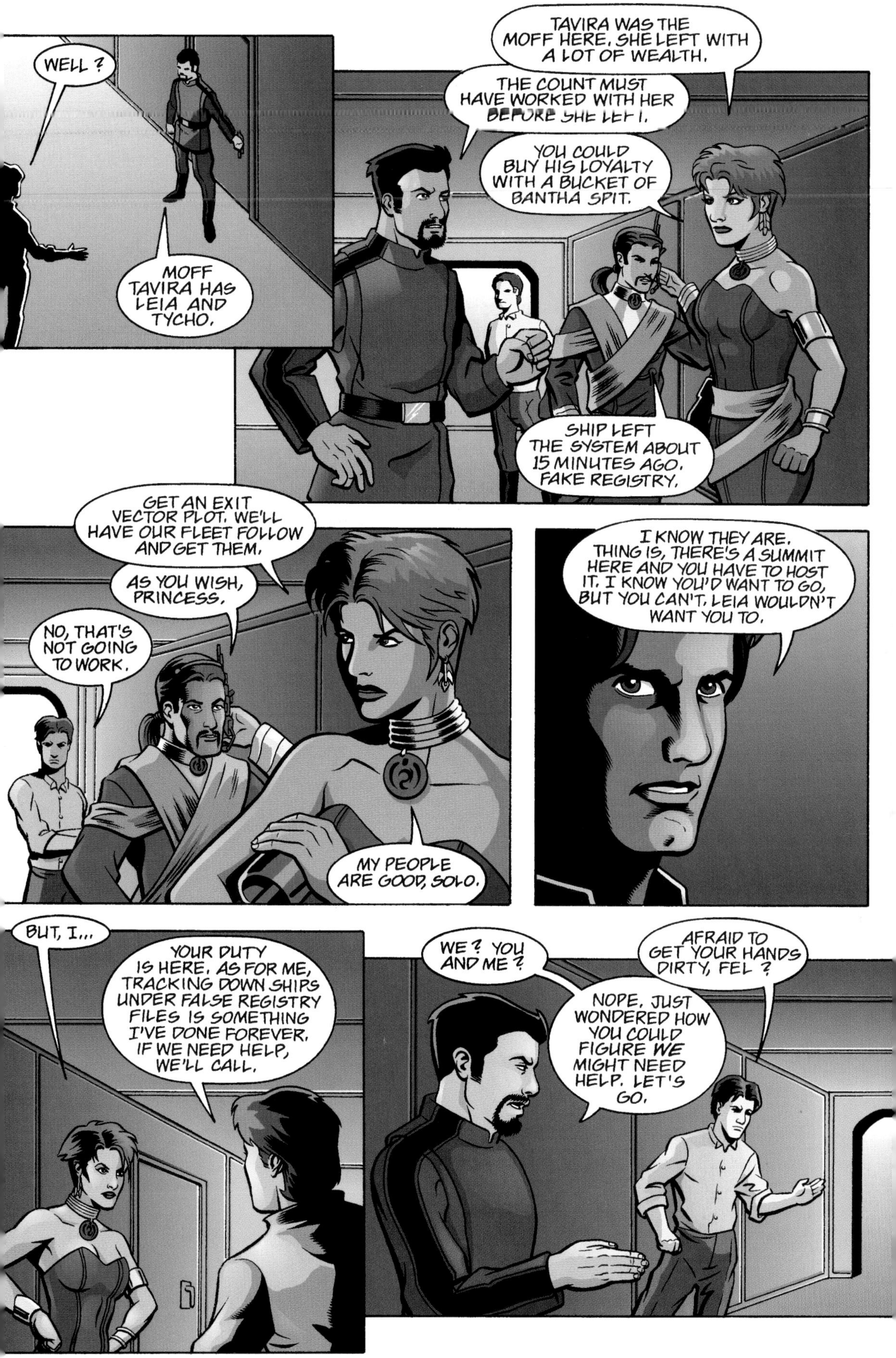
WELL ?
MOFF TAVIRA HAS LEIA AND TYCHO.
TAVIRA WAS THE MOFF HERE. SHE LEFT WITH A LOT OF WEALTH.
THE COUNT MUST HAVE WORKED WITH HER BEFORE SHE LEFT.
YOU COULD BUY HIS LOYALTY WITH A BUCKET OF BANTHA SPIT.
SHIP LEFT THE SYSTEM ABOUT 15 MINUTES AGO. FAKE REGISTRY.
GET AN EXIT VECTOR PLOT. WE'LL HAVE OUR FLEET FOLLOW AND GET THEM.
AS YOU WISH, PRINCESS.
NO, THAT'S NOT GOING TO WORK.
MY PEOPLE ARE GOOD, SOLO.
I KNOW THEY ARE. THING IS, THERE'S A SUMMIT HERE AND YOU HAVE TO HOST IT. I KNOW YOU'D WANT TO GO, BUT YOU CAN'T. LEIA WOULDN'T WANT YOU TO.
BUT, I...
YOUR DUTY IS HERE. AS FOR ME, TRACKING DOWN SHIPS UNDER FALSE REGISTRY FILES IS SOMETHING I'VE DONE FOREVER. IF WE NEED HELP, WE'LL CALL.
WE ? YOU AND ME ?
AFRAID TO GET YOUR HANDS DIRTY, FEL ?
NOPE, JUST WONDERED HOW YOU COULD FIGURE WE MIGHT NEED HELP. LET'S GO.

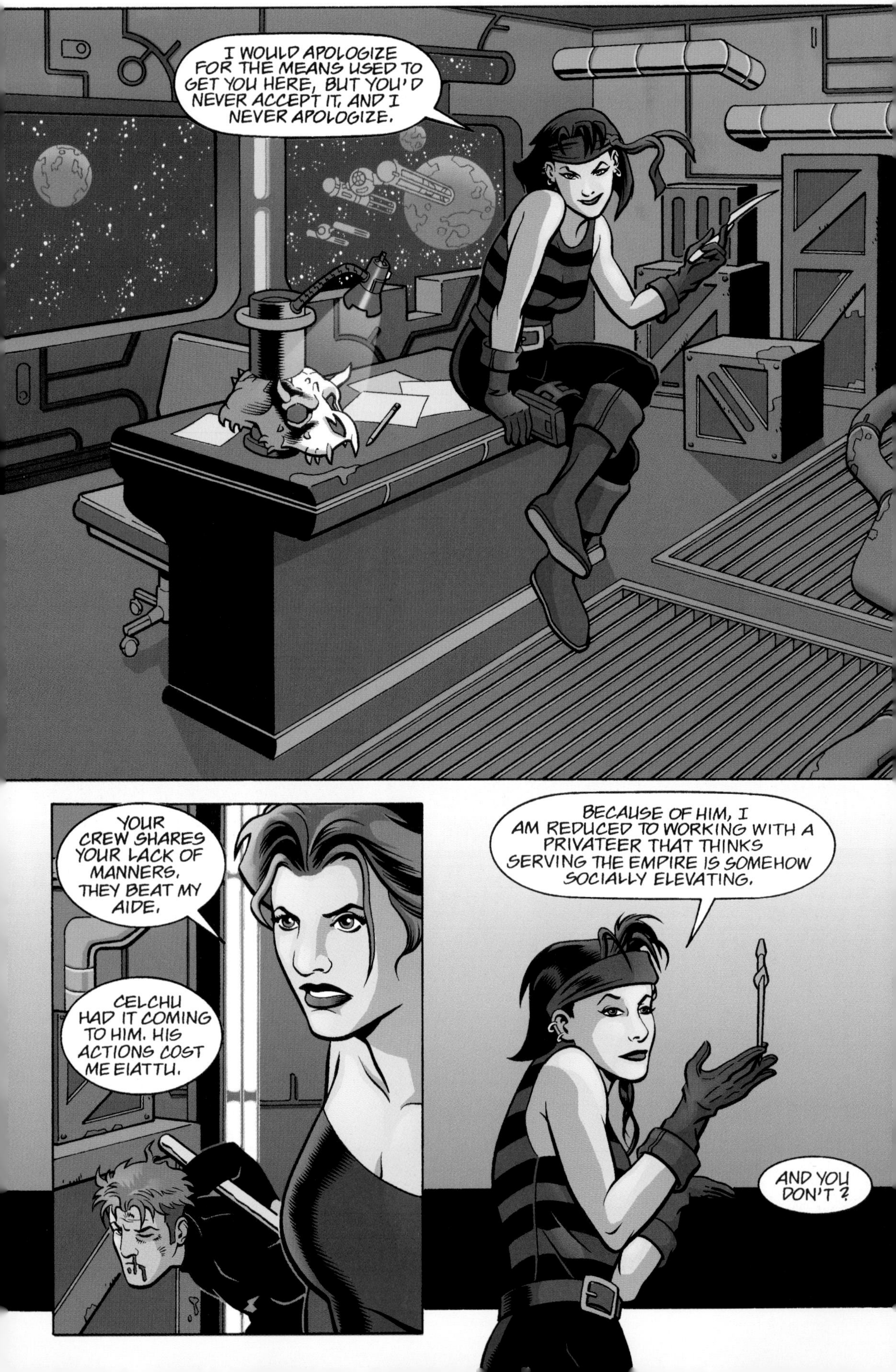
I WOULD APOLOGIZE FOR THE MEANS USED TO GET YOU HERE, BUT YOU'D NEVER ACCEPT IT, AND I NEVER APOLOGIZE.
YOUR CREW SHARES YOUR LACK OF MANNERS. THEY BEAT MY AIDE.
CELCHU HAD IT COMING TO HIM. HIS ACTIONS COST ME EIATTU.
BECAUSE OF HIM, I AM REDUCED TO WORKING WITH A PRIVATEER THAT THINKS SERVING THE EMPIRE IS SOMEHOW SOCIALLY ELEVATING.
AND YOU DON'T?

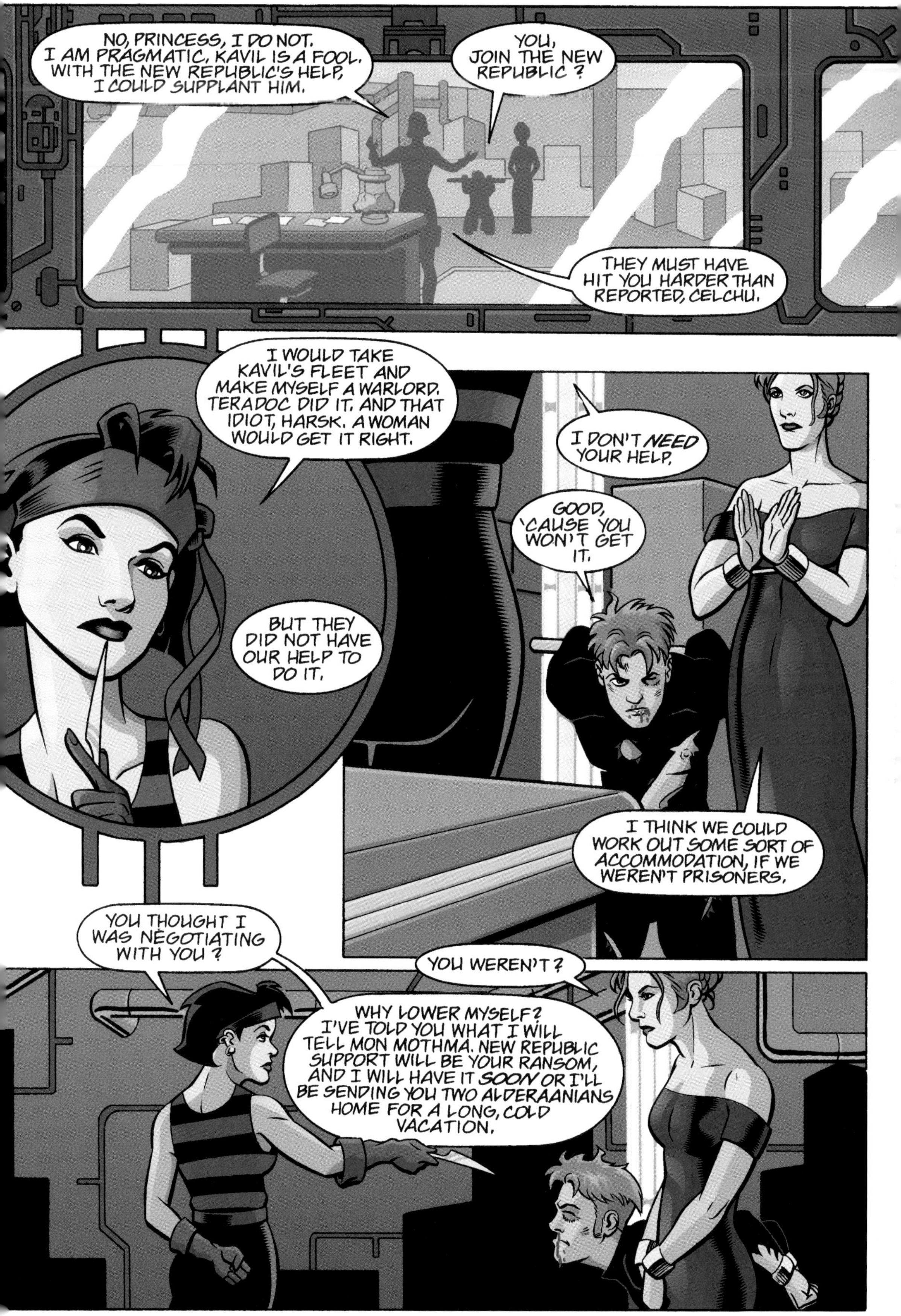
NO, PRINCESS, I DO NOT. I AM PRAGMATIC, KAVIL IS A FOOL. WITH THE NEW REPUBLIC'S HELP, I COULD SUPPLANT HIM.
YOU, JOIN THE NEW REPUBLIC ?
THEY MUST HAVE HIT YOU HARDER THAN REPORTED, CELCHU.
I WOULD TAKE KAVIL'S FLEET AND MAKE MYSELF A WARLORD. TERADOC DID IT, AND THAT IDIOT, HARSK. A WOMAN WOULD GET IT RIGHT.
BUT THEY DID NOT HAVE OUR HELP TO DO IT.
I DON'T NEED YOUR HELP.
GOOD, 'CAUSE YOU WON'T GET IT.
I THINK WE COULD WORK OUT SOME SORT OF ACCOMMODATION, IF WE WEREN'T PRISONERS.
YOU THOUGHT I WAS NEGOTIATING WITH YOU ?
YOU WEREN'T ?
WHY LOWER MYSELF? I'VE TOLD YOU WHAT I WILL TELL MON MOTHMA. NEW REPUBLIC SUPPORT WILL BE YOUR RANSOM, AND I WILL HAVE IT SOON OR I'LL BE SENDING YOU TWO ALDERAANIANS HOME FOR A LONG, COLD VACATION.

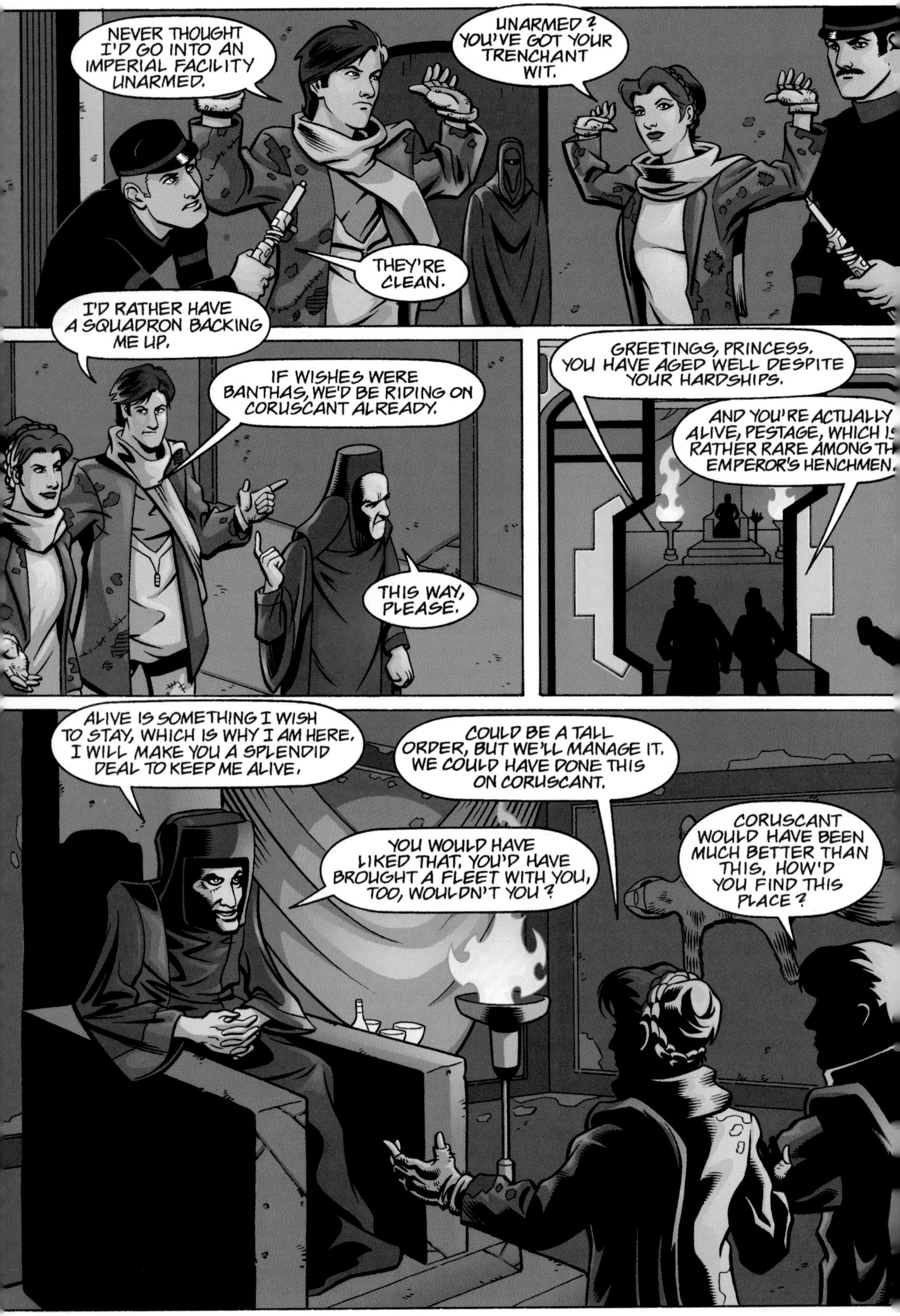
NEVER THOUGHT I'D GO INTO AN IMPERIAL FACILITY UNARMED.
UNARMED? YOU'VE GOT YOUR TRENCHANT WIT.
THEY'RE CLEAN.
I'D RATHER HAVE A SQUADRON BACKING ME UP.
IF WISHES WERE BANTHAS, WE'D BE RIDING ON CORUSCANT ALREADY.
THIS WAY, PLEASE.
GREETINGS, PRINCESS. YOU HAVE AGED WELL DESPITE YOUR HARDSHIPS.
AND YOU'RE ACTUALLY ALIVE, PESTAGE, WHICH IS RATHER RARE AMONG THE EMPEROR'S HENCHMEN.
ALIVE IS SOMETHING I WISH TO STAY, WHICH IS WHY I AM HERE. I WILL MAKE YOU A SPLENDID DEAL TO KEEP ME ALIVE.
COULD BE A TALL ORDER, BUT WE'LL MANAGE IT. WE COULD HAVE DONE THIS ON CORUSCANT.
YOU WOULD HAVE LIKED THAT. YOU'D HAVE BROUGHT A FLEET WITH YOU, TOO, WOULDN'T YOU?
CORUSCANT WOULD HAVE BEEN MUCH BETTER THAN THIS. HOW'D YOU FIND THIS PLACE?

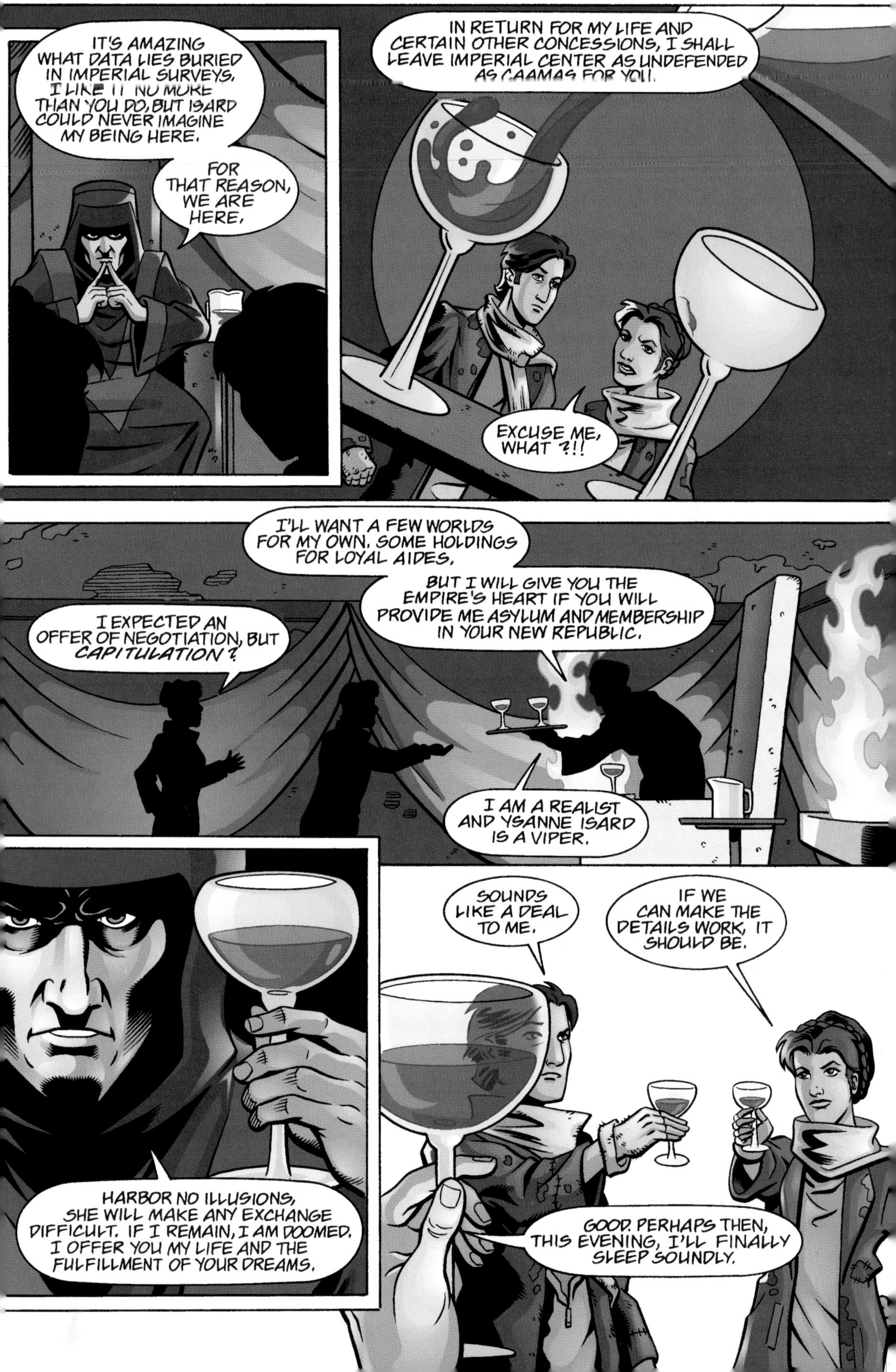
IT'S AMAZING WHAT DATA LIES BURIED IN IMPERIAL SURVEYS. I LIKE IT NO MORE THAN YOU DO, BUT ISARD COULD NEVER IMAGINE MY BEING HERE.
FOR THAT REASON, WE ARE HERE.
IN RETURN FOR MY LIFE AND CERTAIN OTHER CONCESSIONS, I SHALL LEAVE IMPERIAL CENTER AS UNDEFENDED AS CAAMAS FOR YOU.
EXCUSE ME, WHAT ?!!
I'LL WANT A FEW WORLDS FOR MY OWN, SOME HOLDINGS FOR LOYAL AIDES.
BUT I WILL GIVE YOU THE EMPIRE'S HEART IF YOU WILL PROVIDE ME ASYLUM AND MEMBERSHIP IN YOUR NEW REPUBLIC.
I EXPECTED AN OFFER OF NEGOTIATION, BUT *CAPITULATION*?
I AM A REALIST AND YSANNE ISARD IS A VIPER.
HARBOR NO ILLUSIONS, SHE WILL MAKE ANY EXCHANGE DIFFICULT. IF I REMAIN, I AM DOOMED. I OFFER YOU MY LIFE AND THE FULFILLMENT OF YOUR DREAMS.
SOUNDS LIKE A DEAL TO ME.
IF WE CAN MAKE THE DETAILS WORK, IT SHOULD BE.
GOOD. PERHAPS THEN, THIS EVENING, I'LL FINALLY SLEEP SOUNDLY.

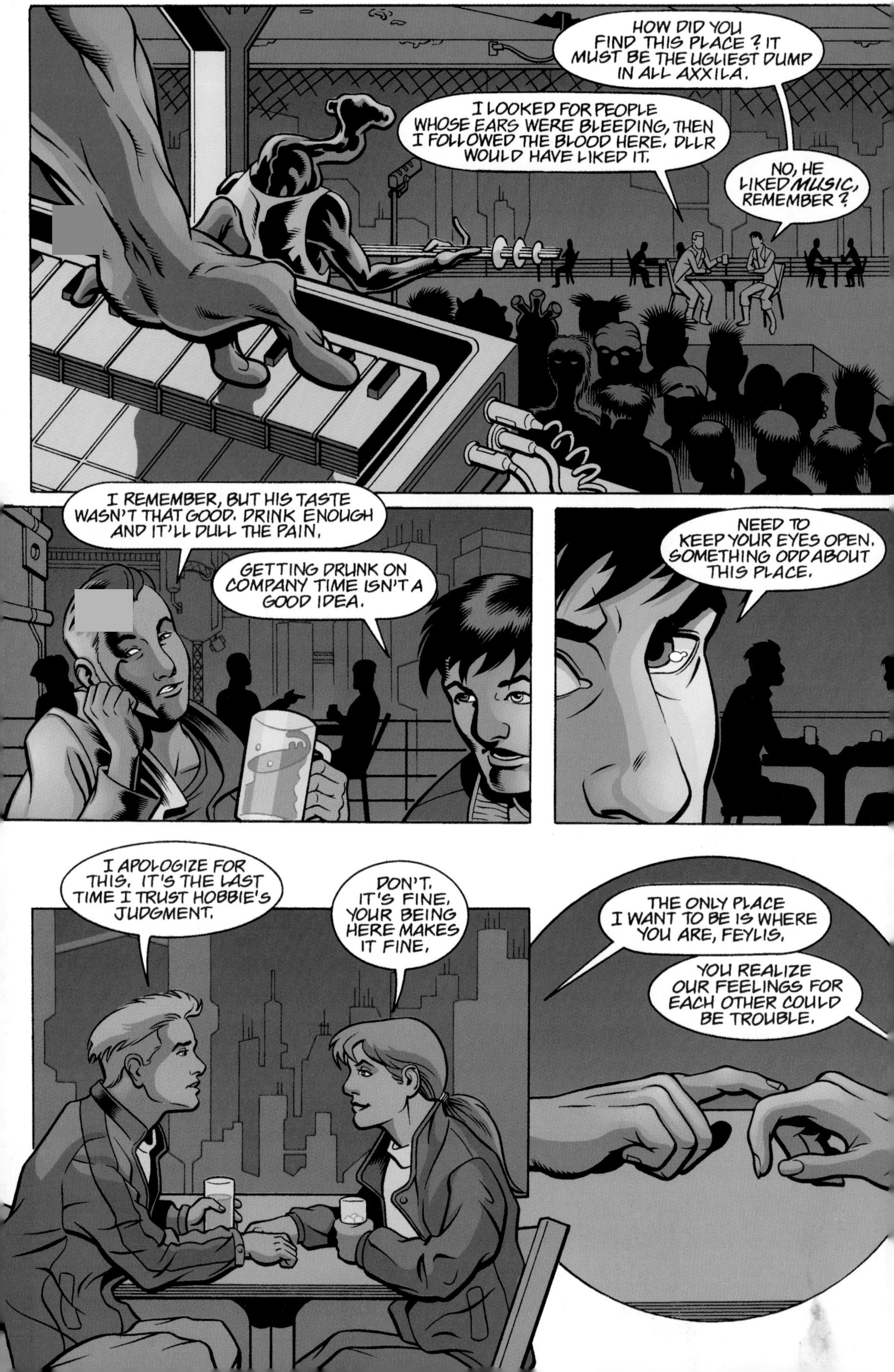

HOW DID YOU FIND THIS PLACE ? IT MUST BE THE UGLIEST DUMP IN ALL AXXILA.
I LOOKED FOR PEOPLE WHOSE EARS WERE BLEEDING, THEN I FOLLOWED THE BLOOD HERE. DLLR WOULD HAVE LIKED IT.
NO, HE LIKED MUSIC, REMEMBER ?
I REMEMBER, BUT HIS TASTE WASN'T THAT GOOD. DRINK ENOUGH AND IT'LL DULL THE PAIN.
GETTING DRUNK ON COMPANY TIME ISN'T A GOOD IDEA.
NEED TO KEEP YOUR EYES OPEN. SOMETHING ODD ABOUT THIS PLACE.
I APOLOGIZE FOR THIS. IT'S THE LAST TIME I TRUST HOBBIE'S JUDGMENT.
DON'T. IT'S FINE. YOUR BEING HERE MAKES IT FINE.
THE ONLY PLACE I WANT TO BE IS WHERE YOU ARE, FEYLIS.
YOU REALIZE OUR FEELINGS FOR EACH OTHER COULD BE TROUBLE.

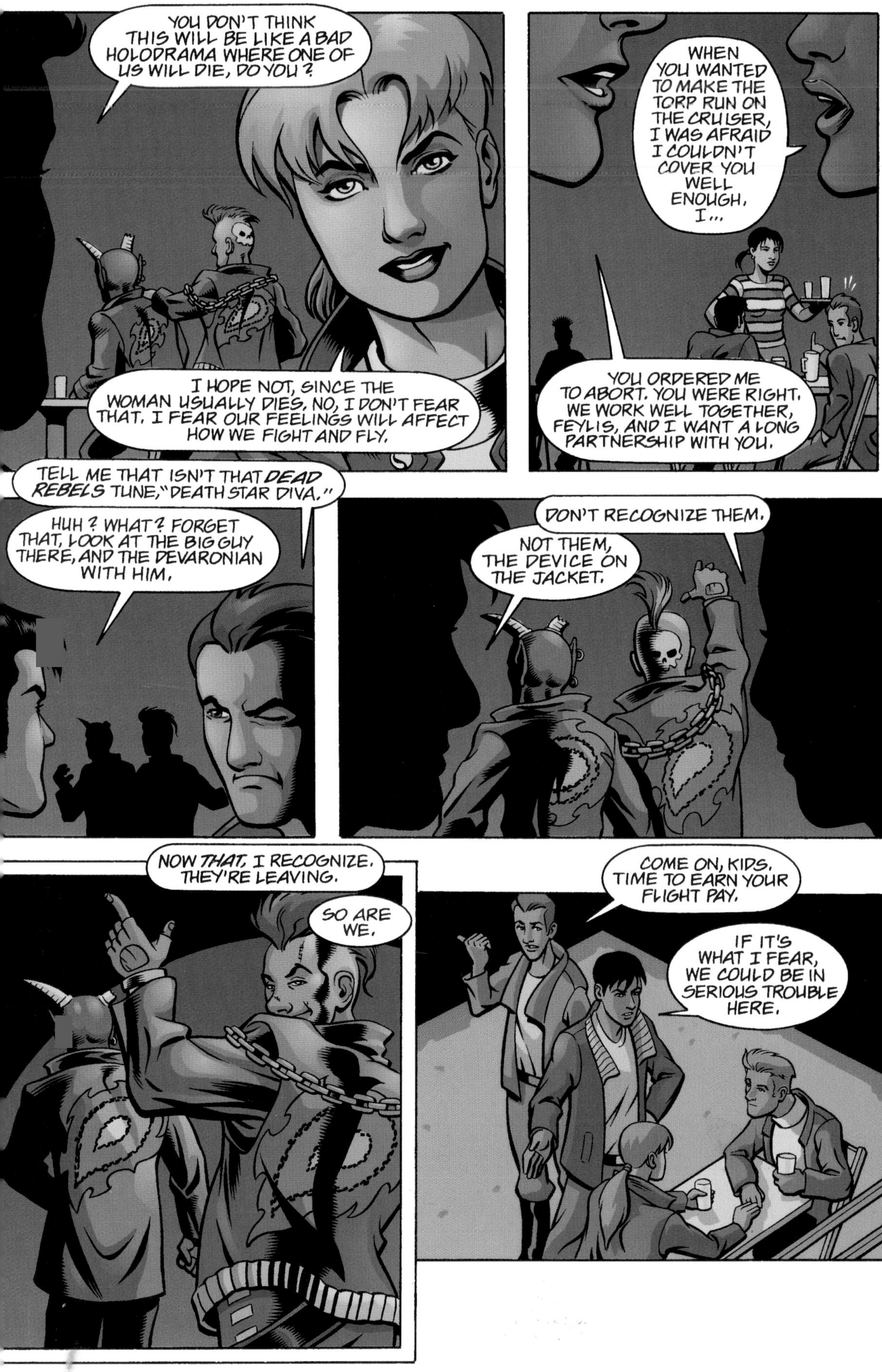
YOU DON'T THINK THIS WILL BE LIKE A BAD HOLODRAMA WHERE ONE OF US WILL DIE, DO YOU?
I HOPE NOT, SINCE THE WOMAN USUALLY DIES. NO, I DON'T FEAR THAT. I FEAR OUR FEELINGS WILL AFFECT HOW WE FIGHT AND FLY.
WHEN YOU WANTED TO MAKE THE TORP RUN ON THE CRUISER, I WAS AFRAID I COULDN'T COVER YOU WELL ENOUGH. I...
YOU ORDERED ME TO ABORT. YOU WERE RIGHT. WE WORK WELL TOGETHER, FEYLIS, AND I WANT A LONG PARTNERSHIP WITH YOU.
TELL ME THAT ISN'T THAT *DEAD REBELS* TUNE, "DEATH STAR DIVA."
HUH? WHAT? FORGET THAT. LOOK AT THE BIG GUY THERE, AND THE DEVARONIAN WITH HIM.
DON'T RECOGNIZE THEM.
NOT THEM, THE DEVICE ON THE JACKET.
NOW *THAT*, I RECOGNIZE. THEY'RE LEAVING.
SO ARE WE.
COME ON, KIDS. TIME TO EARN YOUR FLIGHT PAY.
IF IT'S WHAT I FEAR, WE COULD BE IN SERIOUS TROUBLE HERE.

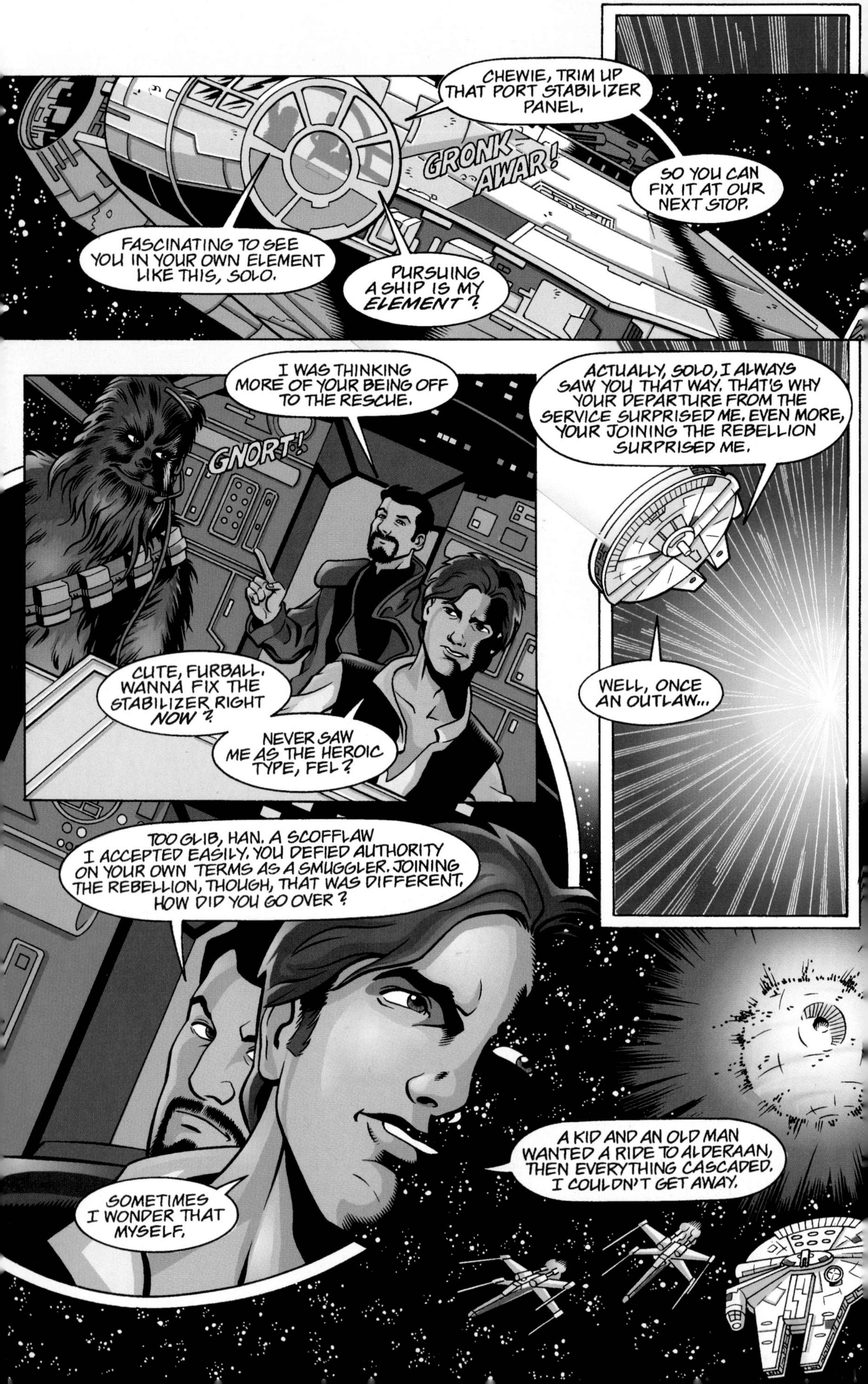
CHEWIE, TRIM UP THAT PORT STABILIZER PANEL.
GRONK AWAR!
SO YOU CAN FIX IT AT OUR NEXT STOP.
FASCINATING TO SEE YOU IN YOUR OWN ELEMENT LIKE THIS, SOLO.
PURSUING A SHIP IS MY ELEMENT?
I WAS THINKING MORE OF YOUR BEING OFF TO THE RESCUE.
GNORT!
CUTE, FURBALL. WANNA FIX THE STABILIZER RIGHT NOW?
NEVER SAW ME AS THE HEROIC TYPE, FEL?
ACTUALLY, SOLO, I ALWAYS SAW YOU THAT WAY. THAT'S WHY YOUR DEPARTURE FROM THE SERVICE SURPRISED ME. EVEN MORE, YOUR JOINING THE REBELLION SURPRISED ME.
WELL, ONCE AN OUTLAW...
TOO GLIB, HAN. A SCOFFLAW I ACCEPTED EASILY. YOU DEFIED AUTHORITY ON YOUR OWN TERMS AS A SMUGGLER. JOINING THE REBELLION, THOUGH, THAT WAS DIFFERENT. HOW DID YOU GO OVER?
SOMETIMES I WONDER THAT MYSELF.
A KID AND AN OLD MAN WANTED A RIDE TO ALDERAAN, THEN EVERYTHING CASCADED. I COULDN'T GET AWAY.

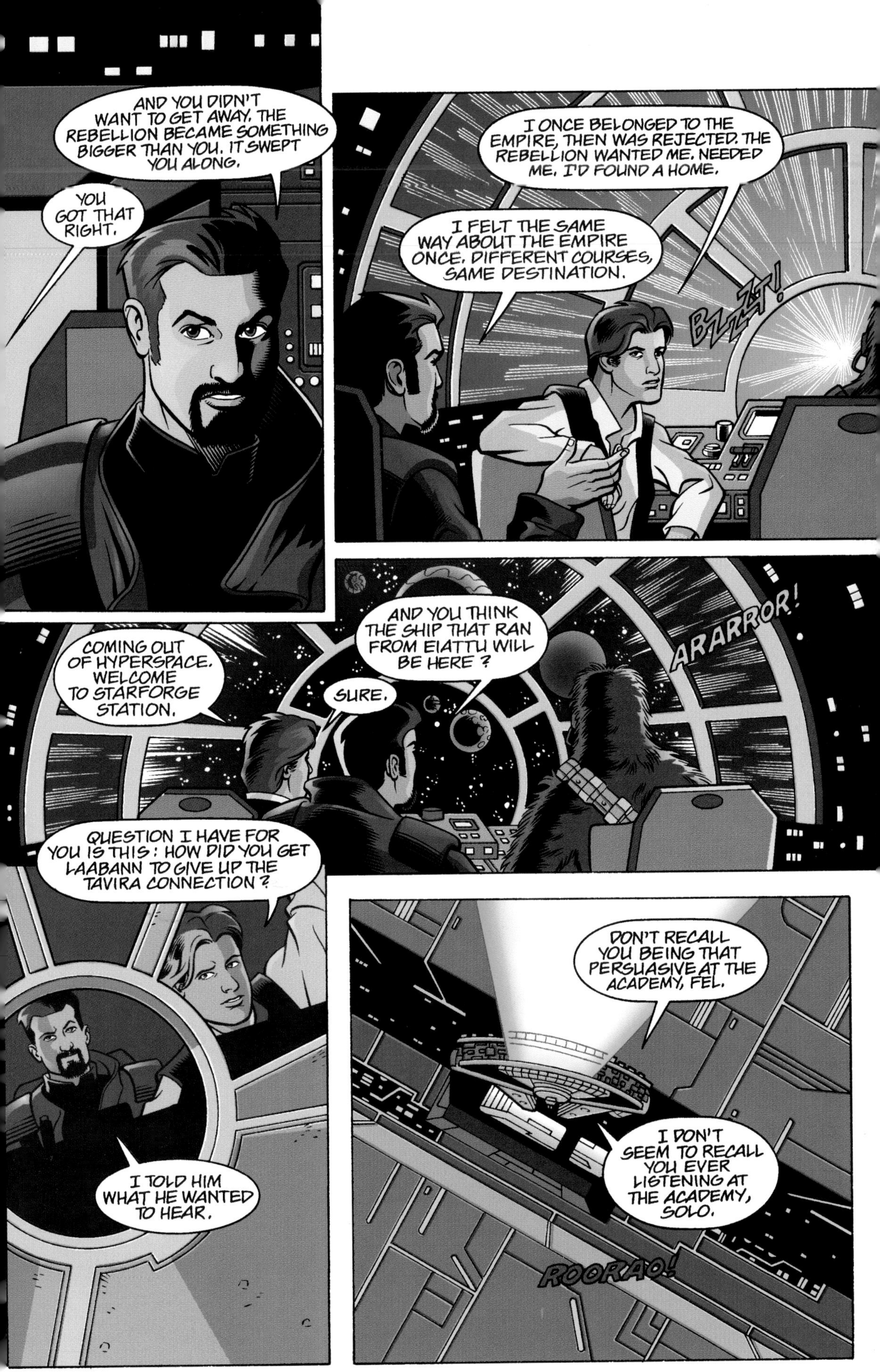
AND YOU DIDN'T WANT TO GET AWAY. THE REBELLION BECAME SOMETHING BIGGER THAN YOU. IT SWEPT YOU ALONG.
YOU GOT THAT RIGHT.
I ONCE BELONGED TO THE EMPIRE, THEN WAS REJECTED. THE REBELLION WANTED ME. NEEDED ME. I'D FOUND A HOME.
I FELT THE SAME WAY ABOUT THE EMPIRE ONCE. DIFFERENT COURSES, SAME DESTINATION.
BZZZT!
COMING OUT OF HYPERSPACE. WELCOME TO STARFORGE STATION.
AND YOU THINK THE SHIP THAT RAN FROM EIATTU WILL BE HERE ?
SURE.
ARARROR!
QUESTION I HAVE FOR YOU IS THIS : HOW DID YOU GET LAABANN TO GIVE UP THE TAVIRA CONNECTION ?
I TOLD HIM WHAT HE WANTED TO HEAR.
DON'T RECALL YOU BEING THAT PERSUASIVE AT THE ACADEMY, FEL.
I DON'T SEEM TO RECALL YOU EVER LISTENING AT THE ACADEMY, SOLO.
ROORAO!

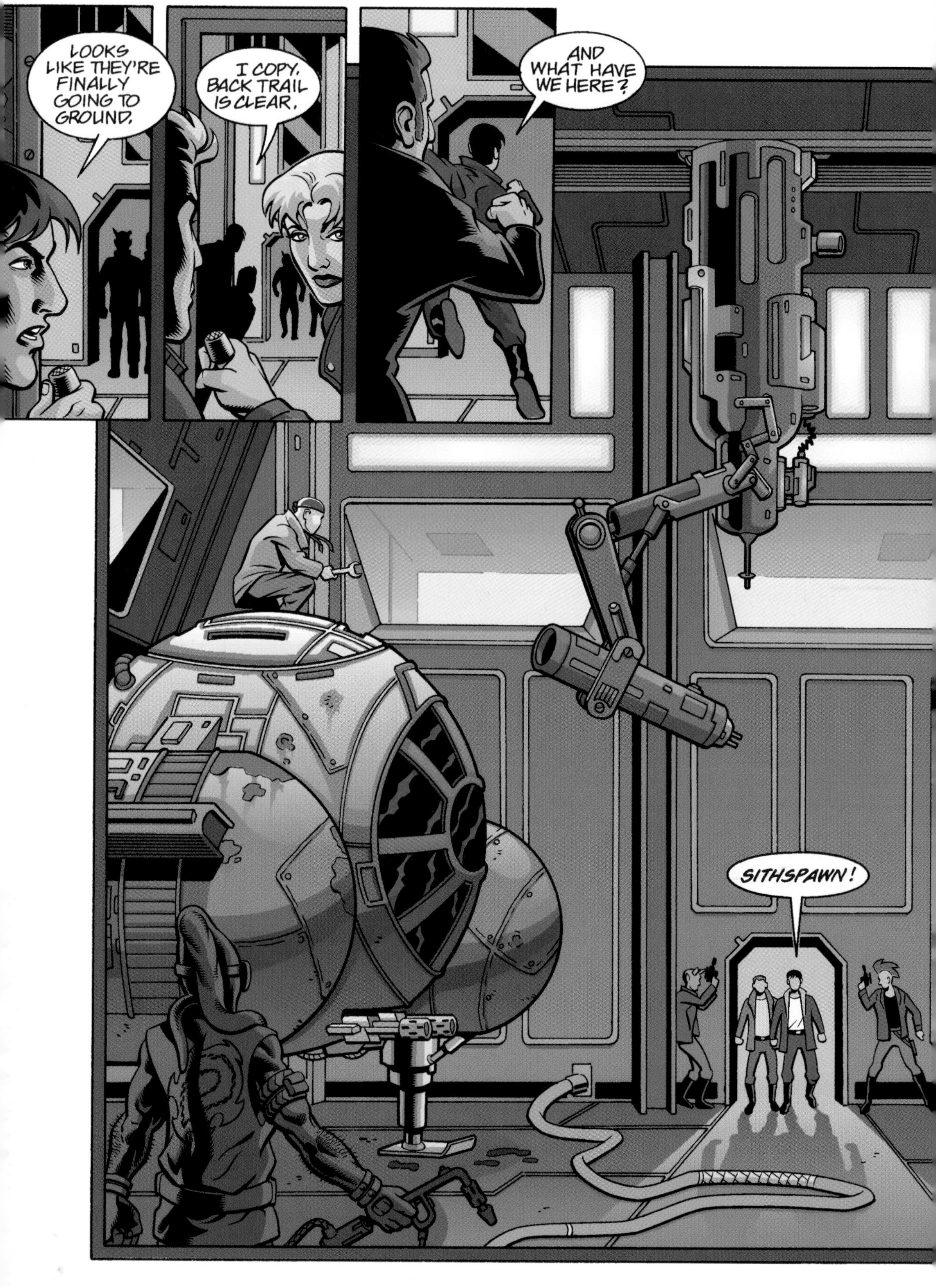
LOOKS LIKE THEY'RE FINALLY GOING TO GROUND.
I COPY. BACK TRAIL IS CLEAR.
AND WHAT HAVE WE HERE?
SITHSPAWN!

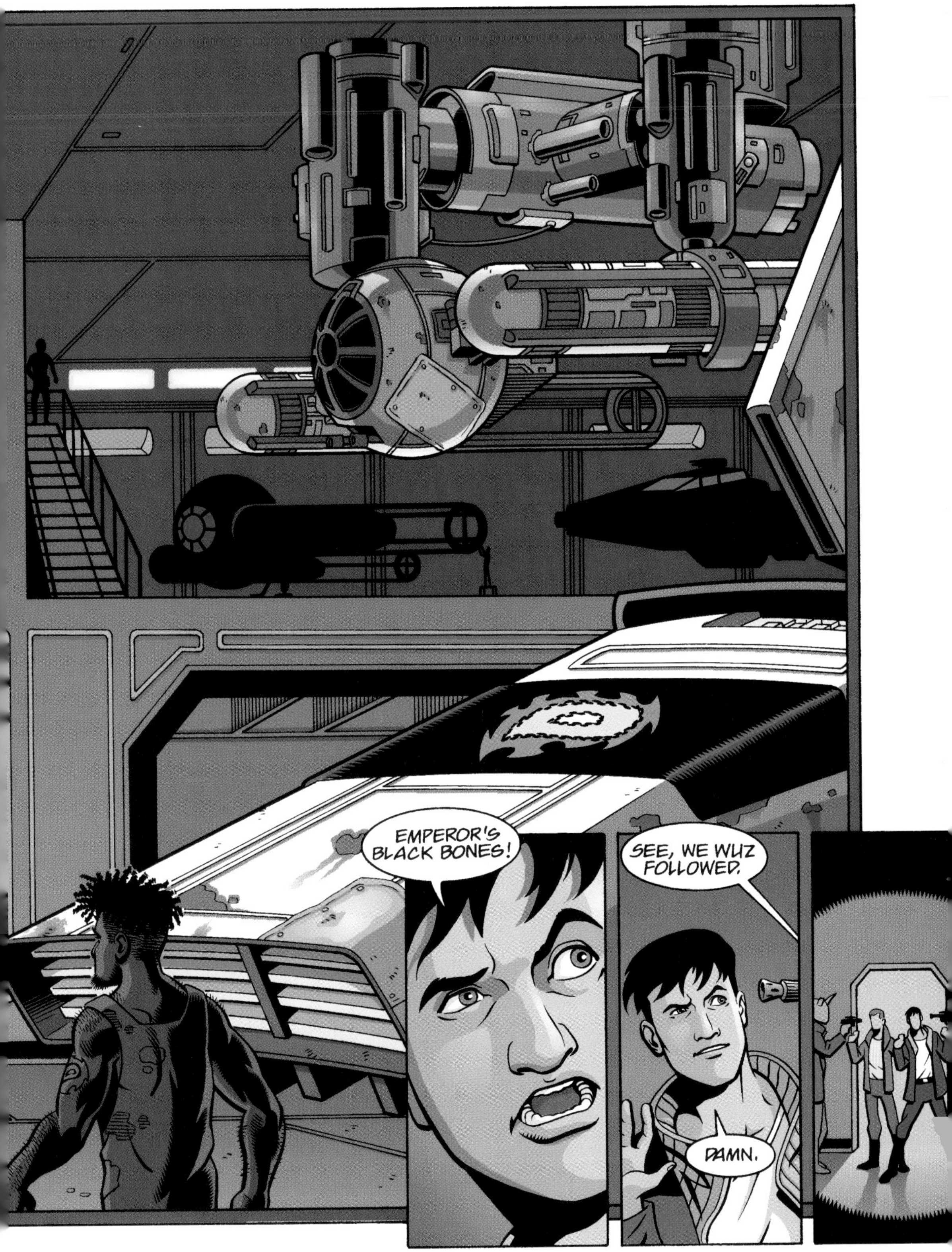
EMPEROR'S BLACK BONES!
SEE, WE WUZ FOLLOWED.
DAMN.

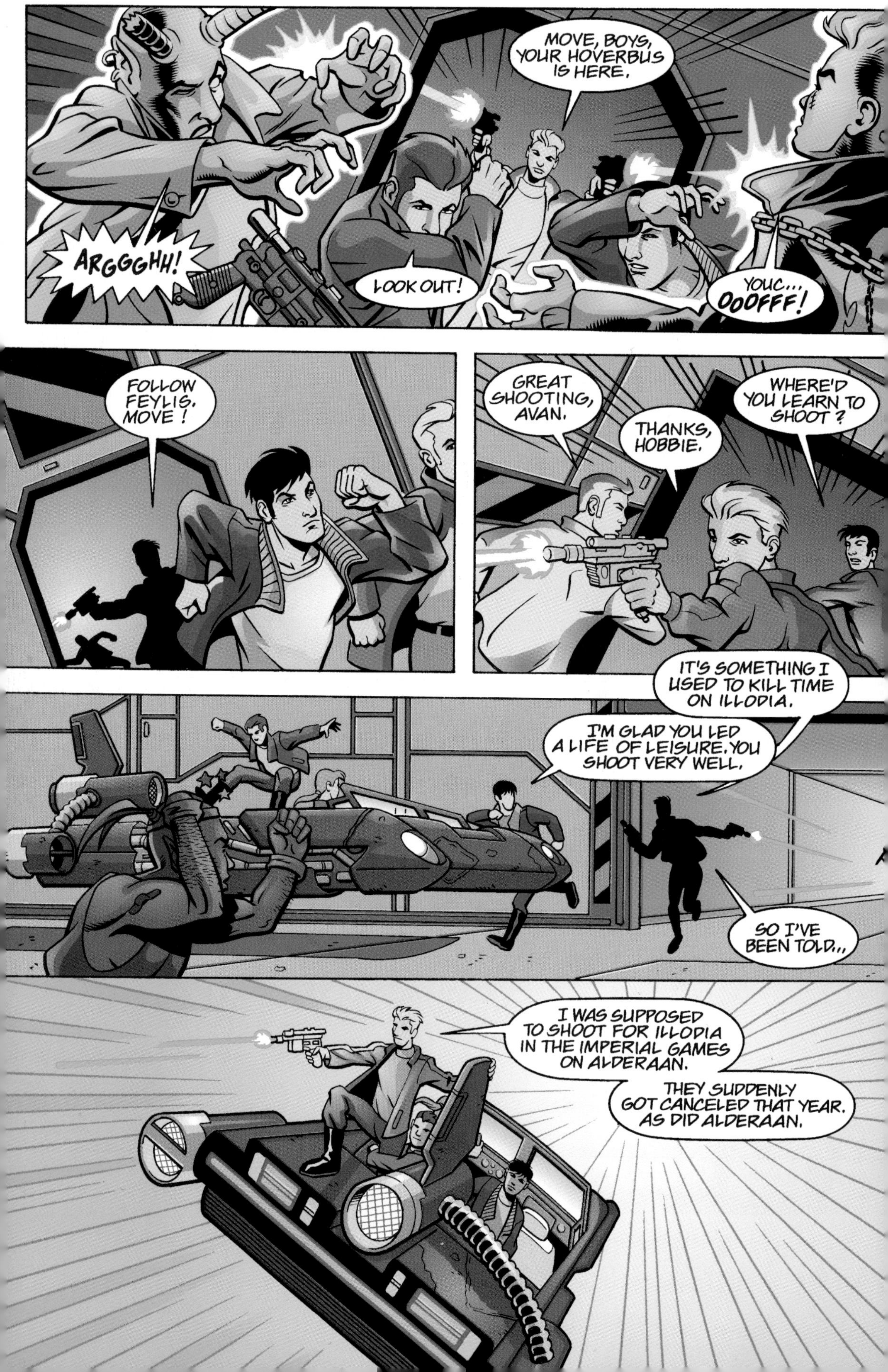
MOVE, BOYS, YOUR HOVERBUS IS HERE.
ARGGGHH!
LOOK OUT!
YOUC... OOOFFF!
FOLLOW FEYLIS. MOVE!
GREAT SHOOTING, AVAN.
THANKS, HOBBIE.
WHERE'D YOU LEARN TO SHOOT?
IT'S SOMETHING I USED TO KILL TIME ON ILLODIA.
I'M GLAD YOU LED A LIFE OF LEISURE. YOU SHOOT VERY WELL.
SO I'VE BEEN TOLD...
I WAS SUPPOSED TO SHOOT FOR ILLODIA IN THE IMPERIAL GAMES ON ALDERAAN.
THEY SUDDENLY GOT CANCELED THAT YEAR. AS DID ALDERAAN.

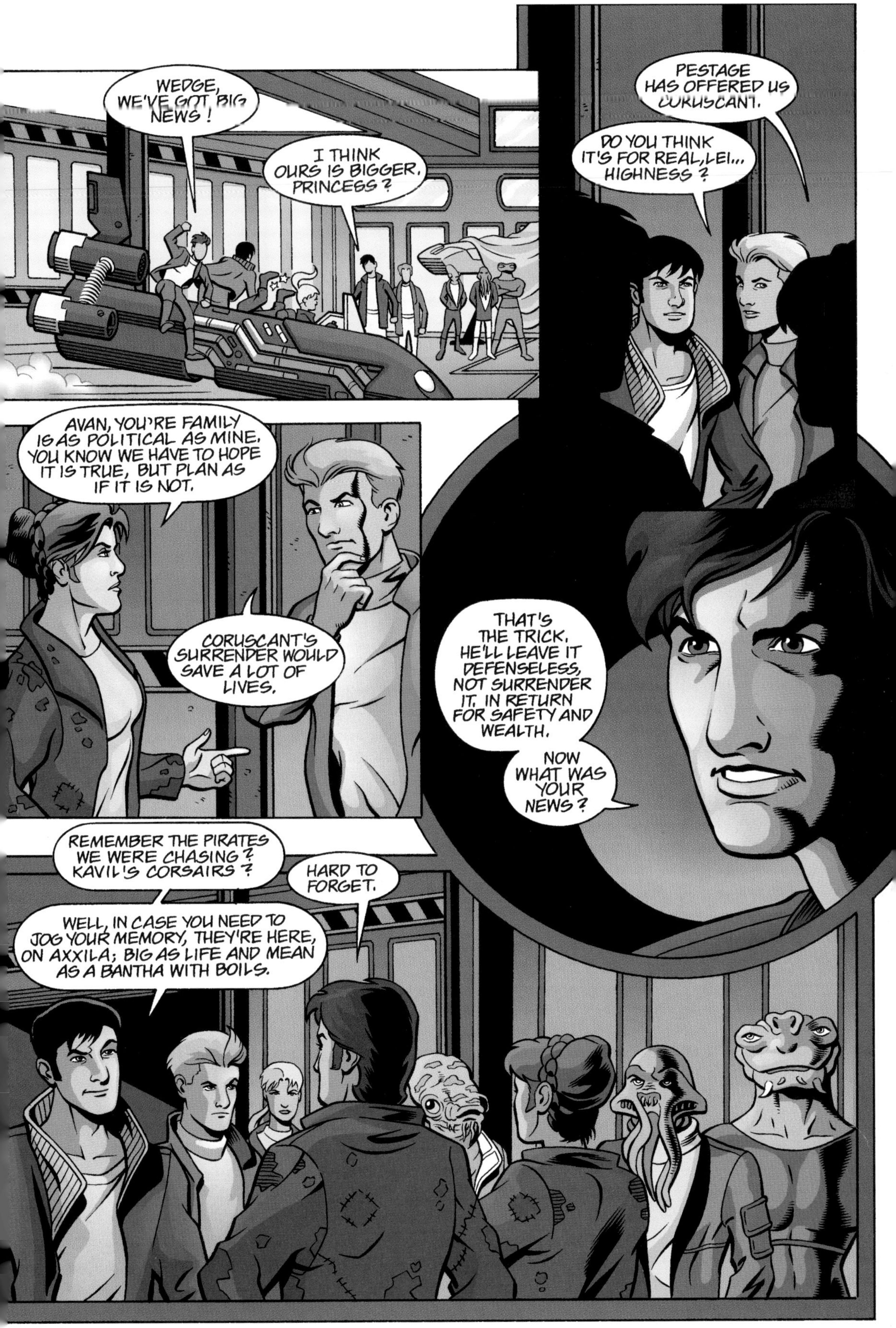
WEDGE, WE'VE GOT BIG NEWS !
I THINK OURS IS BIGGER, PRINCESS ?
PESTAGE HAS OFFERED US CORUSCANT.
DO YOU THINK IT'S FOR REAL, LEI... HIGHNESS ?
AVAN, YOU'RE FAMILY IS AS POLITICAL AS MINE. YOU KNOW WE HAVE TO HOPE IT IS TRUE, BUT PLAN AS IF IT IS NOT.
CORUSCANT'S SURRENDER WOULD SAVE A LOT OF LIVES.
THAT'S THE TRICK, HE'LL LEAVE IT DEFENSELESS, NOT SURRENDER IT, IN RETURN FOR SAFETY AND WEALTH.
NOW WHAT WAS YOUR NEWS ?
REMEMBER THE PIRATES WE WERE CHASING ? KAVIL'S CORSAIRS ?
HARD TO FORGET.
WELL, IN CASE YOU NEED TO JOG YOUR MEMORY, THEY'RE HERE, ON AXXILA; BIG AS LIFE AND MEAN AS A BANTHA WITH BOILS.

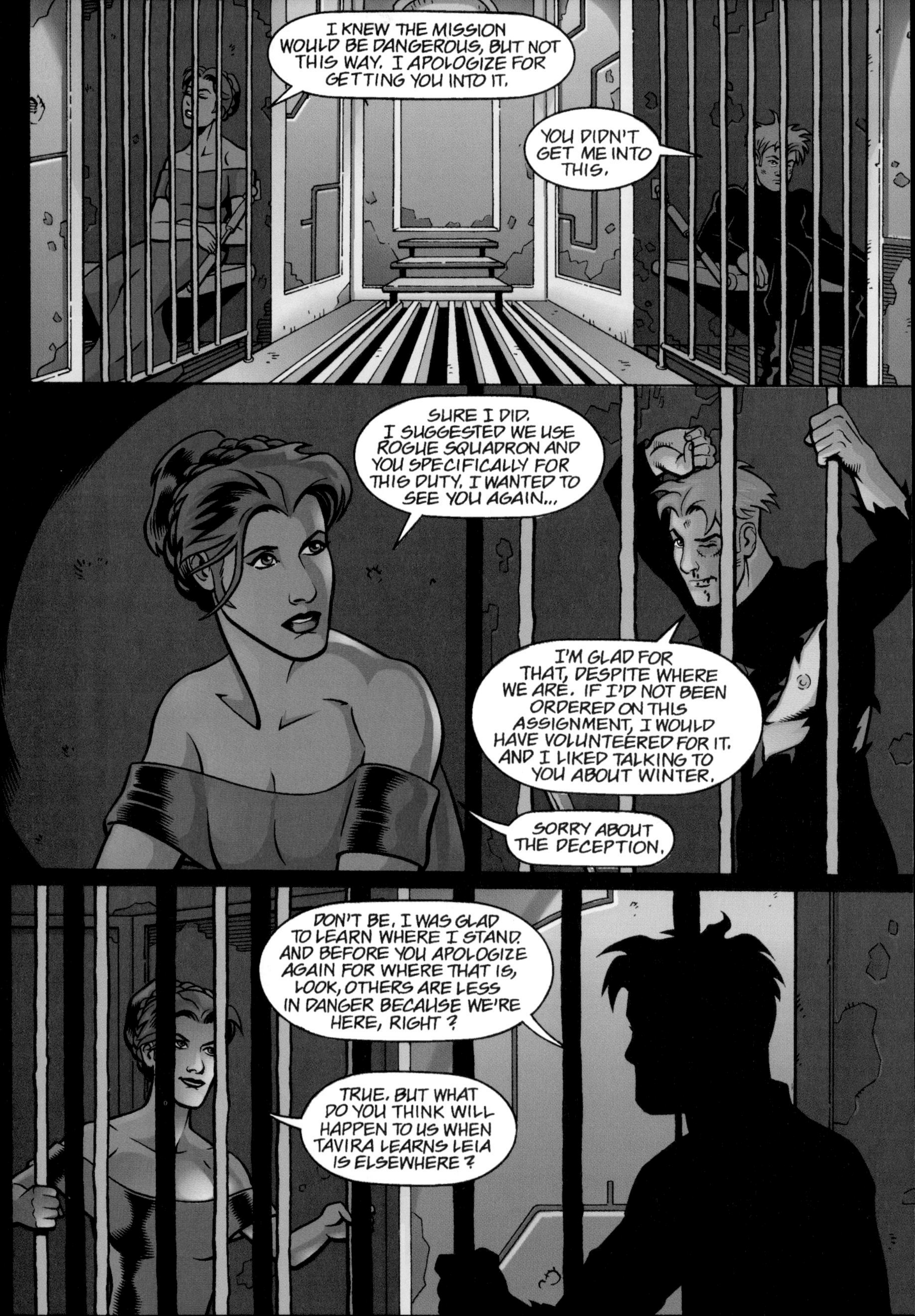
I KNEW THE MISSION WOULD BE DANGEROUS, BUT NOT THIS WAY. I APOLOGIZE FOR GETTING YOU INTO IT.
YOU DIDN'T GET ME INTO THIS.
SURE I DID. I SUGGESTED WE USE ROGUE SQUADRON AND YOU SPECIFICALLY FOR THIS DUTY. I WANTED TO SEE YOU AGAIN...
I'M GLAD FOR THAT, DESPITE WHERE WE ARE. IF I'D NOT BEEN ORDERED ON THIS ASSIGNMENT, I WOULD HAVE VOLUNTEERED FOR IT. AND I LIKED TALKING TO YOU ABOUT WINTER.
SORRY ABOUT THE DECEPTION.
DON'T BE. I WAS GLAD TO LEARN WHERE I STAND. AND BEFORE YOU APOLOGIZE AGAIN FOR WHERE THAT IS, LOOK, OTHERS ARE LESS IN DANGER BECAUSE WE'RE HERE, RIGHT?
TRUE. BUT WHAT DO YOU THINK WILL HAPPEN TO US WHEN TAVIRA LEARNS LEIA IS ELSEWHERE?

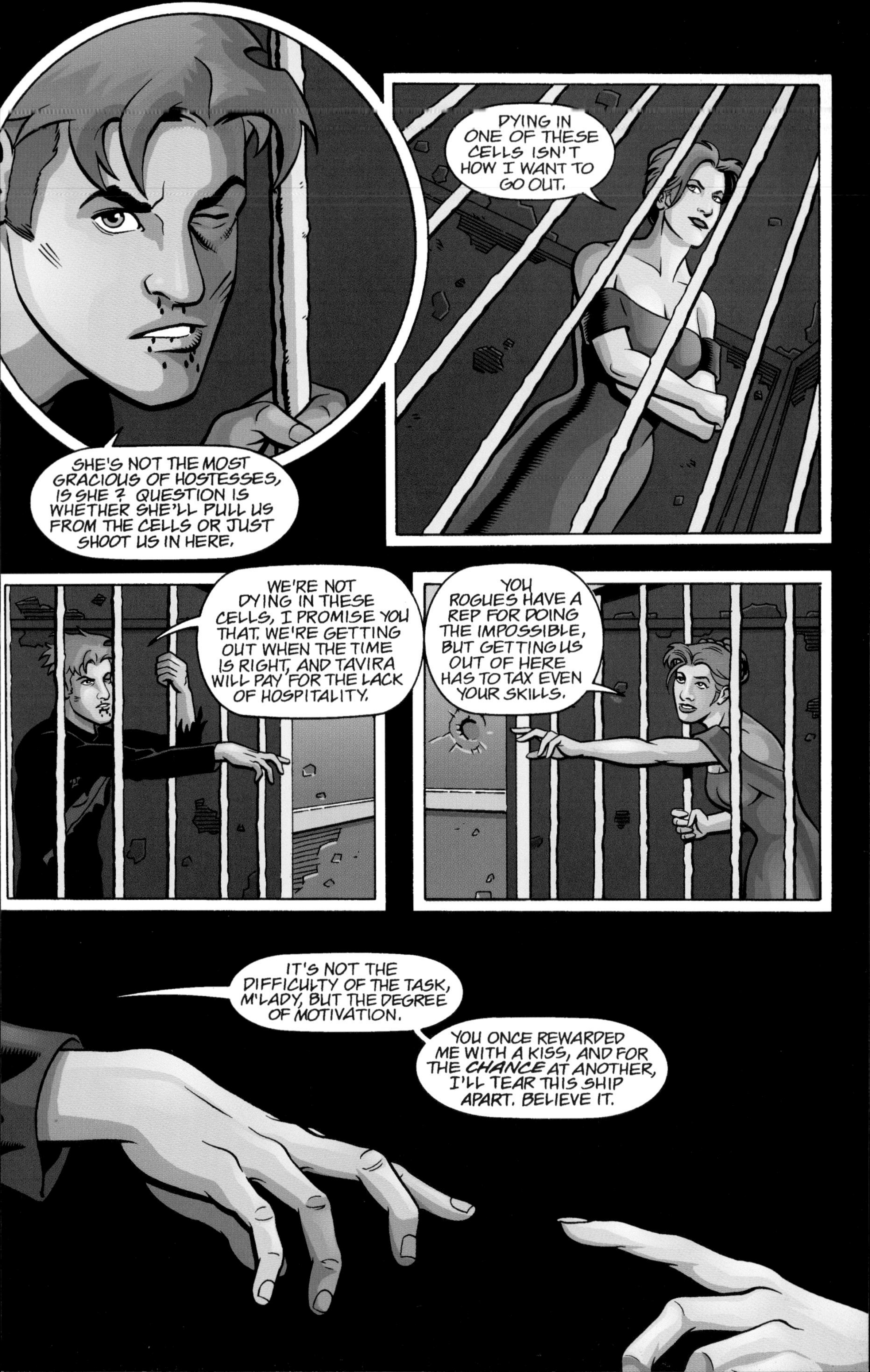
DYING IN ONE OF THESE CELLS ISN'T HOW I WANT TO GO OUT.
SHE'S NOT THE MOST GRACIOUS OF HOSTESSES, IS SHE? QUESTION IS WHETHER SHE'LL PULL US FROM THE CELLS OR JUST SHOOT US IN HERE.
WE'RE NOT DYING IN THESE CELLS, I PROMISE YOU THAT. WE'RE GETTING OUT WHEN THE TIME IS RIGHT, AND TAVIRA WILL PAY FOR THE LACK OF HOSPITALITY.
YOU ROGUES HAVE A REP FOR DOING THE IMPOSSIBLE, BUT GETTING US OUT OF HERE HAS TO TAX EVEN YOUR SKILLS.
IT'S NOT THE DIFFICULTY OF THE TASK, M'LADY, BUT THE DEGREE OF MOTIVATION.
YOU ONCE REWARDED ME WITH A KISS, AND FOR THE *CHANCE* AT ANOTHER, I'LL TEAR THIS SHIP APART. BELIEVE IT.

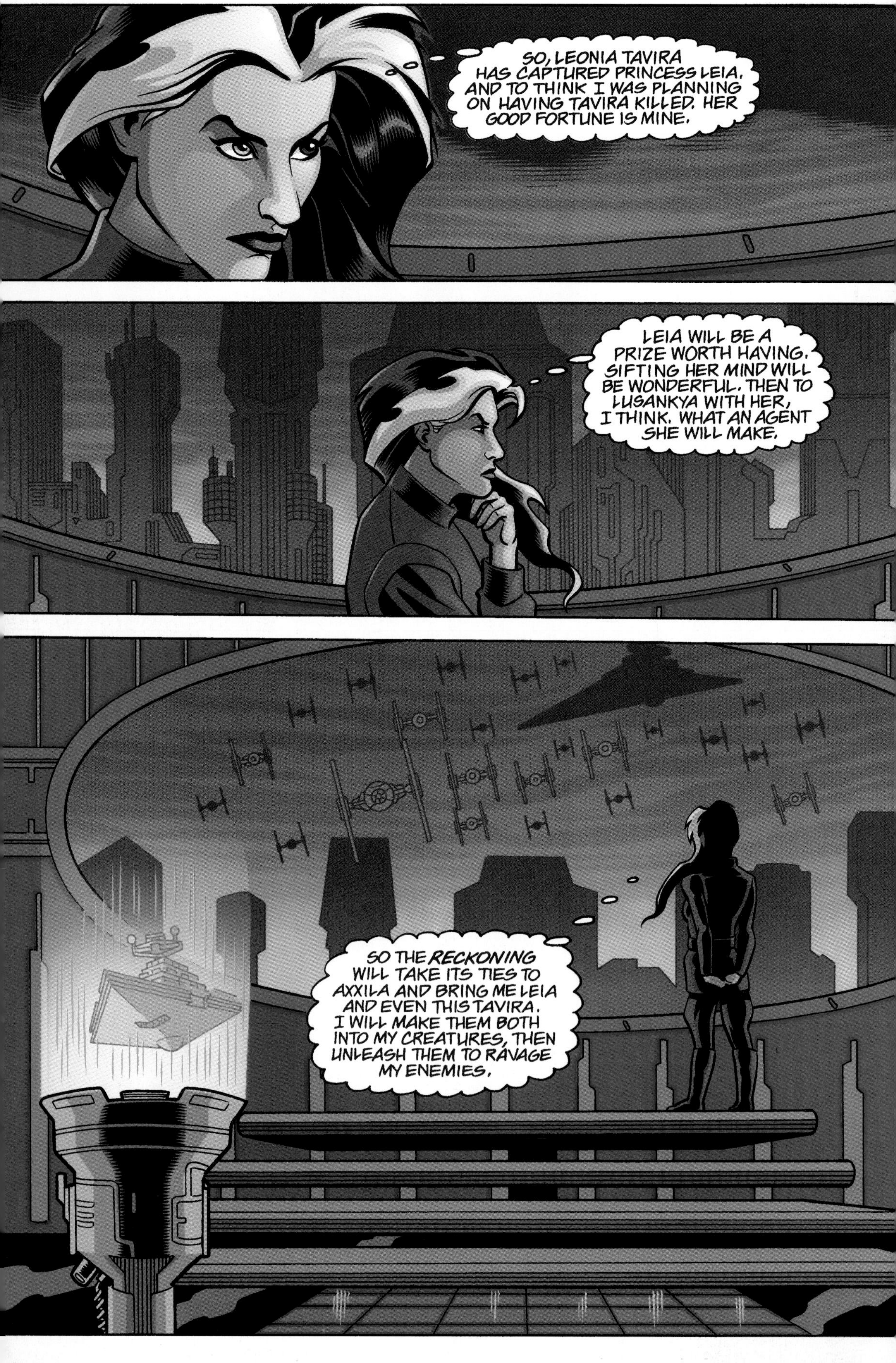
SO, LEONIA TAVIRA HAS CAPTURED PRINCESS LEIA. AND TO THINK I WAS PLANNING ON HAVING TAVIRA KILLED. HER GOOD FORTUNE IS MINE.
LEIA WILL BE A PRIZE WORTH HAVING. SIFTING HER MIND WILL BE WONDERFUL. THEN TO LUSANKYA WITH HER, I THINK. WHAT AN AGENT SHE WILL MAKE.
SO THE *RECKONING* WILL TAKE ITS TIES TO AXXILA AND BRING ME LEIA AND EVEN THIS TAVIRA. I WILL MAKE THEM BOTH INTO MY CREATURES, THEN UNLEASH THEM TO RAVAGE MY ENEMIES.

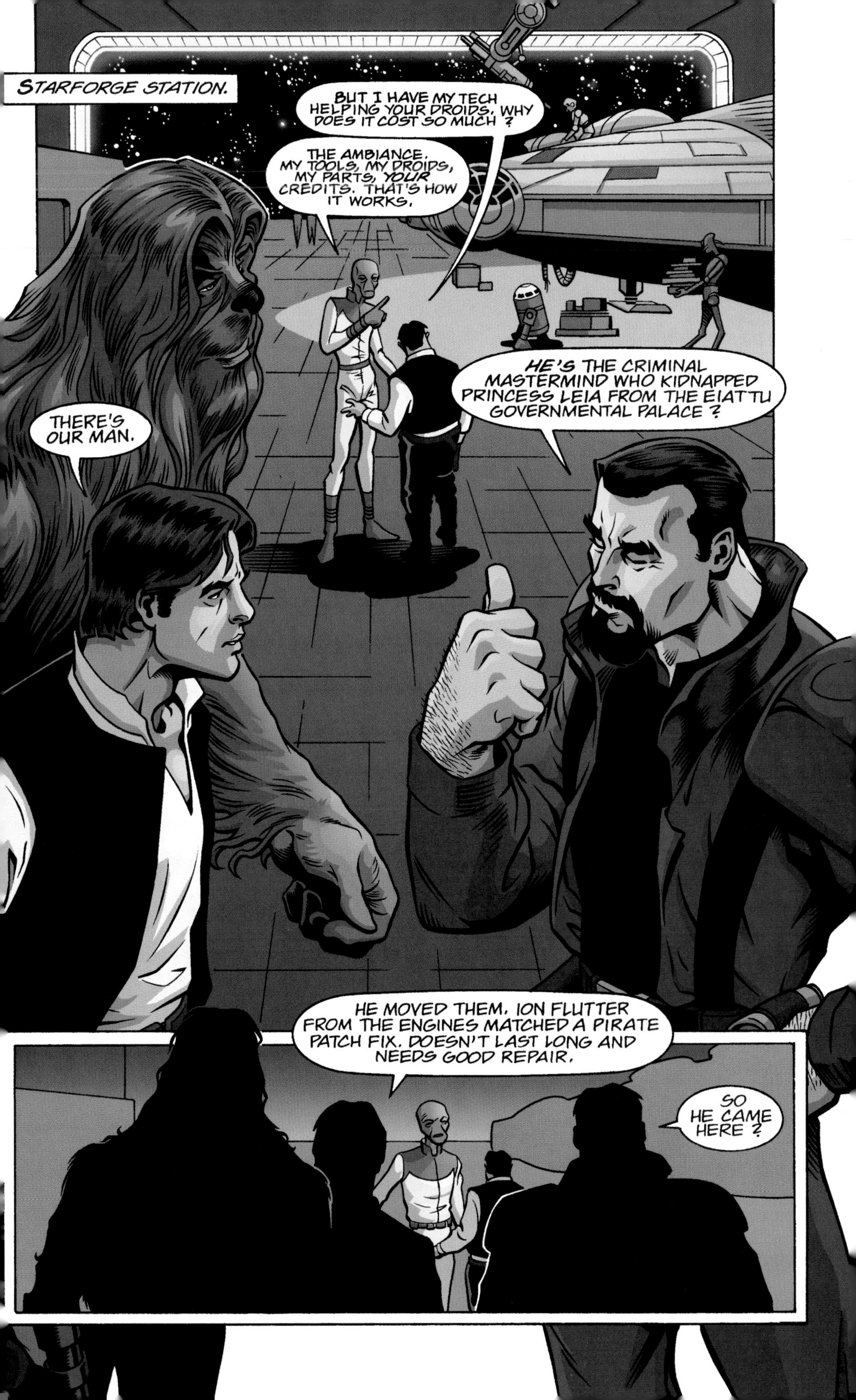
STARFORGE STATION.
BUT I HAVE MY TECH HELPING YOUR DROIDS. WHY DOES IT COST SO MUCH?
THE AMBIANCE. MY TOOLS, MY DROIDS, MY PARTS, YOUR CREDITS. THAT'S HOW IT WORKS.
THERE'S OUR MAN.
HE'S THE CRIMINAL MASTERMIND WHO KIDNAPPED PRINCESS LEIA FROM THE EIATTU GOVERNMENTAL PALACE?
HE MOVED THEM. ION FLUTTER FROM THE ENGINES MATCHED A PIRATE PATCH FIX. DOESN'T LAST LONG AND NEEDS GOOD REPAIR.
SO HE CAME HERE?

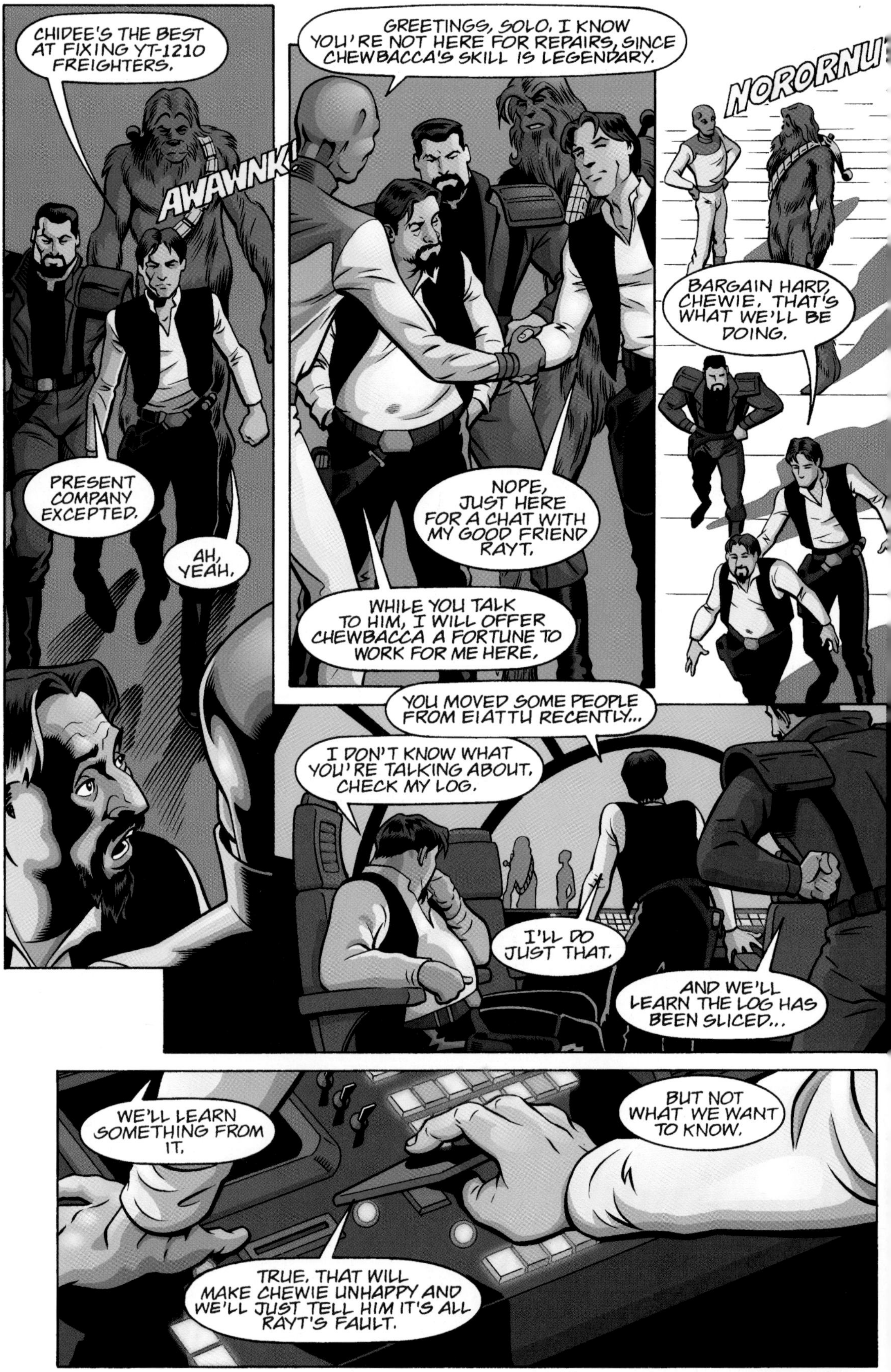
CHIDEE'S THE BEST AT FIXING YT-1210 FREIGHTERS.
AWAWNK!
PRESENT COMPANY EXCEPTED.
AH, YEAH.
GREETINGS, SOLO. I KNOW YOU'RE NOT HERE FOR REPAIRS, SINCE CHEWBACCA'S SKILL IS LEGENDARY.
NOPE, JUST HERE FOR A CHAT WITH MY GOOD FRIEND RAYT.
WHILE YOU TALK TO HIM, I WILL OFFER CHEWBACCA A FORTUNE TO WORK FOR ME HERE.
NORORNU
BARGAIN HARD, CHEWIE. THAT'S WHAT WE'LL BE DOING.
YOU MOVED SOME PEOPLE FROM EIATTU RECENTLY...
I DON'T KNOW WHAT YOU'RE TALKING ABOUT. CHECK MY LOG.
I'LL DO JUST THAT.
AND WE'LL LEARN THE LOG HAS BEEN SLICED...
WE'LL LEARN SOMETHING FROM IT.
BUT NOT WHAT WE WANT TO KNOW.
TRUE. THAT WILL MAKE CHEWIE UNHAPPY AND WE'LL JUST TELL HIM IT'S ALL RAYT'S FAULT.

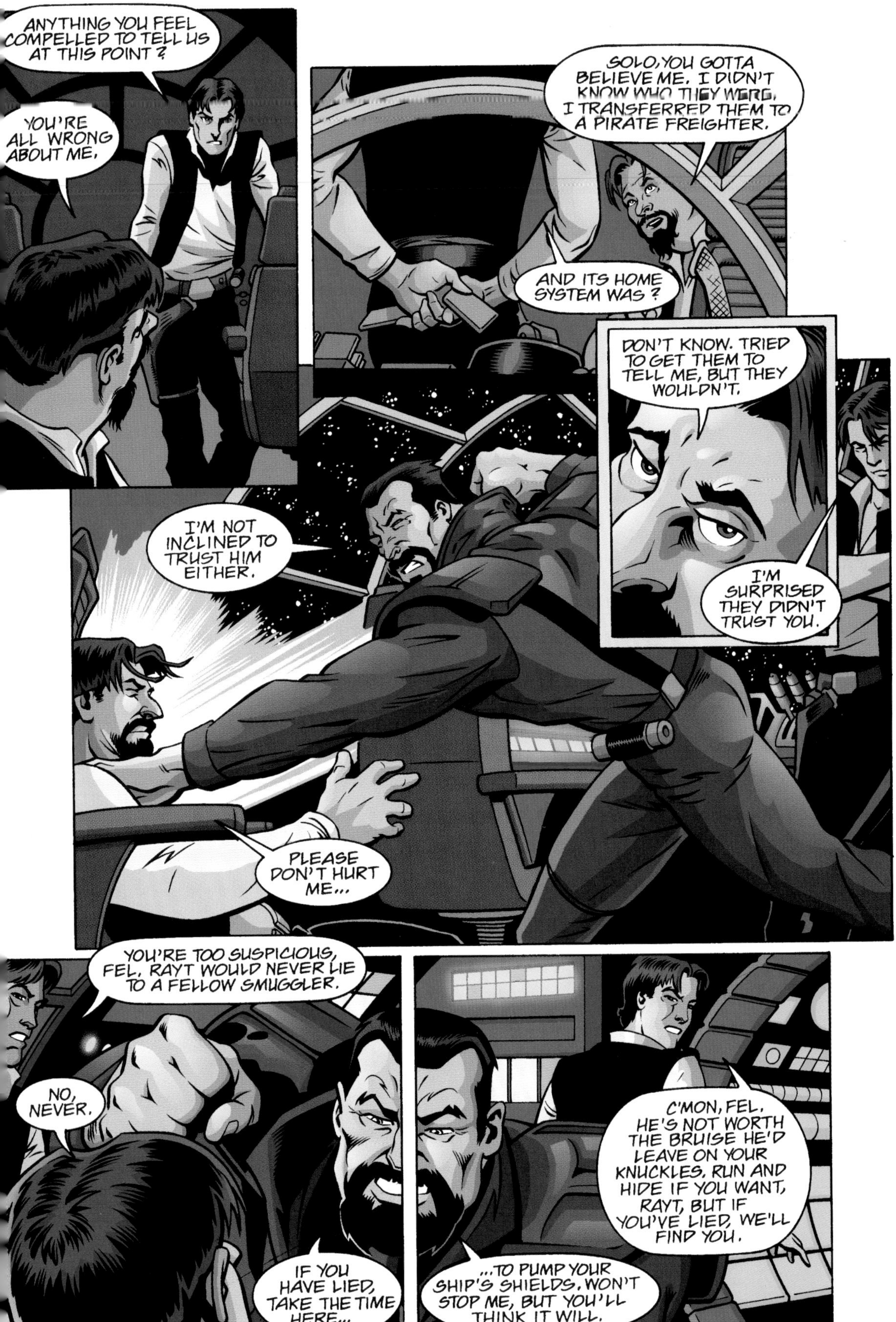
ANYTHING YOU FEEL COMPELLED TO TELL US AT THIS POINT ?
YOU'RE ALL WRONG ABOUT ME.
SOLO, YOU GOTTA BELIEVE ME. I DIDN'T KNOW WHO THEY WERE. I TRANSFERRED THEM TO A PIRATE FREIGHTER.
AND ITS HOME SYSTEM WAS ?
DON'T KNOW. TRIED TO GET THEM TO TELL ME, BUT THEY WOULDN'T.
I'M SURPRISED THEY DIDN'T TRUST YOU.
I'M NOT INCLINED TO TRUST HIM EITHER.
PLEASE DON'T HURT ME...
YOU'RE TOO SUSPICIOUS, FEL. RAYT WOULD NEVER LIE TO A FELLOW SMUGGLER.
NO, NEVER.
IF YOU HAVE LIED, TAKE THE TIME HERE...
...TO PUMP YOUR SHIP'S SHIELDS. WON'T STOP ME, BUT YOU'LL THINK IT WILL.
C'MON, FEL, HE'S NOT WORTH THE BRUISE HE'D LEAVE ON YOUR KNUCKLES. RUN AND HIDE IF YOU WANT, RAYT, BUT IF YOU'VE LIED, WE'LL FIND YOU.

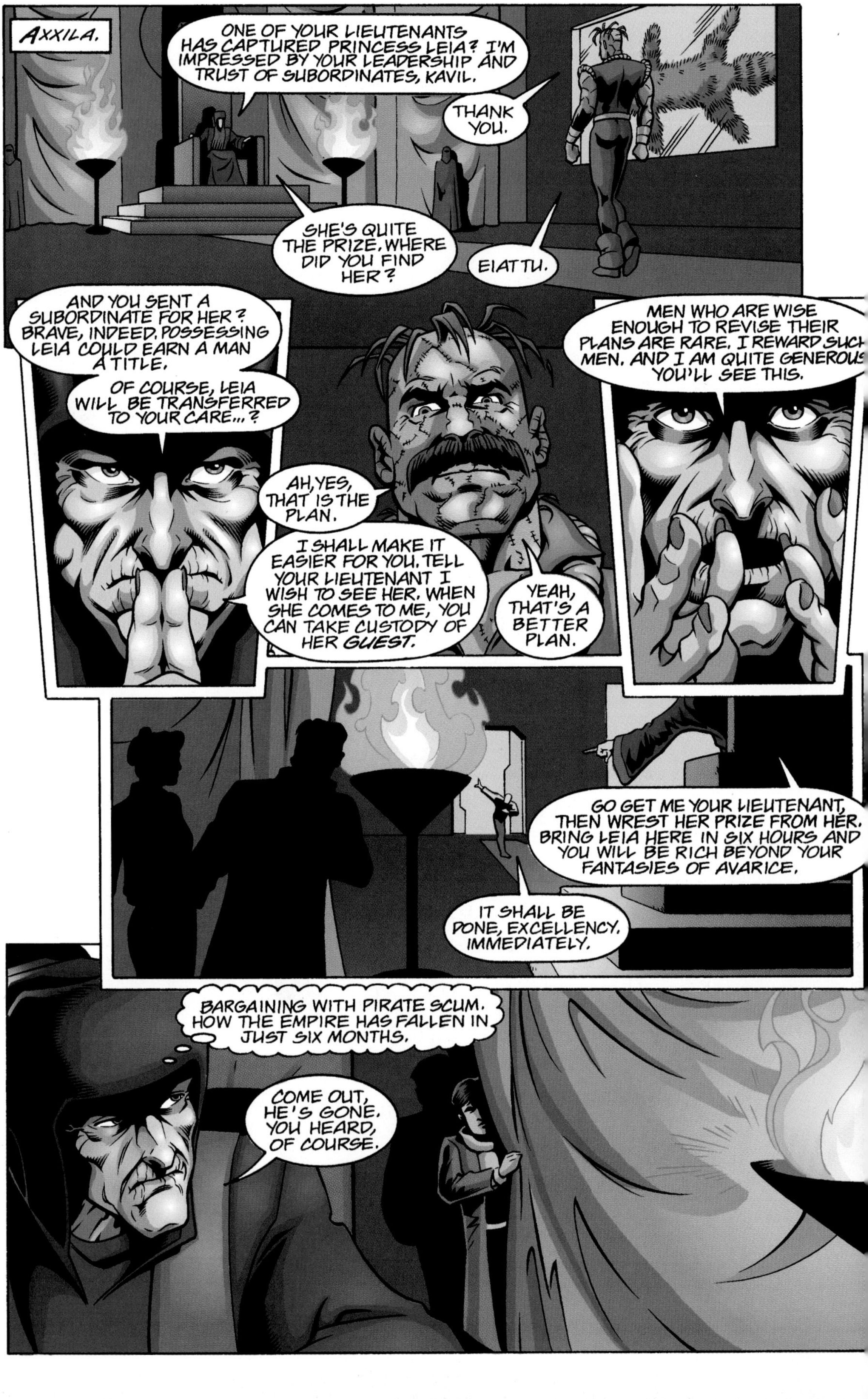
AXXILA.
ONE OF YOUR LIEUTENANTS HAS CAPTURED PRINCESS LEIA? I'M IMPRESSED BY YOUR LEADERSHIP AND TRUST OF SUBORDINATES, KAVIL.
THANK YOU.
SHE'S QUITE THE PRIZE. WHERE DID YOU FIND HER?
EIATTU.
AND YOU SENT A SUBORDINATE FOR HER? BRAVE, INDEED. POSSESSING LEIA COULD EARN A MAN A TITLE.
OF COURSE, LEIA WILL BE TRANSFERRED TO YOUR CARE...?
AH, YES, THAT IS THE PLAN.
I SHALL MAKE IT EASIER FOR YOU. TELL YOUR LIEUTENANT I WISH TO SEE HER. WHEN SHE COMES TO ME, YOU CAN TAKE CUSTODY OF HER GUEST.
YEAH, THAT'S A BETTER PLAN.
MEN WHO ARE WISE ENOUGH TO REVISE THEIR PLANS ARE RARE. I REWARD SUCH MEN. AND I AM QUITE GENEROUS. YOU'LL SEE THIS.
GO GET ME YOUR LIEUTENANT, THEN WREST HER PRIZE FROM HER. BRING LEIA HERE IN SIX HOURS AND YOU WILL BE RICH BEYOND YOUR FANTASIES OF AVARICE.
IT SHALL BE DONE, EXCELLENCY. IMMEDIATELY.
BARGAINING WITH PIRATE SCUM. HOW THE EMPIRE HAS FALLEN IN JUST SIX MONTHS.
COME OUT, HE'S GONE. YOU HEARD, OF COURSE.

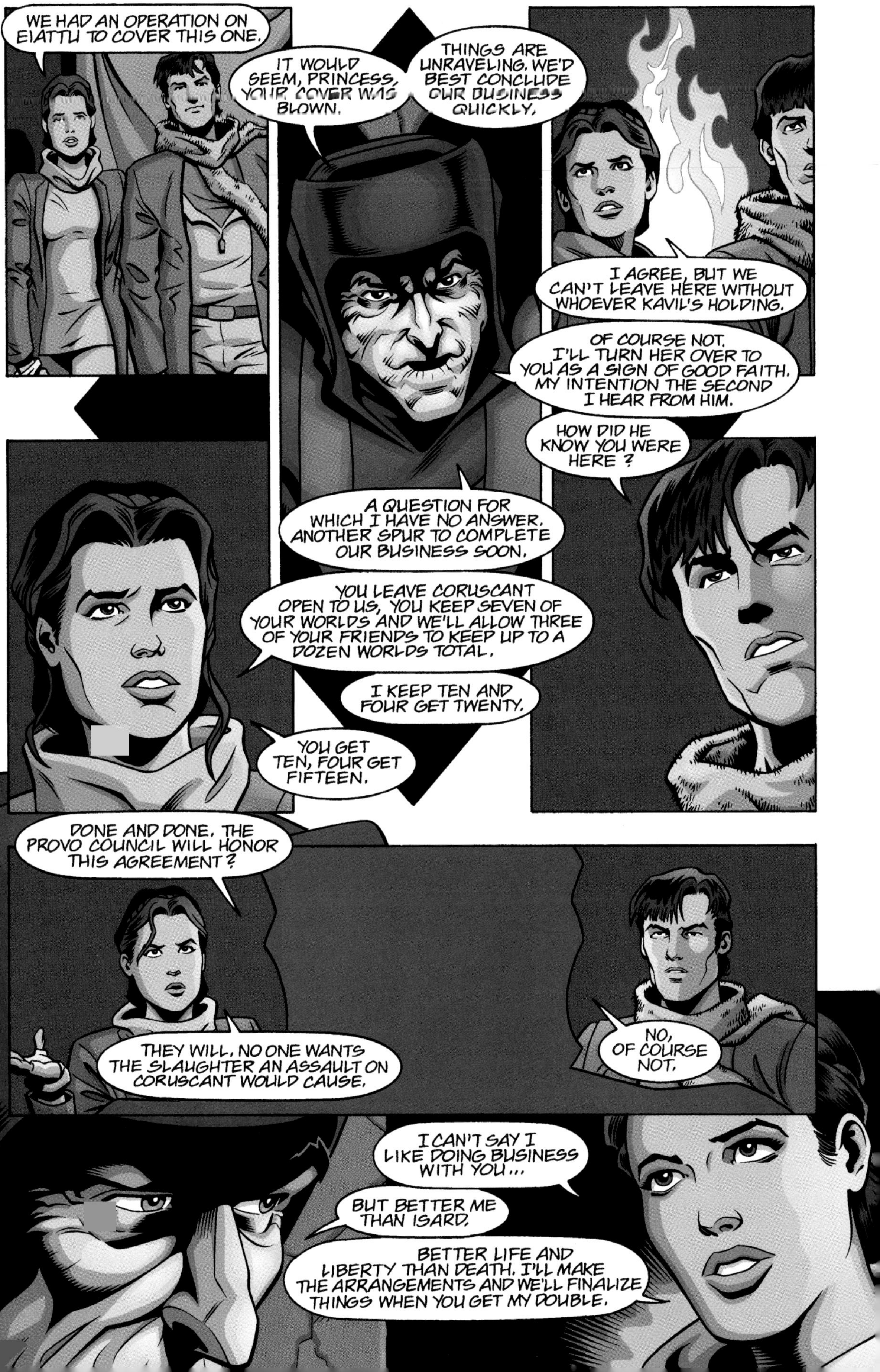

WE HAD AN OPERATION ON EIATTU TO COVER THIS ONE.
IT WOULD SEEM, PRINCESS, YOUR COVER WAS BLOWN.
THINGS ARE UNRAVELING. WE'D BEST CONCLUDE OUR BUSINESS QUICKLY.
I AGREE, BUT WE CAN'T LEAVE HERE WITHOUT WHOEVER KAVIL'S HOLDING.
OF COURSE NOT. I'LL TURN HER OVER TO YOU AS A SIGN OF GOOD FAITH. MY INTENTION THE SECOND I HEAR FROM HIM.
HOW DID HE KNOW YOU WERE HERE?
A QUESTION FOR WHICH I HAVE NO ANSWER. ANOTHER SPUR TO COMPLETE OUR BUSINESS SOON.
YOU LEAVE CORUSCANT OPEN TO US, YOU KEEP SEVEN OF YOUR WORLDS AND WE'LL ALLOW THREE OF YOUR FRIENDS TO KEEP UP TO A DOZEN WORLDS TOTAL.
I KEEP TEN AND FOUR GET TWENTY.
YOU GET TEN, FOUR GET FIFTEEN.
DONE AND DONE. THE PROVO COUNCIL WILL HONOR THIS AGREEMENT?
THEY WILL. NO ONE WANTS THE SLAUGHTER AN ASSAULT ON CORUSCANT WOULD CAUSE.
NO, OF COURSE NOT.
I CAN'T SAY I LIKE DOING BUSINESS WITH YOU...
BUT BETTER ME THAN ISARD.
BETTER LIFE AND LIBERTY THAN DEATH. I'LL MAKE THE ARRANGEMENTS AND WE'LL FINALIZE THINGS WHEN YOU GET MY DOUBLE.

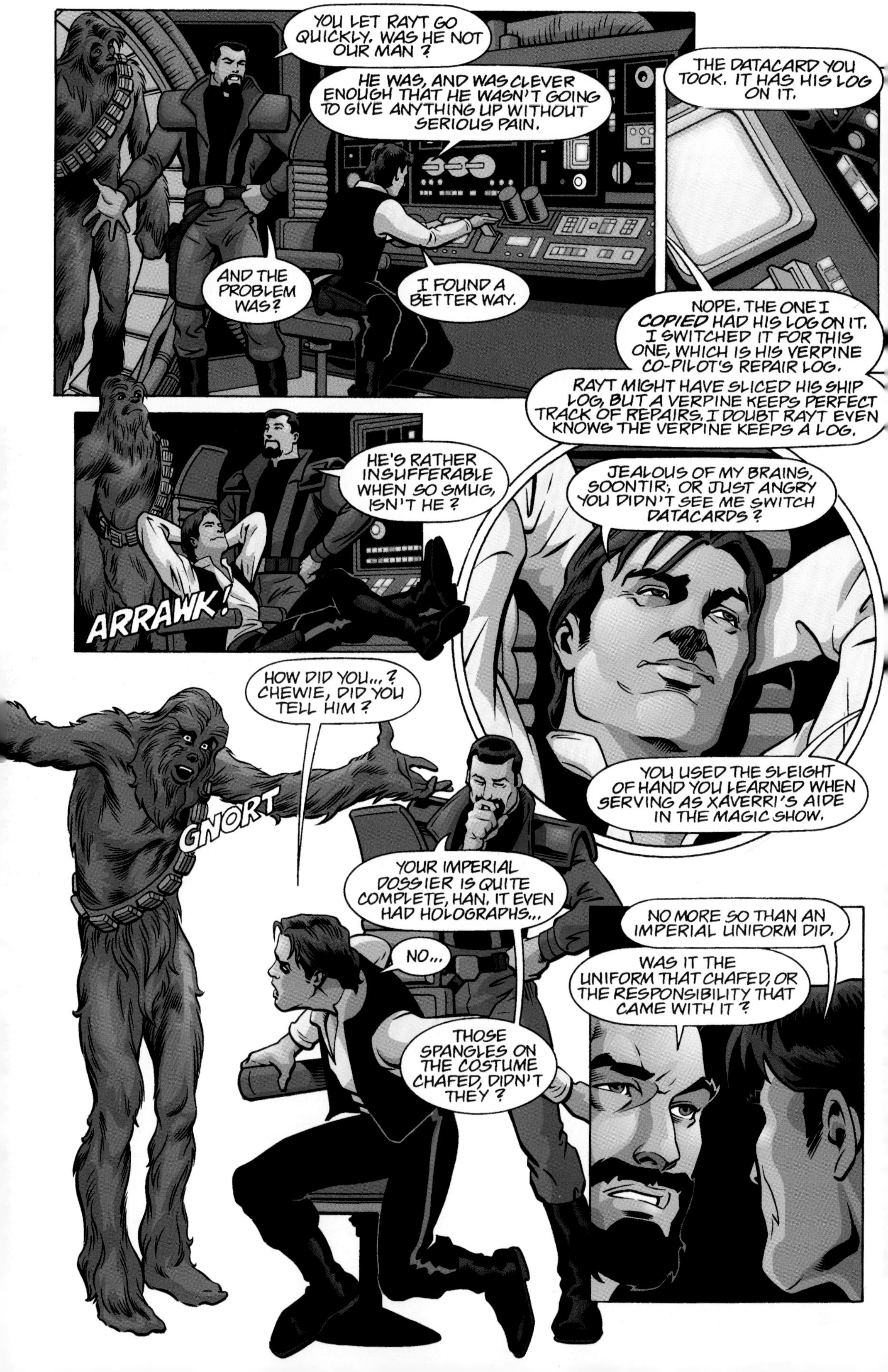
YOU LET RAYT GO QUICKLY. WAS HE NOT OUR MAN ?
HE WAS, AND WAS CLEVER ENOUGH THAT HE WASN'T GOING TO GIVE ANYTHING UP WITHOUT SERIOUS PAIN.
AND THE PROBLEM WAS?
I FOUND A BETTER WAY.
THE DATACARD YOU TOOK. IT HAS HIS LOG ON IT.
NOPE. THE ONE I COPIED HAD HIS LOG ON IT. I SWITCHED IT FOR THIS ONE, WHICH IS HIS VERPINE CO-PILOT'S REPAIR LOG.
RAYT MIGHT HAVE SLICED HIS SHIP LOG, BUT A VERPINE KEEPS PERFECT TRACK OF REPAIRS. I DOUBT RAYT EVEN KNOWS THE VERPINE KEEPS A LOG.
HE'S RATHER INSUFFERABLE WHEN SO SMUG, ISN'T HE ?
ARRAWK!
JEALOUS OF MY BRAINS, SOONTIR; OR JUST ANGRY YOU DIDN'T SEE ME SWITCH DATACARDS ?
YOU USED THE SLEIGHT OF HAND YOU LEARNED WHEN SERVING AS XAVERRI'S AIDE IN THE MAGIC SHOW.
HOW DID YOU...? CHEWIE, DID YOU TELL HIM ?
GNORT
YOUR IMPERIAL DOSSIER IS QUITE COMPLETE, HAN. IT EVEN HAD HOLOGRAPHS...
NO...
THOSE SPANGLES ON THE COSTUME CHAFED, DIDN'T THEY ?
NO MORE SO THAN AN IMPERIAL UNIFORM DID.
WAS IT THE UNIFORM THAT CHAFED, OR THE RESPONSIBILITY THAT CAME WITH IT ?

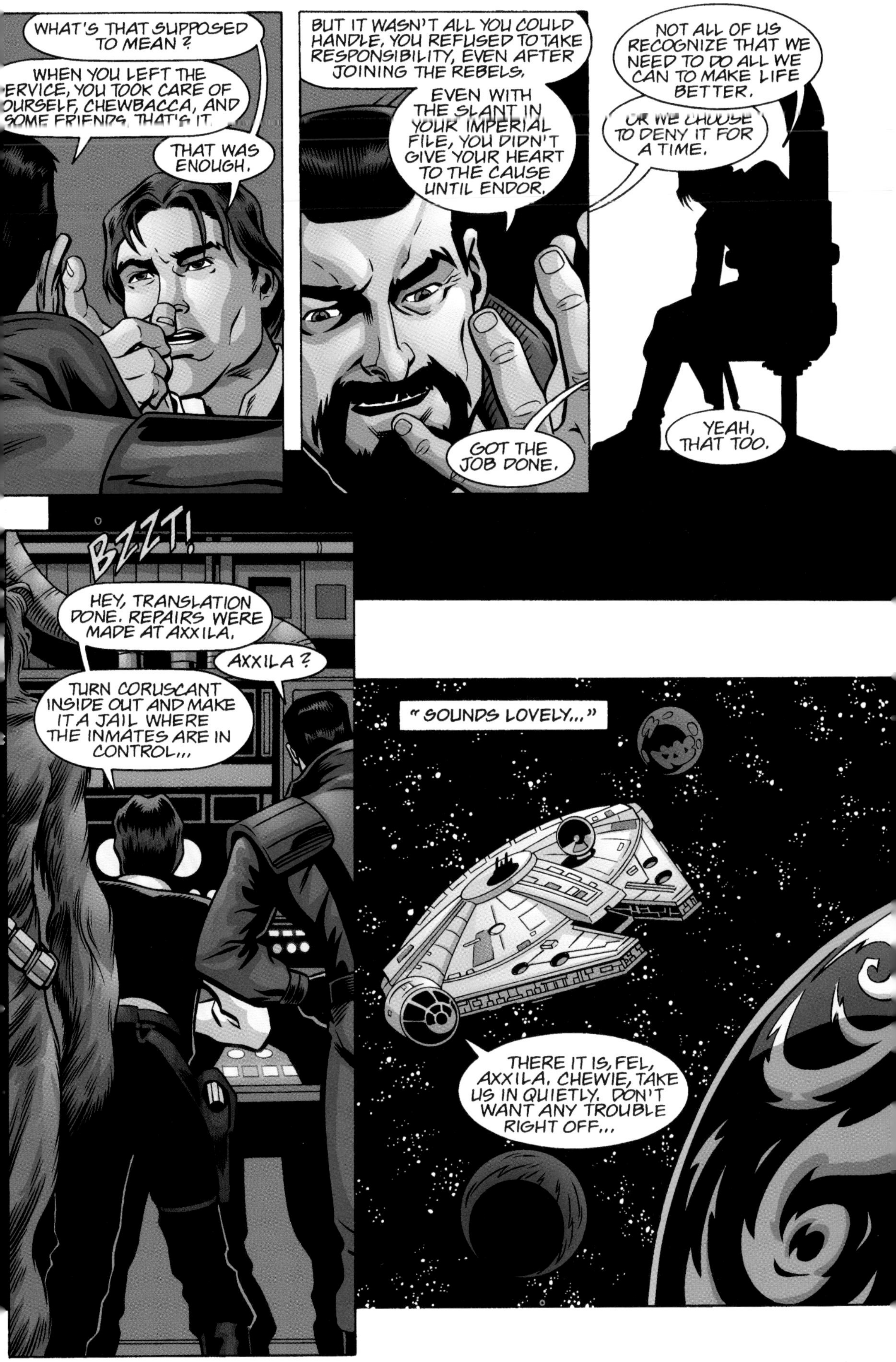
WHAT'S THAT SUPPOSED TO MEAN?
WHEN YOU LEFT THE ERVICE, YOU TOOK CARE OF OURSELF, CHEWBACCA, AND SOME FRIENDS, THAT'S IT.
THAT WAS ENOUGH.
BUT IT WASN'T ALL YOU COULD HANDLE, YOU REFUSED TO TAKE RESPONSIBILITY, EVEN AFTER JOINING THE REBELS.
EVEN WITH THE SLANT IN YOUR IMPERIAL FILE, YOU DIDN'T GIVE YOUR HEART TO THE CAUSE UNTIL ENDOR.
GOT THE JOB DONE.
NOT ALL OF US RECOGNIZE THAT WE NEED TO DO ALL WE CAN TO MAKE LIFE BETTER.
OR WE CHOOSE TO DENY IT FOR A TIME.
YEAH, THAT TOO.
BZZZT!
HEY, TRANSLATION DONE. REPAIRS WERE MADE AT AXXILA.
AXXILA?
TURN CORUSCANT INSIDE OUT AND MAKE IT A JAIL WHERE THE INMATES ARE IN CONTROL...
"SOUNDS LOVELY..."
THERE IT IS, FEL, AXXILA. CHEWIE, TAKE US IN QUIETLY. DON'T WANT ANY TROUBLE RIGHT OFF...

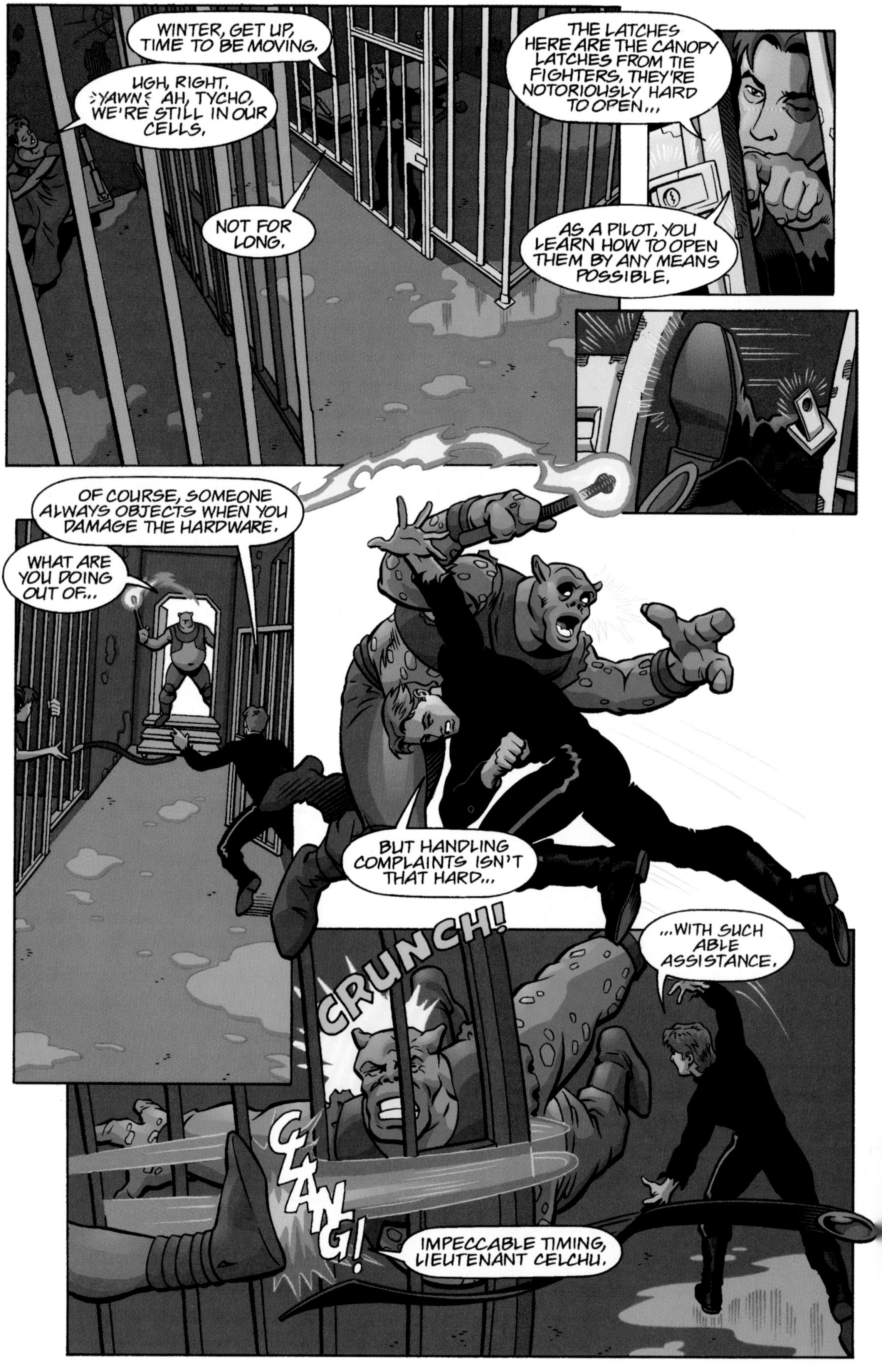
WINTER, GET UP, TIME TO BE MOVING.
UGH, RIGHT. YAWN AH, TYCHO, WE'RE STILL IN OUR CELLS.
NOT FOR LONG.
THE LATCHES HERE ARE THE CANOPY LATCHES FROM TIE FIGHTERS, THEY'RE NOTORIOUSLY HARD TO OPEN...
AS A PILOT, YOU LEARN HOW TO OPEN THEM BY ANY MEANS POSSIBLE.
OF COURSE, SOMEONE ALWAYS OBJECTS WHEN YOU DAMAGE THE HARDWARE.
WHAT ARE YOU DOING OUT OF...
BUT HANDLING COMPLAINTS ISN'T THAT HARD...
CRUNCH!
...WITH SUCH ABLE ASSISTANCE.
CLANG!
IMPECCABLE TIMING, LIEUTENANT CELCHU.

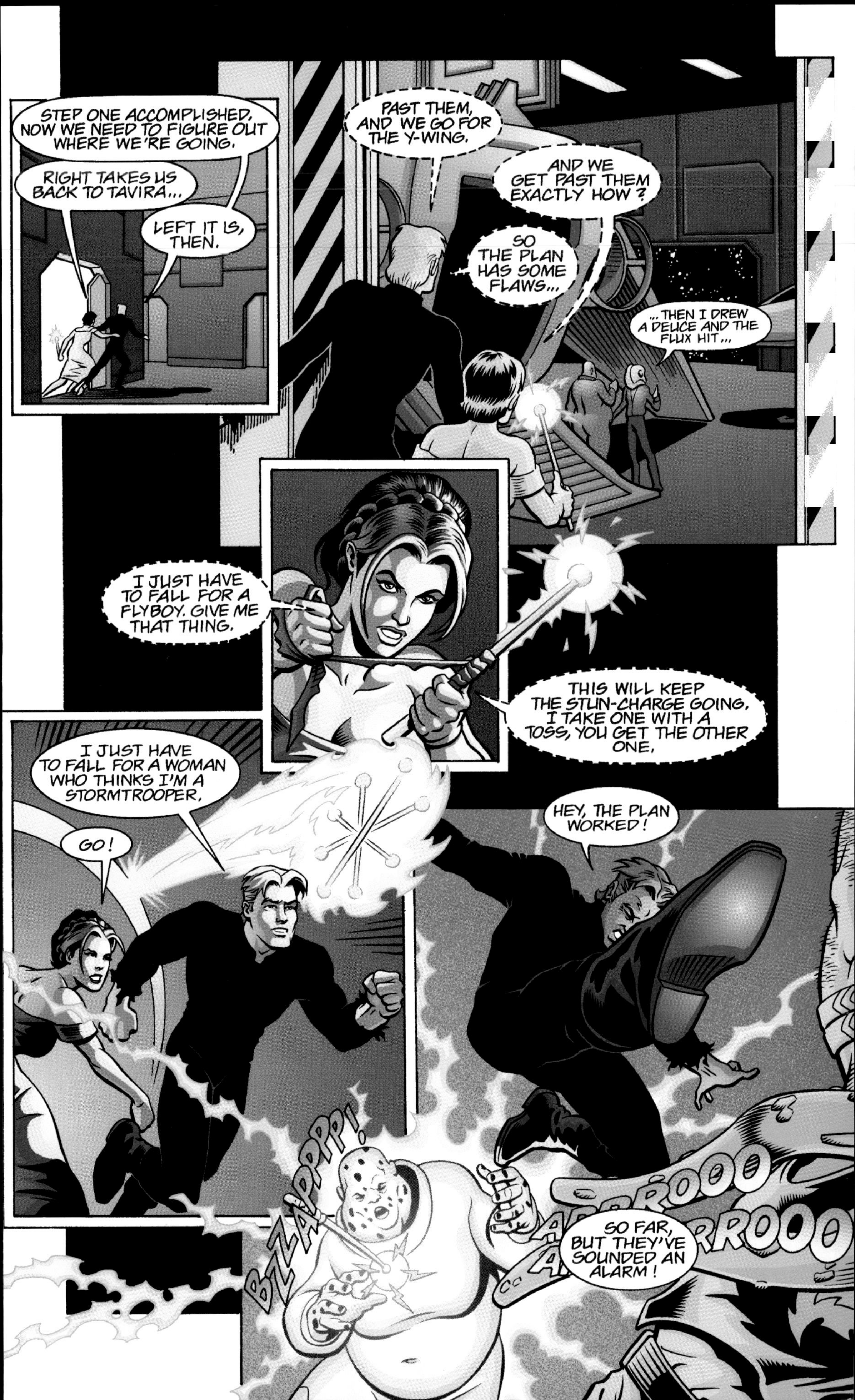
STEP ONE ACCOMPLISHED. NOW WE NEED TO FIGURE OUT WHERE WE'RE GOING.
RIGHT TAKES US BACK TO TAVIRA...
LEFT IT IS, THEN.
PAST THEM, AND WE GO FOR THE Y-WING.
AND WE GET PAST THEM EXACTLY HOW?
SO THE PLAN HAS SOME FLAWS...
...THEN I DREW A DEUCE AND THE FLUX HIT...
I JUST HAVE TO FALL FOR A FLYBOY. GIVE ME THAT THING.
THIS WILL KEEP THE STUN-CHARGE GOING. I TAKE ONE WITH A TOSS, YOU GET THE OTHER ONE.
I JUST HAVE TO FALL FOR A WOMAN WHO THINKS I'M A STORMTROOPER.
GO!
HEY, THE PLAN WORKED!
BZZAPPPP!
SO FAR, BUT THEY'VE SOUNDED AN ALARM!

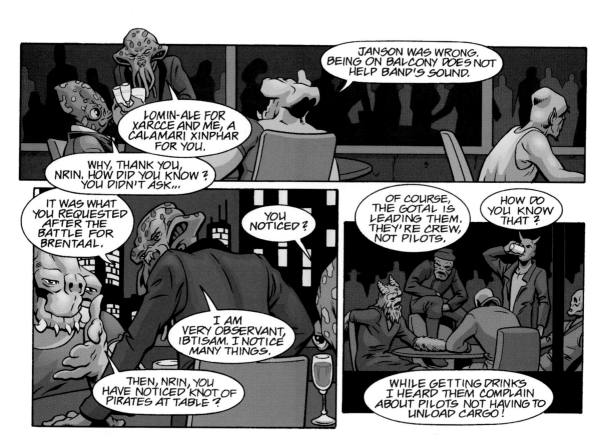

JANSON WAS WRONG. BEING ON BALCONY DOES NOT HELP BAND'S SOUND.

LOMIN-ALE FOR XARCCE AND ME, A CALAMARI XINPHAR FOR YOU.

WHY, THANK YOU, NRIN, HOW DID YOU KNOW? YOU DIDN'T ASK...

IT WAS WHAT YOU REQUESTED AFTER THE BATTLE FOR BRENTAAL.

YOU NOTICED?

I AM VERY OBSERVANT, IBTISAM. I NOTICE MANY THINGS.

THEN, NRIN, YOU HAVE NOTICED KNOT OF PIRATES AT TABLE?

OF COURSE, THE GOTAL IS LEADING THEM. THEY'RE CREW, NOT PILOTS.

HOW DO YOU KNOW THAT?

WHILE GETTING DRINKS I HEARD THEM COMPLAIN ABOUT PILOTS NOT HAVING TO UNLOAD CARGO!

I SALUTE YOUR DEDUCTIVE ABILITY.

TO THE FORCE BEING WITH US.

AND OUR SAFETY.

ESPECIALLY THAT.

CLINK-CLINK

I DON'T KNOW, NRIN, I SEEM TO SENSE A CHANGE IN YOU.

CHANGE? ME? YOU MUST BE MISTAKEN.

REALLY. I WOULD HATE TO THINK I AM, FOR I LIKE THIS CHANGE.

EVEN I SEE CHANGE, NRIN, YOU NO LONGER MOPE.
NRIN WAS MOPING ?!
I WAS NOT !
WHILE YOU WERE ON GROUND, IBTISAM, HE MOPED.
THAT IS BASE SLANDER.
YOU WERE WORRIED WHILE I WAS GONE ? I'M, AH, I'M TOUCHED, I DIDN'T KNOW...
TOUCHED ?
THE ANIMOSITY BETWEEN US... I'VE HATED IT. OUR PEOPLE DO NOT GET ALONG, BUT WE DON'T HAVE TO BE OUR PEOPLE, DO WE ?
TELL ME WE DON'T, NRIN, PLEASE.
I COPY. WE'RE COMING.
NO, IBTISAM, WE CAN RISE ABOVE OLD RIVALRIES.
THEY'RE ON THE MOVE.
YOU TWO REPORT BACK TO WEDGE. I'LL FOLLOW THEM...

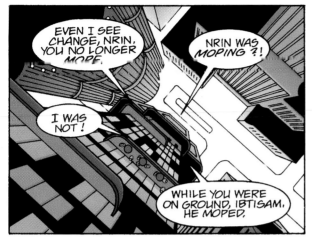

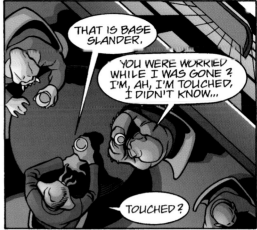

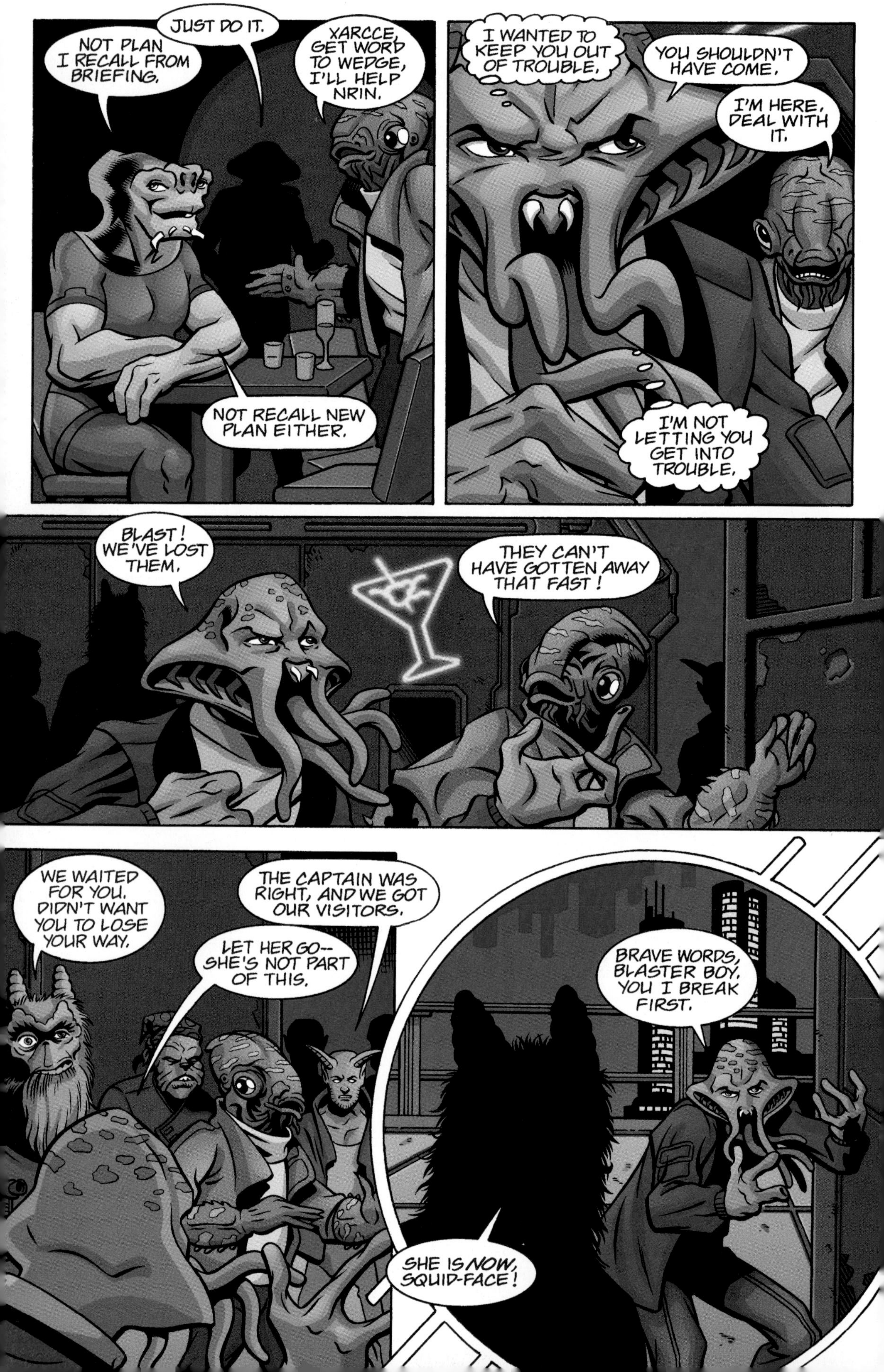
NOT PLAN I RECALL FROM BRIEFING.
JUST DO IT.
XARCCE, GET WORD TO WEDGE. I'LL HELP NRIN.
NOT RECALL NEW PLAN EITHER.
I WANTED TO KEEP YOU OUT OF TROUBLE.
YOU SHOULDN'T HAVE COME.
I'M HERE. DEAL WITH IT.
I'M NOT LETTING YOU GET INTO TROUBLE.
BLAST! WE'VE LOST THEM.
THEY CAN'T HAVE GOTTEN AWAY THAT FAST!
WE WAITED FOR YOU. DIDN'T WANT YOU TO LOSE YOUR WAY.
THE CAPTAIN WAS RIGHT, AND WE GOT OUR VISITORS.
LET HER GO-- SHE'S NOT PART OF THIS.
BRAVE WORDS, BLASTER BOY. YOU I BREAK FIRST.
SHE IS *NOW*, SQUID-FACE!

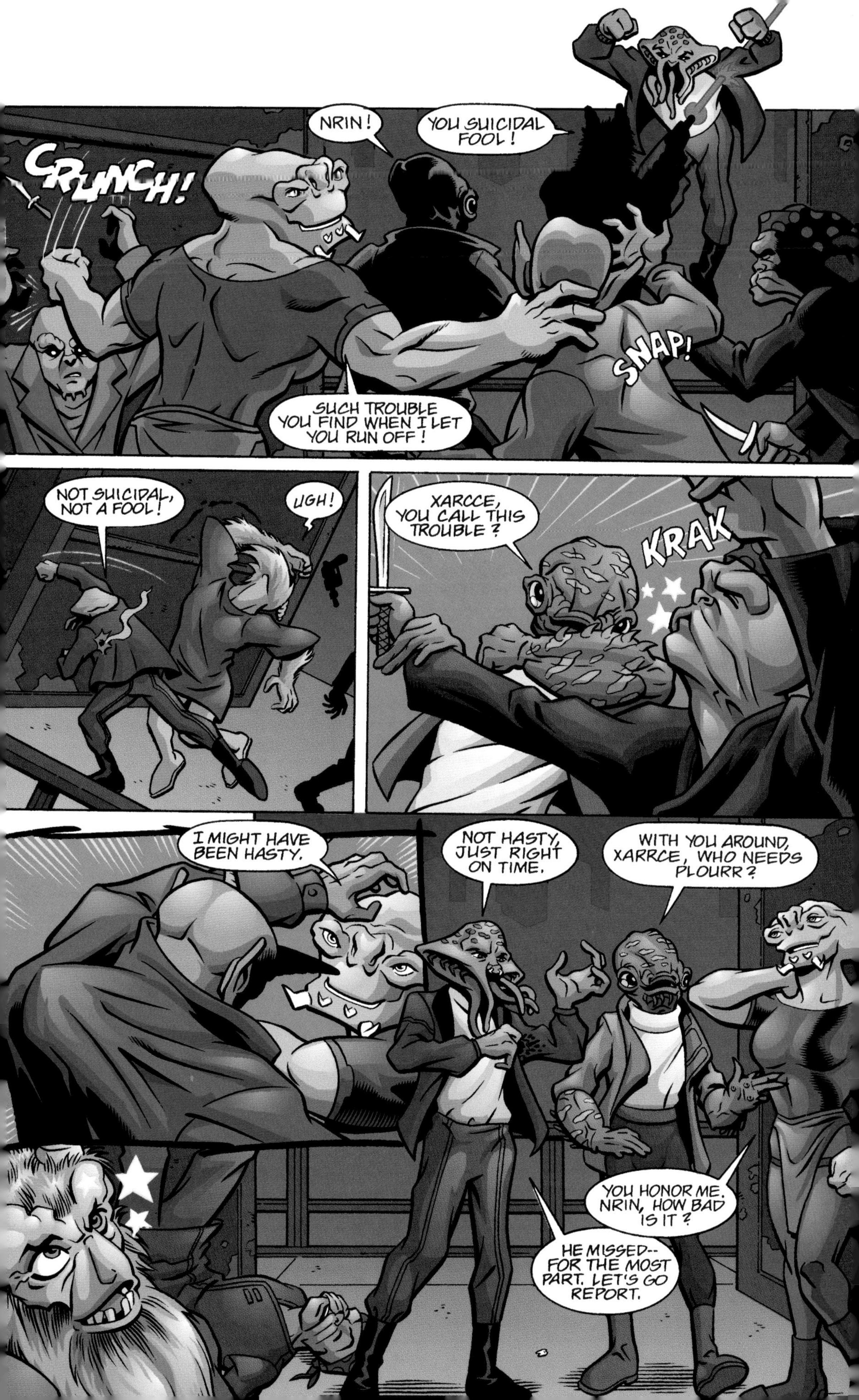
CRUNCH!
NRIN!
YOU SUICIDAL FOOL!
SUCH TROUBLE YOU FIND WHEN I LET YOU RUN OFF!
SNAP!
NOT SUICIDAL, NOT A FOOL!
UGH!
XARCCE, YOU CALL THIS TROUBLE?
KRAK
I MIGHT HAVE BEEN HASTY.
NOT HASTY, JUST RIGHT ON TIME.
WITH YOU AROUND, XARRCE, WHO NEEDS PLOURR?
YOU HONOR ME. NRIN, HOW BAD IS IT?
HE MISSED-- FOR THE MOST PART. LET'S GO REPORT.

WHY'D A Y-WING HAVE TO BE THE ONLY TWO SEATER HERE?

WHY A TWO SEATER? I THOUGHT YOU LIKED THE IDEA OF SNUGGLING.

IF WE LIVE TO GET OUT OF THIS, I'LL REMIND YOU OF THAT REMARK.

DO THAT, FLYBOY. I'M IN AND LOCKED. MOVE THIS THING.

AS ORDERED. I HAVE ENGINE START, SHUNTING POWER TO WEAPONS.

WE ARE GREEN ON LASERS AND ION CANNONS, RED ON MISSILES, SHIELDS COMING UP... NOW!

WE'RE DOING MORE SITTING THAN WE ARE FLYING, TYCHO.

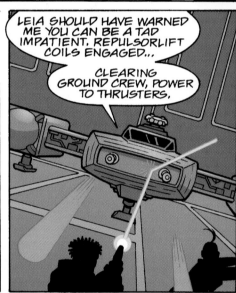

LEIA SHOULD HAVE WARNED ME YOU CAN BE A TAD IMPATIENT. REPULSORLIFT COILS ENGAGED...

CLEARING GROUND CREW, POWER TO THRUSTERS.

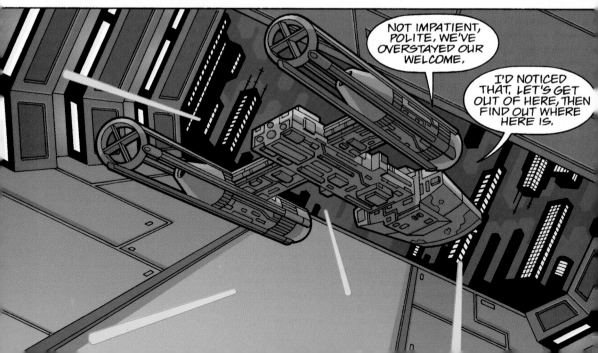

NOT IMPATIENT, POLITE. WE'VE OVERSTAYED OUR WELCOME.

I'D NOTICED THAT. LET'S GET OUT OF HERE, THEN FIND OUT WHERE HERE IS.

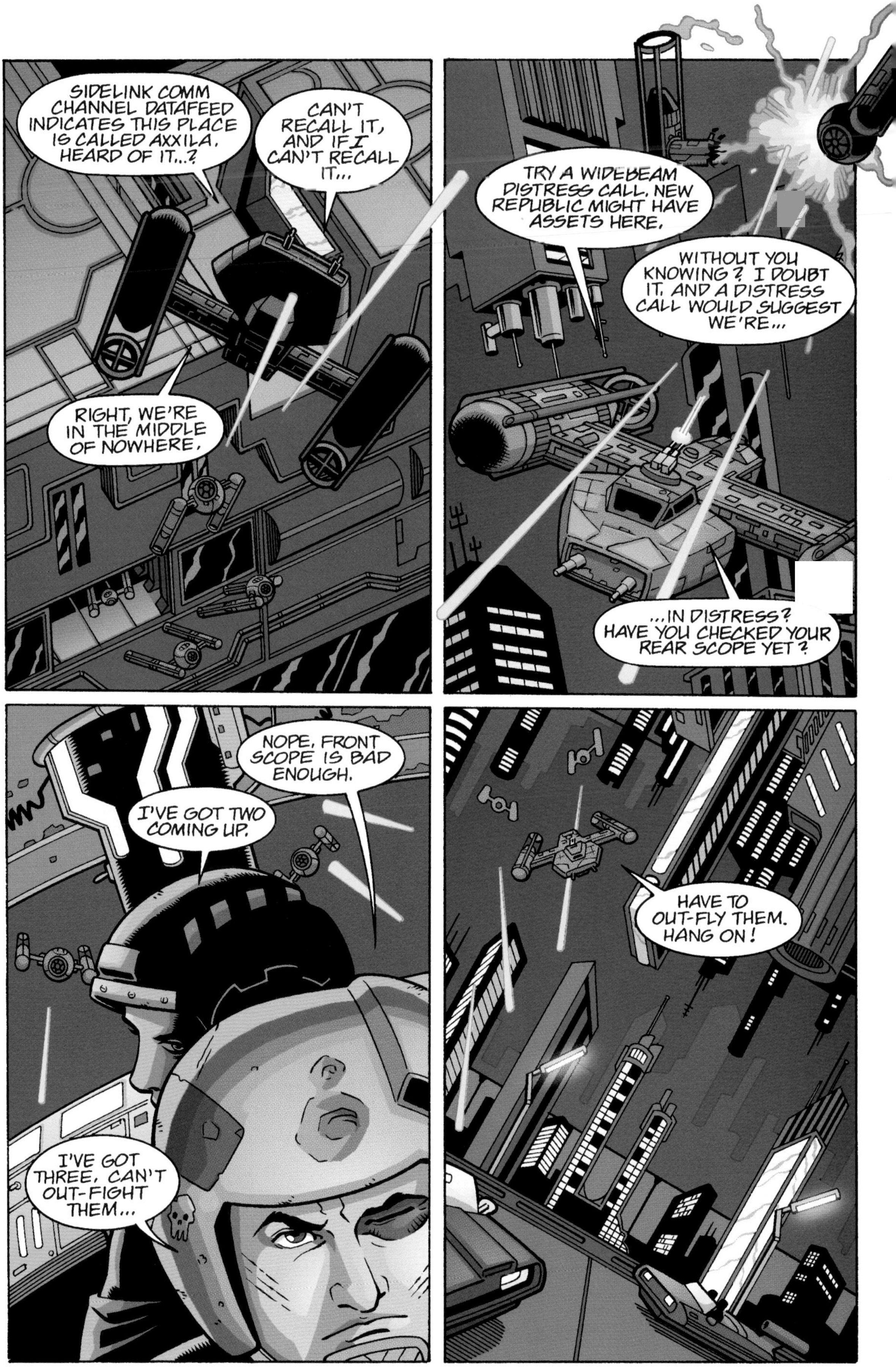
SIDELINK COMM CHANNEL DATAFEED INDICATES THIS PLACE IS CALLED AXXILA. HEARD OF IT...?
CAN'T RECALL IT, AND IF I CAN'T RECALL IT...
RIGHT, WE'RE IN THE MIDDLE OF NOWHERE.
TRY A WIDEBEAM DISTRESS CALL. NEW REPUBLIC MIGHT HAVE ASSETS HERE.
WITHOUT YOU KNOWING? I DOUBT IT. AND A DISTRESS CALL WOULD SUGGEST WE'RE...
...IN DISTRESS? HAVE YOU CHECKED YOUR REAR SCOPE YET?
NOPE, FRONT SCOPE IS BAD ENOUGH.
I'VE GOT TWO COMING UP.
I'VE GOT THREE. CAN'T OUT-FIGHT THEM...
HAVE TO OUT-FLY THEM. HANG ON!

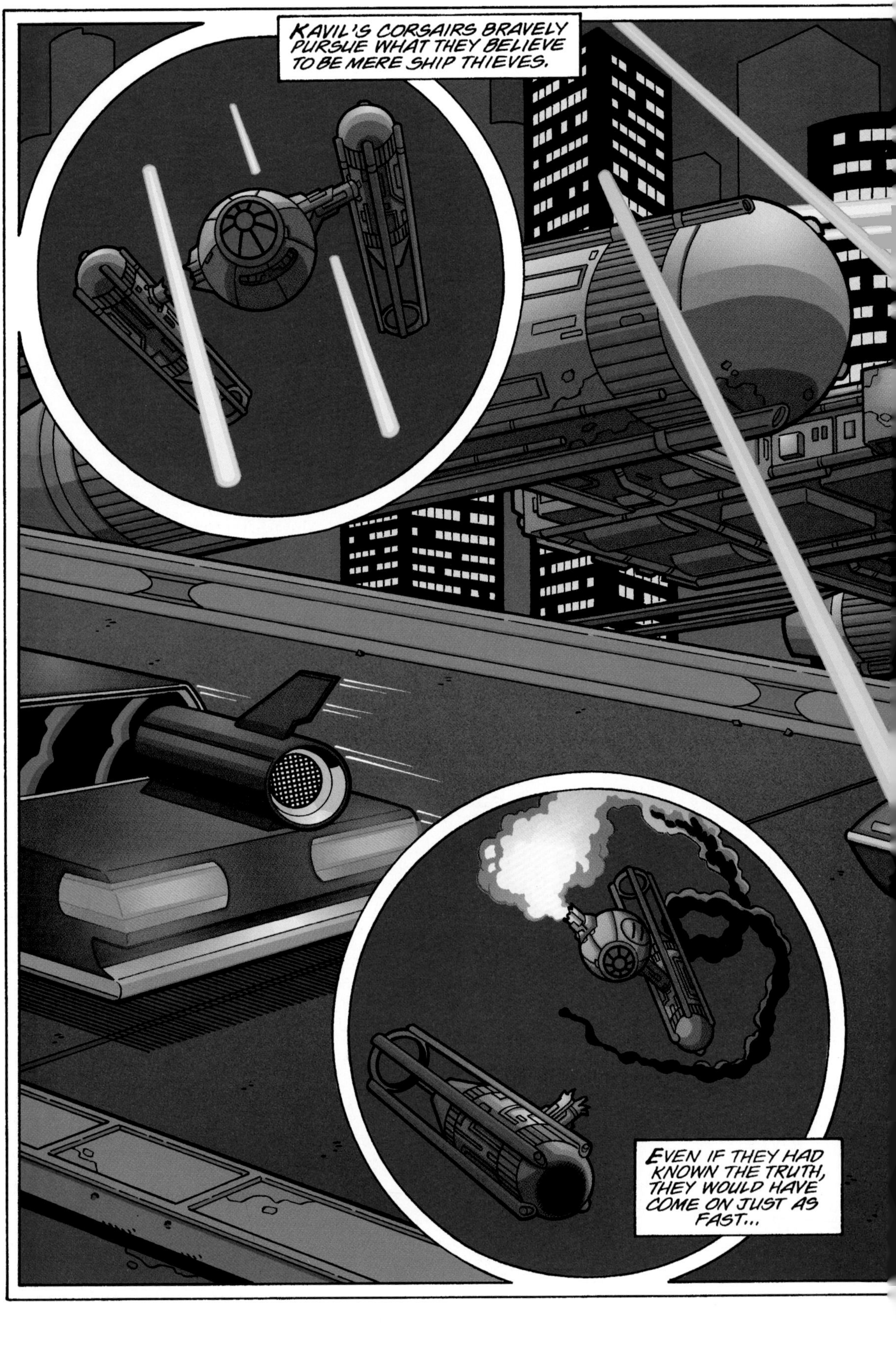
KAVIL'S CORSAIRS BRAVELY PURSUE WHAT THEY BELIEVE TO BE MERE SHIP THIEVES.
EVEN IF THEY HAD KNOWN THE TRUTH, THEY WOULD HAVE COME ON JUST AS FAST...

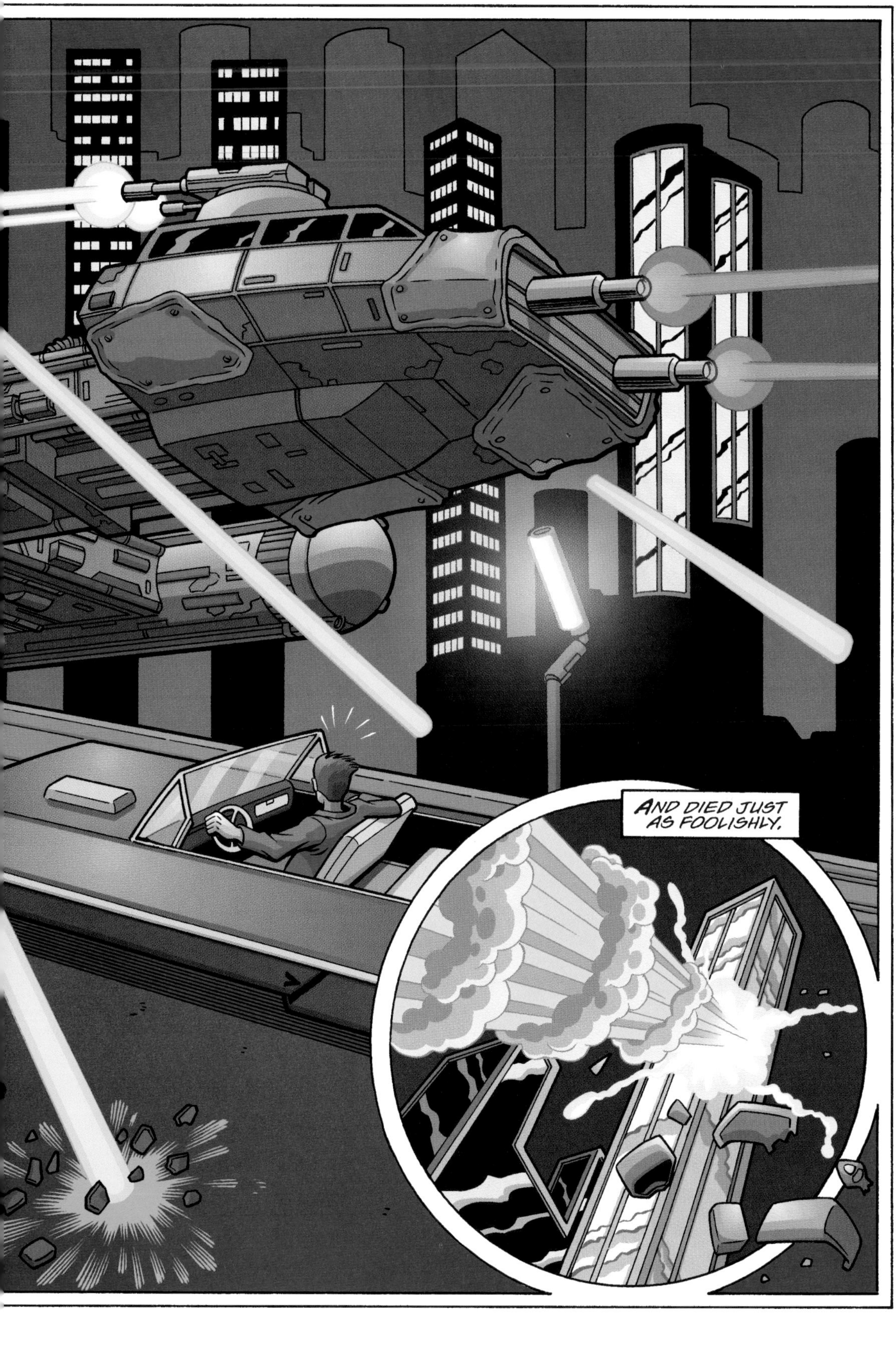
AND DIED JUST
AS FOOLISHLY.

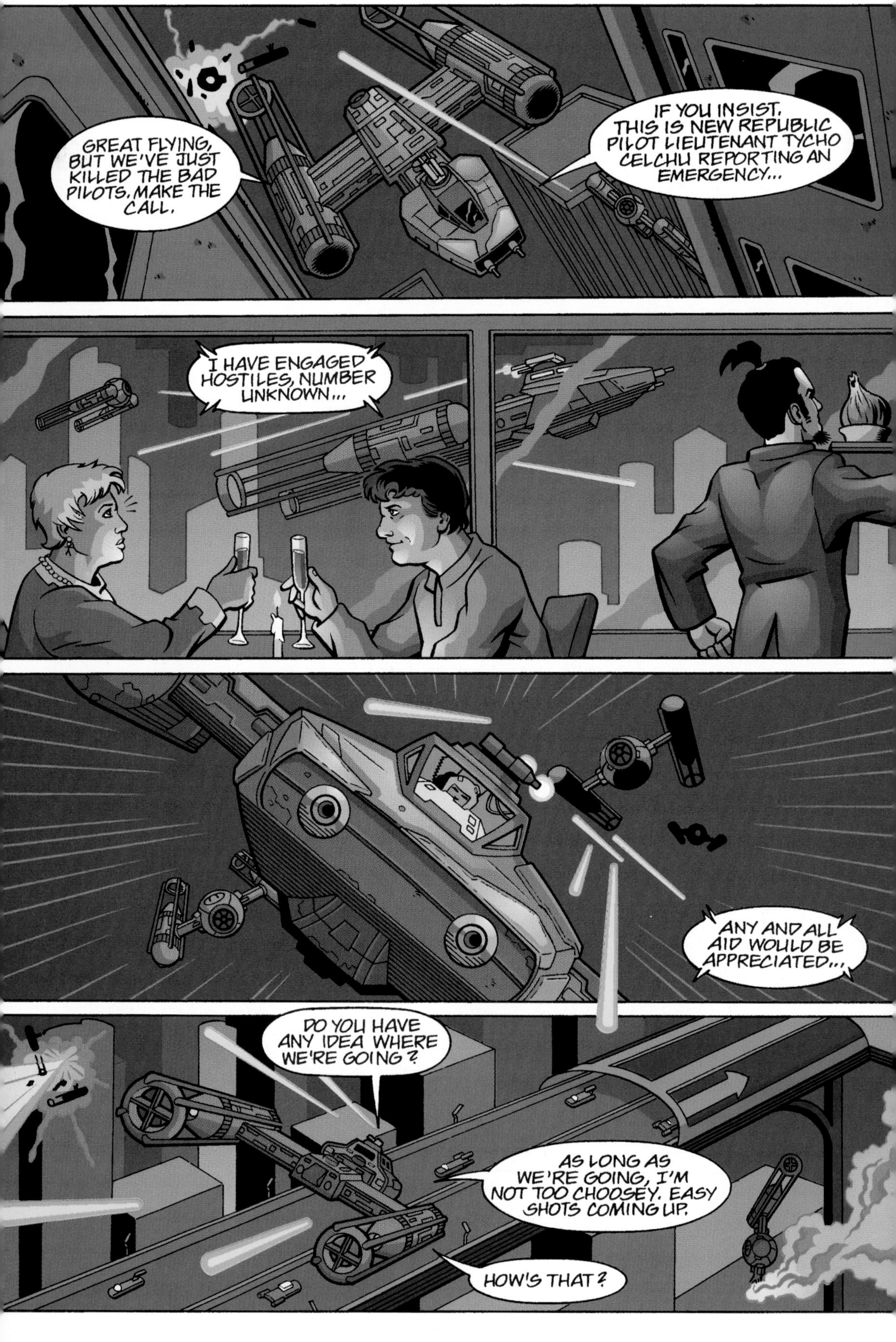
GREAT FLYING, BUT WE'VE JUST KILLED THE BAD PILOTS. MAKE THE CALL.
IF YOU INSIST. THIS IS NEW REPUBLIC PILOT LIEUTENANT TYCHO CELCHU REPORTING AN EMERGENCY...
I HAVE ENGAGED HOSTILES, NUMBER UNKNOWN...
ANY AND ALL AID WOULD BE APPRECIATED...
DO YOU HAVE ANY IDEA WHERE WE'RE GOING?
AS LONG AS WE'RE GOING, I'M NOT TOO CHOOSEY. EASY SHOTS COMING UP.
HOW'S THAT?

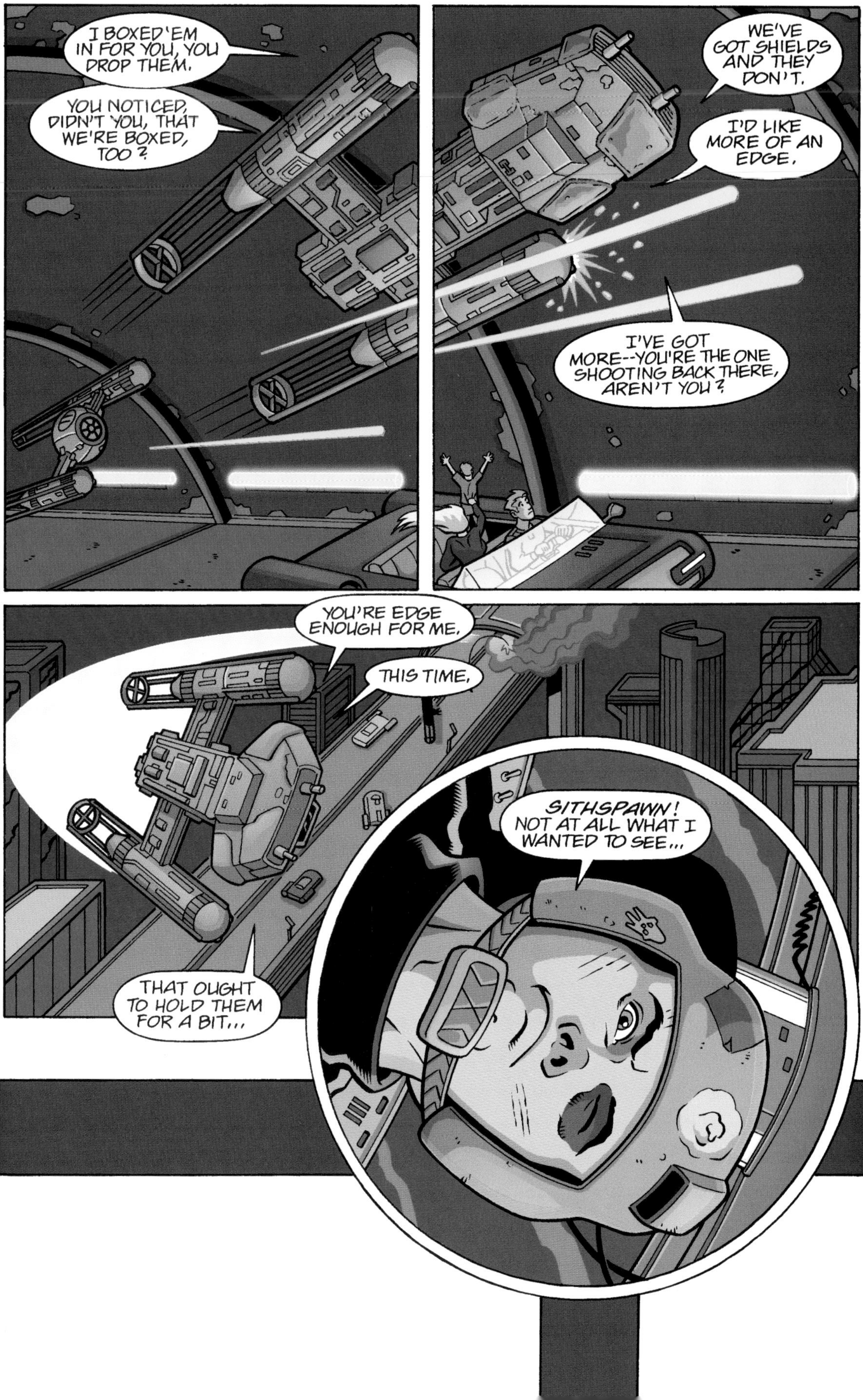
I BOXED 'EM IN FOR YOU, YOU DROP THEM.
YOU NOTICED, DIDN'T YOU, THAT WE'RE BOXED, TOO?
WE'VE GOT SHIELDS AND THEY DON'T.
I'D LIKE MORE OF AN EDGE.
I'VE GOT MORE--YOU'RE THE ONE SHOOTING BACK THERE, AREN'T YOU?
YOU'RE EDGE ENOUGH FOR ME.
THIS TIME.
THAT OUGHT TO HOLD THEM FOR A BIT...
SITHSPAWN! NOT AT ALL WHAT I WANTED TO SEE...

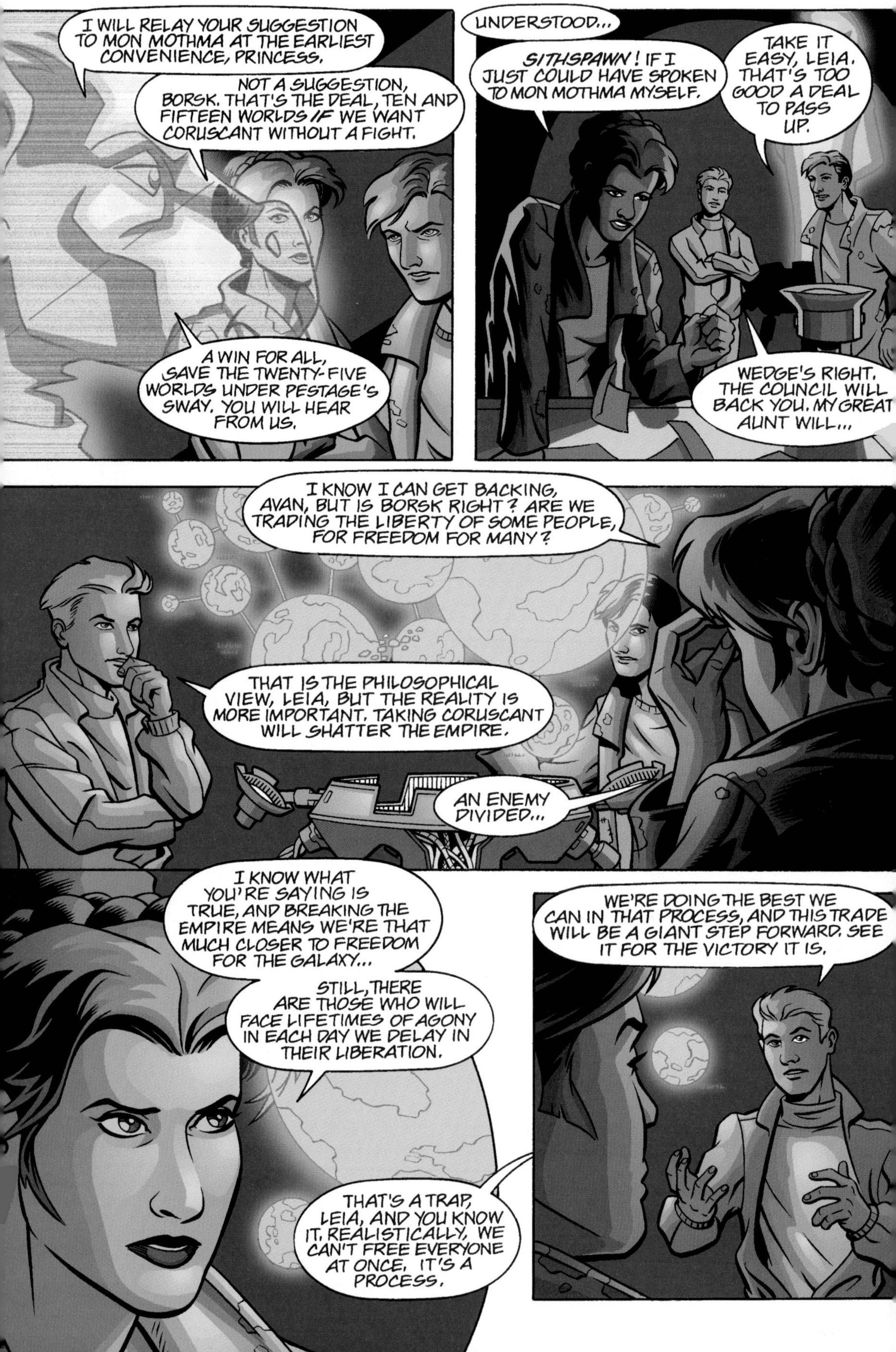
I WILL RELAY YOUR SUGGESTION TO MON MOTHMA AT THE EARLIEST CONVENIENCE, PRINCESS.
NOT A SUGGESTION, BORSK. THAT'S THE DEAL, TEN AND FIFTEEN WORLDS *IF* WE WANT CORUSCANT WITHOUT A FIGHT.
A WIN FOR ALL, SAVE THE TWENTY-FIVE WORLDS UNDER PESTAGE'S SWAY. YOU WILL HEAR FROM US.
UNDERSTOOD...
SITHSPAWN! IF I JUST COULD HAVE SPOKEN TO MON MOTHMA MYSELF.
TAKE IT EASY, LEIA. THAT'S TOO GOOD A DEAL TO PASS UP.
WEDGE'S RIGHT. THE COUNCIL WILL BACK YOU. MY GREAT AUNT WILL...
I KNOW I CAN GET BACKING, AVAN, BUT IS BORSK RIGHT? ARE WE TRADING THE LIBERTY OF SOME PEOPLE, FOR FREEDOM FOR MANY?
THAT IS THE PHILOSOPHICAL VIEW, LEIA, BUT THE REALITY IS MORE IMPORTANT. TAKING CORUSCANT WILL SHATTER THE EMPIRE.
AN ENEMY DIVIDED...
I KNOW WHAT YOU'RE SAYING IS TRUE, AND BREAKING THE EMPIRE MEANS WE'RE THAT MUCH CLOSER TO FREEDOM FOR THE GALAXY...
STILL, THERE ARE THOSE WHO WILL FACE LIFETIMES OF AGONY IN EACH DAY WE DELAY IN THEIR LIBERATION.
THAT'S A TRAP, LEIA, AND YOU KNOW IT. REALISTICALLY, WE CAN'T FREE EVERYONE AT ONCE. IT'S A PROCESS.
WE'RE DOING THE BEST WE CAN IN THAT PROCESS, AND THIS TRADE WILL BE A GIANT STEP FORWARD. SEE IT FOR THE VICTORY IT IS.

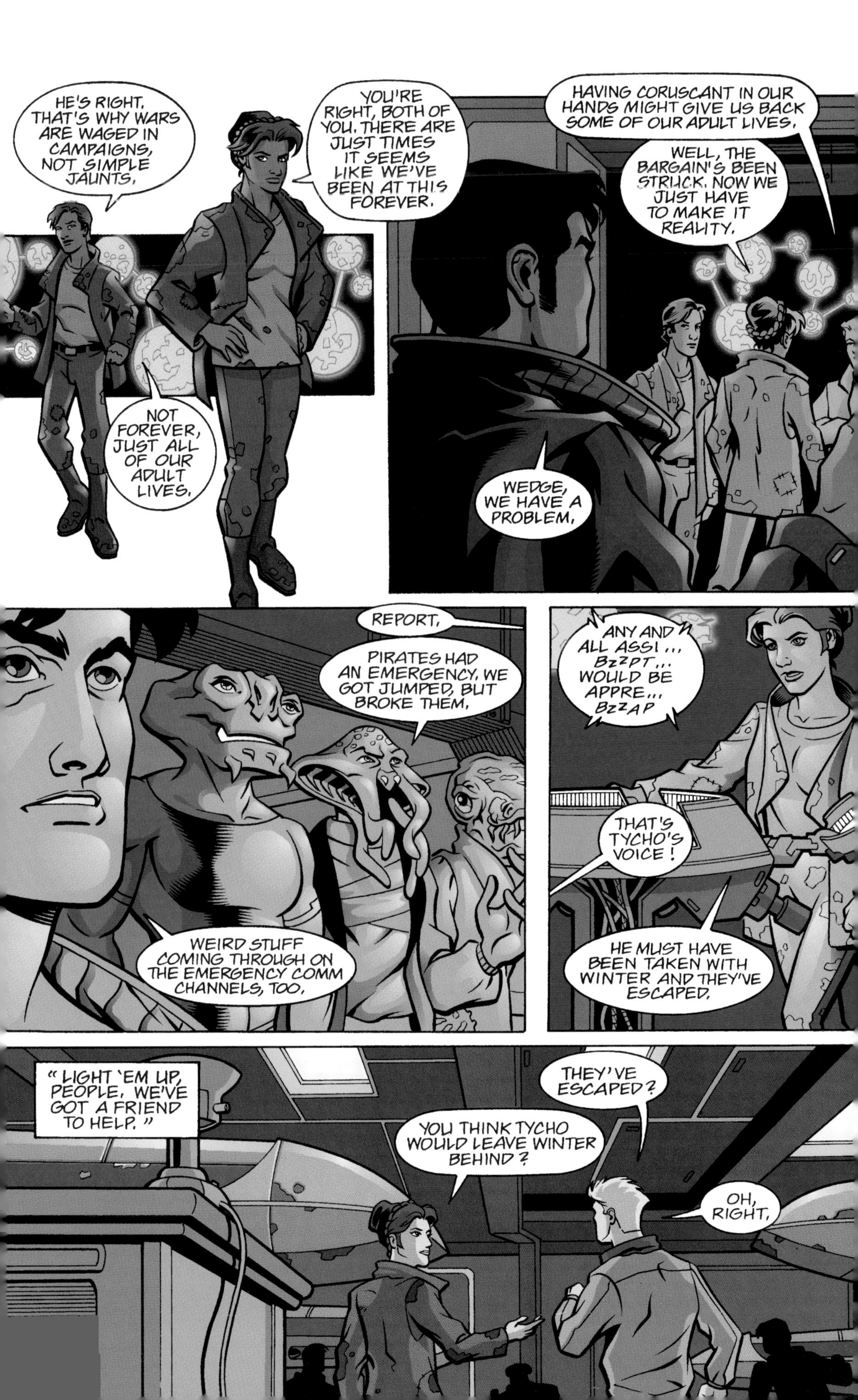
HE'S RIGHT. THAT'S WHY WARS ARE WAGED IN CAMPAIGNS, NOT SIMPLE JAUNTS.
YOU'RE RIGHT, BOTH OF YOU. THERE ARE JUST TIMES IT SEEMS LIKE WE'VE BEEN AT THIS FOREVER.
NOT FOREVER, JUST ALL OF OUR ADULT LIVES.
HAVING CORUSCANT IN OUR HANDS MIGHT GIVE US BACK SOME OF OUR ADULT LIVES.
WELL, THE BARGAIN'S BEEN STRUCK. NOW WE JUST HAVE TO MAKE IT REALITY.
WEDGE, WE HAVE A PROBLEM.
REPORT.
PIRATES HAD AN EMERGENCY. WE GOT JUMPED, BUT BROKE THEM.
WEIRD STUFF COMING THROUGH ON THE EMERGENCY COMM CHANNELS, TOO.
ANY AND ALL ASSI... BZZPT... WOULD BE APPRE... BZZAP
THAT'S TYCHO'S VOICE!
HE MUST HAVE BEEN TAKEN WITH WINTER AND THEY'VE ESCAPED.
"LIGHT 'EM UP, PEOPLE. WE'VE GOT A FRIEND TO HELP."
THEY'VE ESCAPED?
YOU THINK TYCHO WOULD LEAVE WINTER BEHIND?
OH, RIGHT.

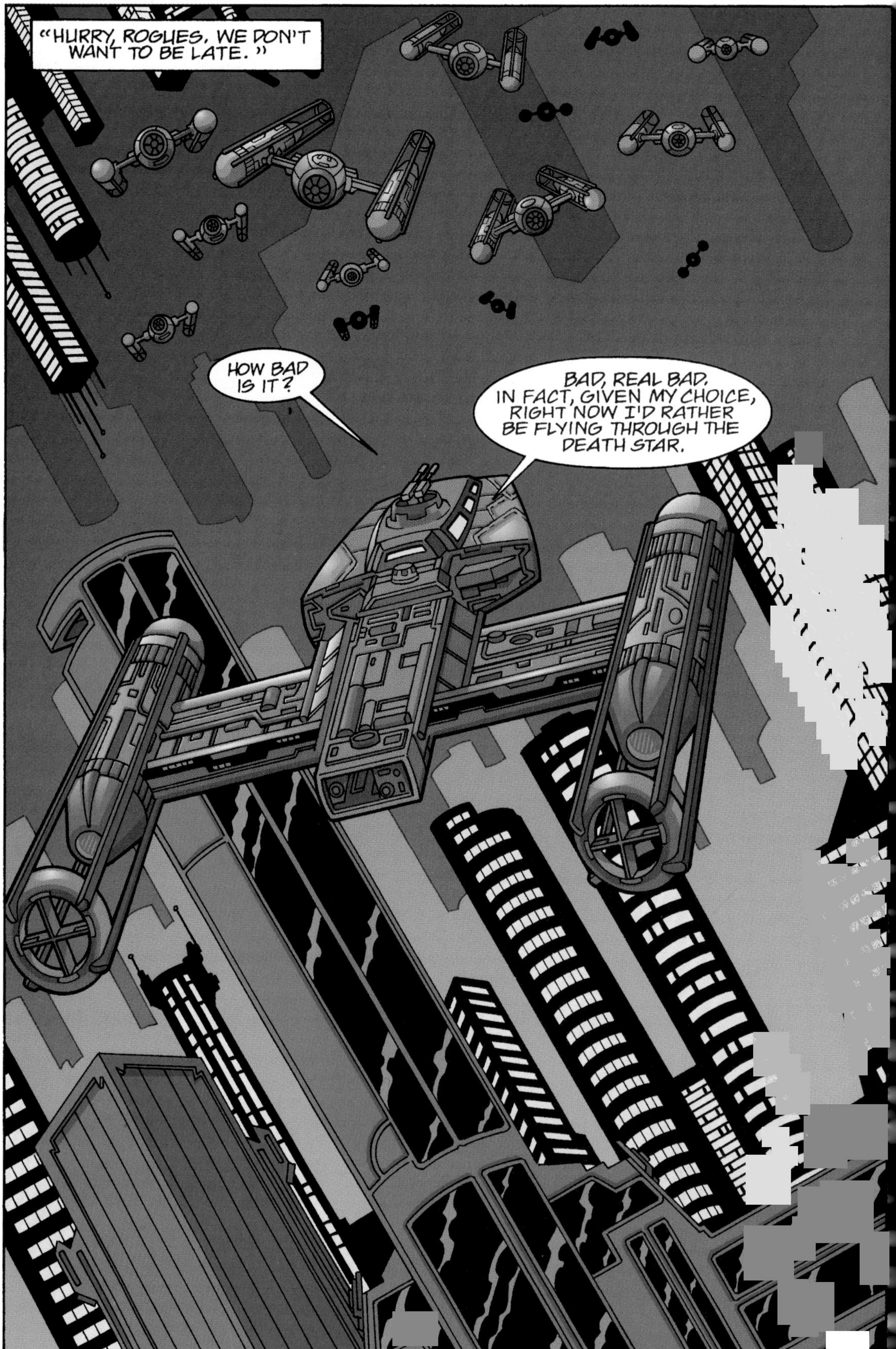
"HURRY, ROGUES, WE DON'T WANT TO BE LATE."
HOW BAD IS IT?
BAD, REAL BAD. IN FACT, GIVEN MY CHOICE, RIGHT NOW I'D RATHER BE FLYING THROUGH THE DEATH STAR.

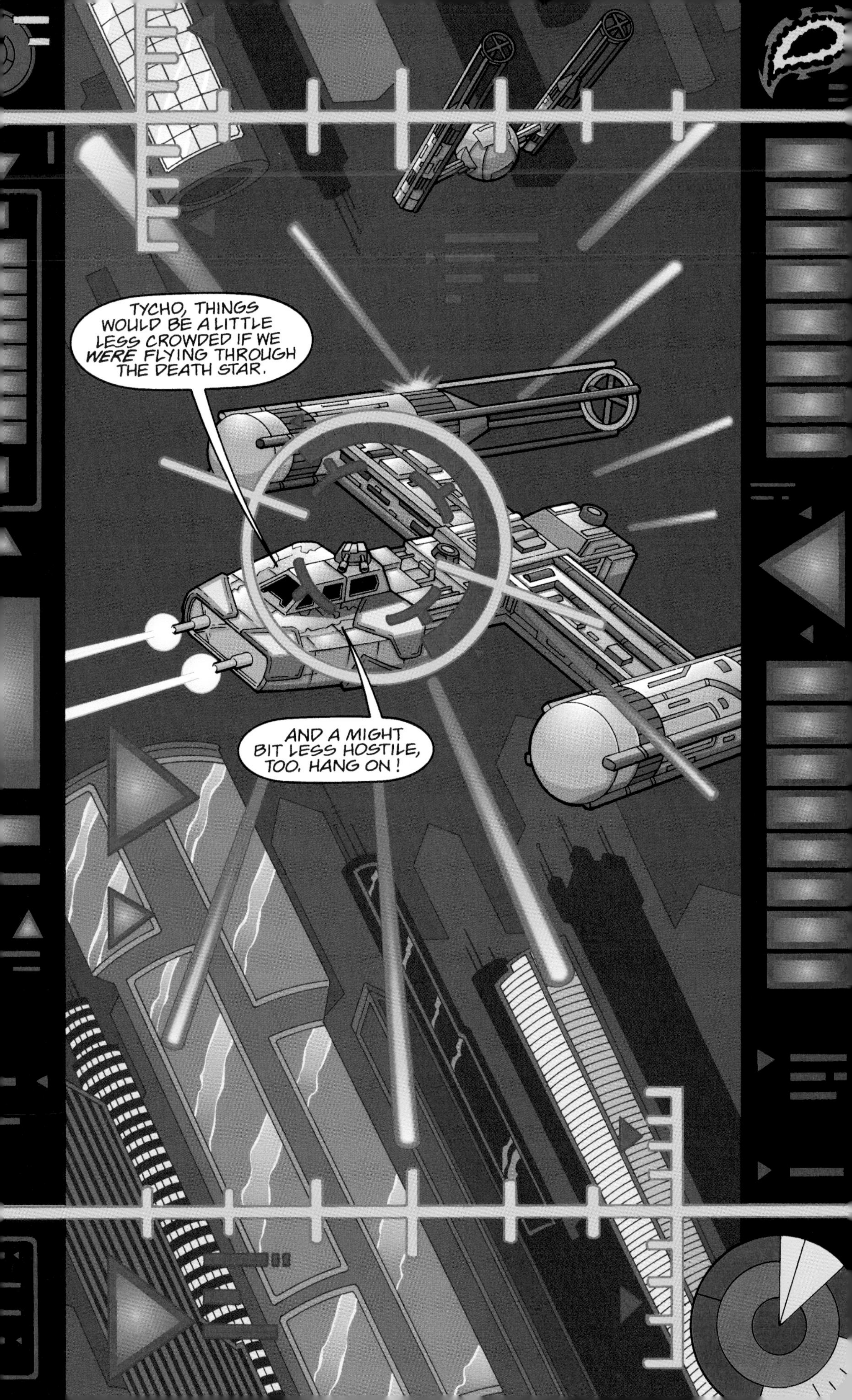
TYCHO, THINGS WOULD BE A LITTLE LESS CROWDED IF WE *WERE* FLYING THROUGH THE DEATH STAR.
AND A MIGHT BIT LESS HOSTILE, TOO. HANG ON!

YOUR MOVE DIDN'T FOOL THEM.
SUCH GENEROSITY...
NOT DESIGNED TO-- I WANTED TO GIVE YOU BETTER TARGETS.
WELL, YOU DESERVE THE BEST, WINTER.
I'LL SETTLE FOR CLEAR SCOPES.
WISH I COULD COMPLY, LOVE, BUT MY SCOPE JUST PICKED UP INCOMING.
AND I SHOW A HEAVIER SHIP HERE. IT WAS FUN, WASN'T IT?
AND ABOUT TO BECOME MORE SO...
WHAT?
YOU HAVEN'T FINISHED THESE GUYS YET, TYCHO?

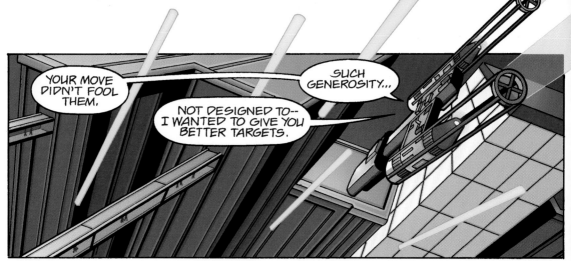

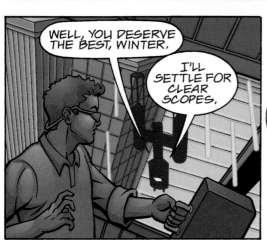

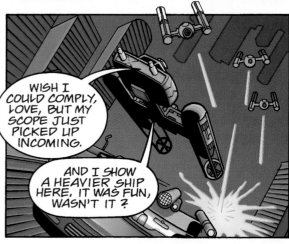

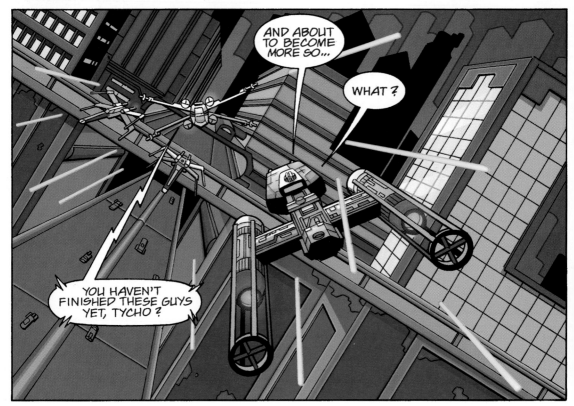

WELL, YOU KNOW, THESE Y-WINGS ARE SLOW AND I WANTED TO LEAVE A FEW FOR WINTER TO SHOOT.

YOU'LL REGRET THAT REMARK, CELCHU.

GET CLEAR. WE HAVE THEM.

LOTS OF THEM, SEVEN OF YOU, WE HAVE SHIELDS, WE'LL COME BACK INTO THE FIGHT, THANKS.

MOVE FAST, MAY NOT BE THAT MUCH FIGHT LEFT FOR YOU.

LEAD, FOUR HAS Z-INTERCEPTOR SQUADRON COMING IN AT 318 MARK 35.

I COPY, FOUR.

TWO HAS YOUR BACK, FOUR.

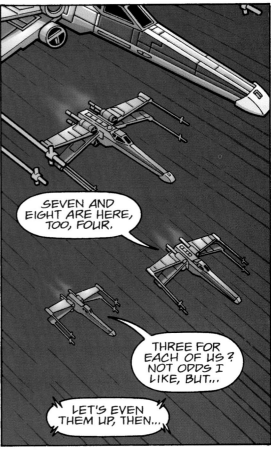

SEVEN AND EIGHT ARE HERE, TOO, FOUR.

THREE FOR EACH OF US? NOT ODDS I LIKE, BUT...

LET'S EVEN THEM UP, THEN...

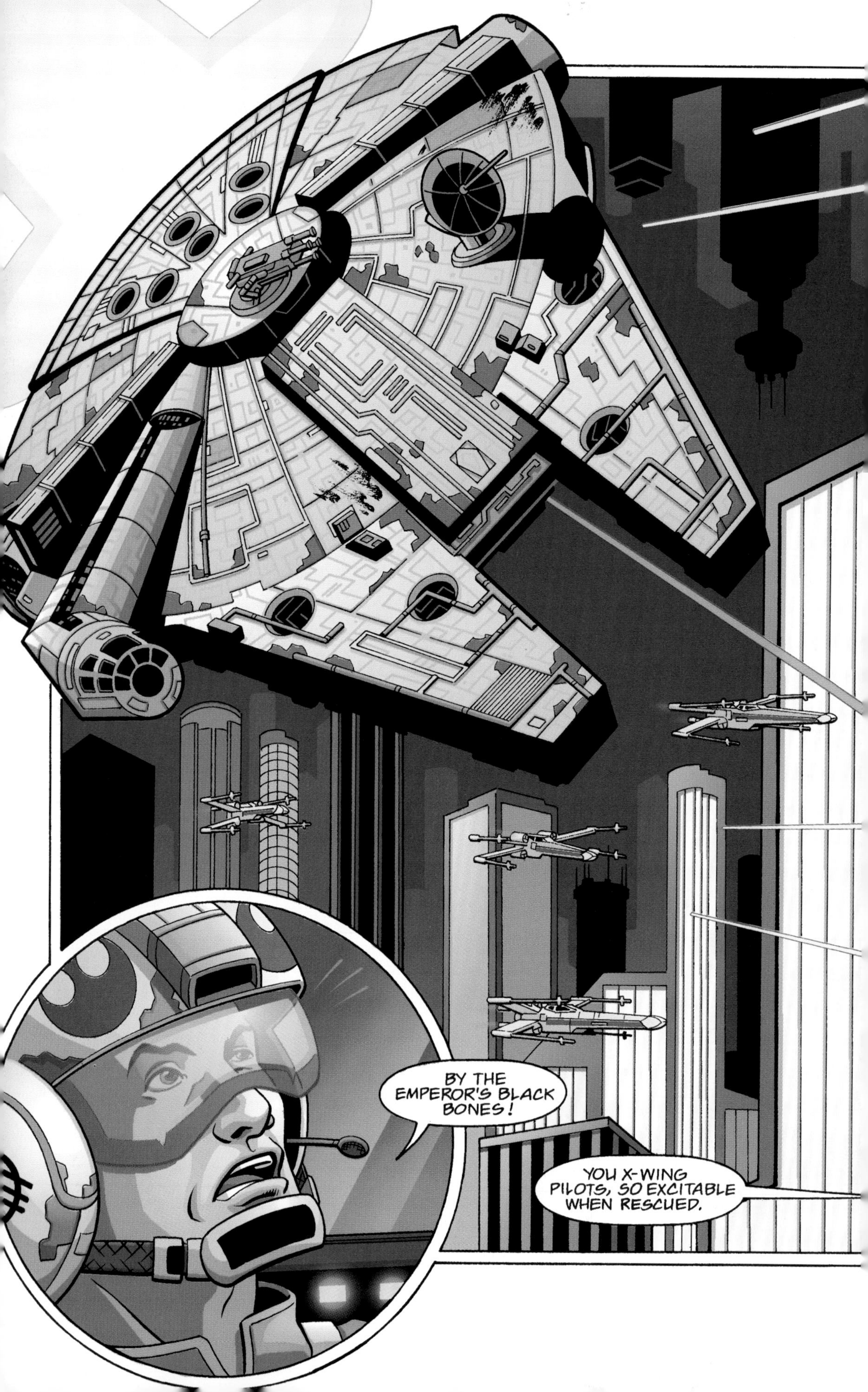
BY THE EMPEROR'S BLACK BONES!
YOU X-WING PILOTS, SO EXCITABLE WHEN RESCUED.

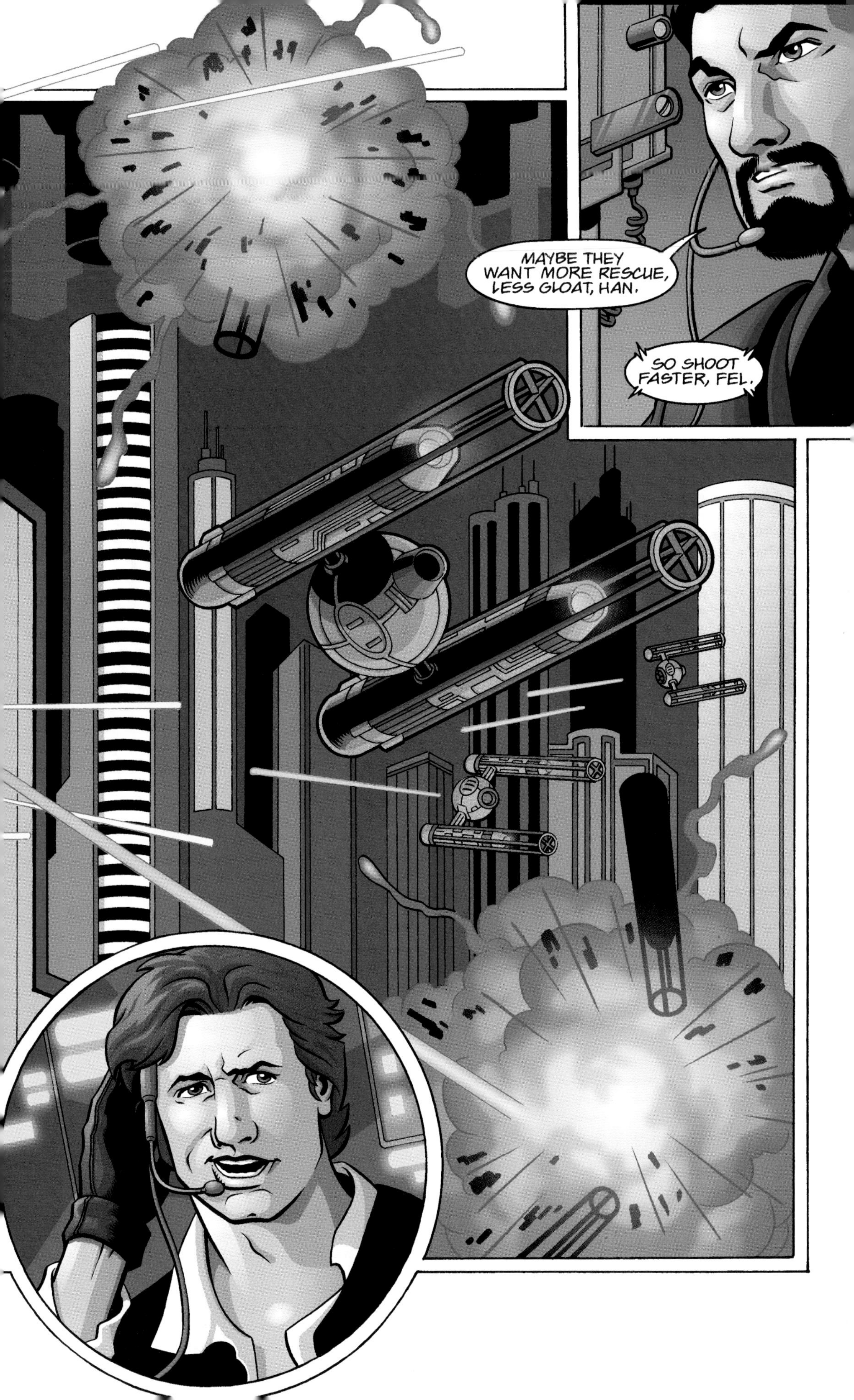
MAYBE THEY WANT MORE RESCUE, LESS GLOAT, HAN.
SO SHOOT FASTER, FEL.

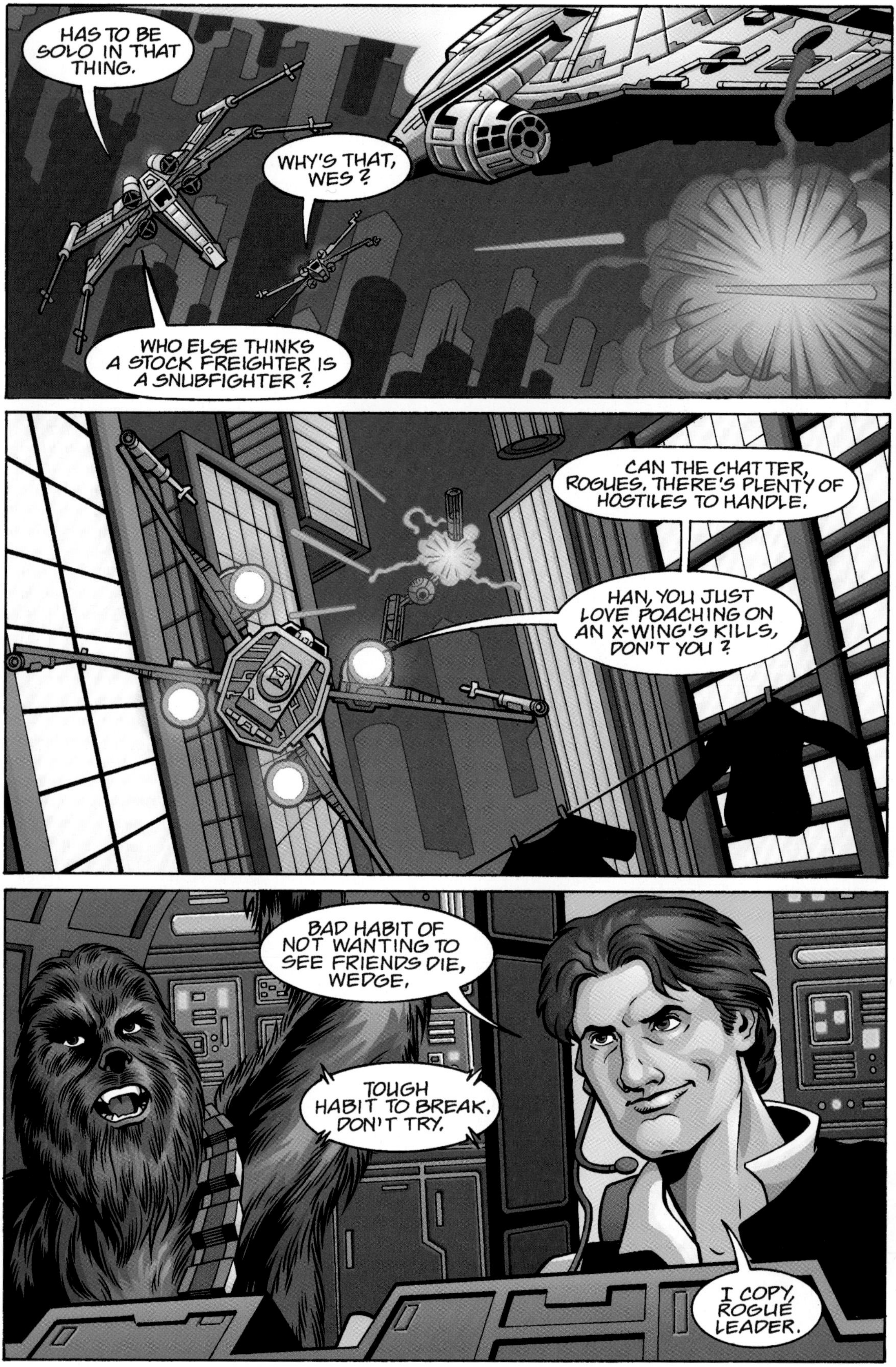
HAS TO BE SOLO IN THAT THING.
WHY'S THAT, WES?
WHO ELSE THINKS A STOCK FREIGHTER IS A SNUBFIGHTER?
CAN THE CHATTER, ROGUES. THERE'S PLENTY OF HOSTILES TO HANDLE.
HAN, YOU JUST LOVE POACHING ON AN X-WING'S KILLS, DON'T YOU?
BAD HABIT OF NOT WANTING TO SEE FRIENDS DIE, WEDGE.
TOUGH HABIT TO BREAK. DON'T TRY.
I COPY, ROGUE LEADER.

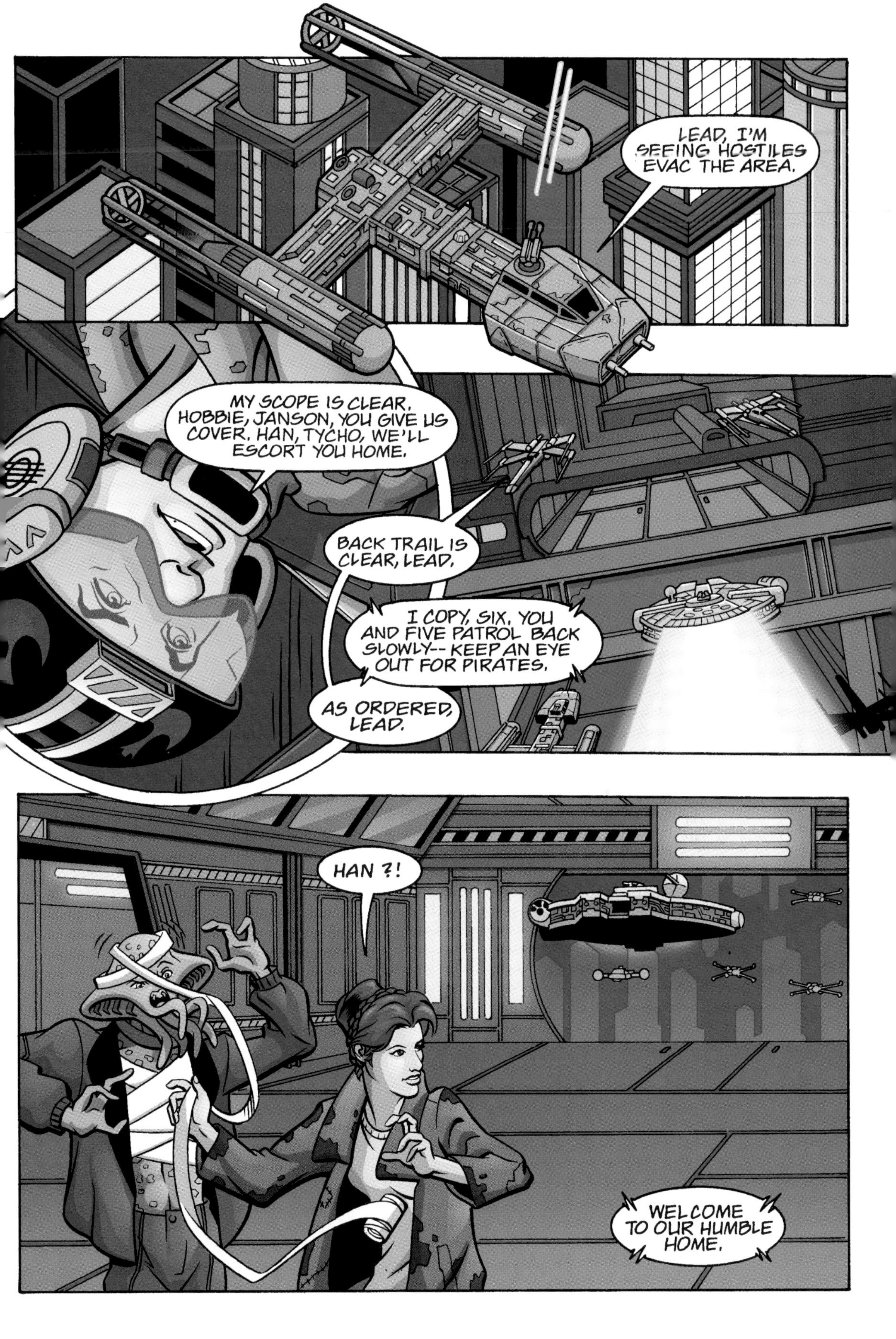
LEAD, I'M SEEING HOSTILES EVAC THE AREA.
MY SCOPE IS CLEAR. HOBBIE, JANSON, YOU GIVE US COVER. HAN, TYCHO, WE'LL ESCORT YOU HOME.
BACK TRAIL IS CLEAR, LEAD.
I COPY, SIX. YOU AND FIVE PATROL BACK SLOWLY-- KEEP AN EYE OUT FOR PIRATES.
AS ORDERED, LEAD.
HAN ?!
WELCOME TO OUR HUMBLE HOME.

YOU FLY WING COVER WELL, IBTISAM.

YOU'RE HARD TO KEEP UP WITH, XARCCE.

I'M TELLING YOU, CAPTAIN, THAT FREIGHTER CAME OUT OF NOWHERE.

THE FALCON DOES THAT SORT OF THING PRETTY WELL.

NRIN, YOU MISSED A BATTLE!

YOU'RE UNHURT?

THE BOTH OF US, YES.

I HATED BEING HERE, WAITING.

YOU'RE REFERRING TO THE DEATH STAR AT YAVIN, RIGHT?

THEN DO NOT GET SHOT NEXT TIME...

SOLO AND THE FALCON SAVED LUKE SKYWALKER AND THE REBELLION DOING LESS THAN TODAY.

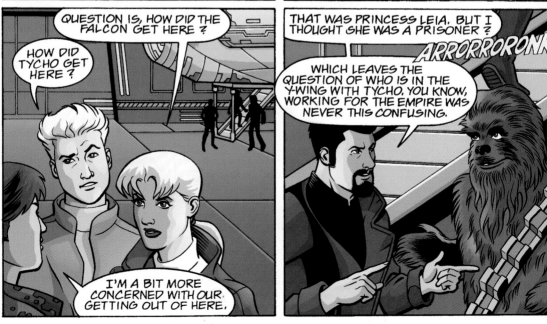

QUESTION IS, HOW DID THE FALCON GET HERE?

HOW DID TYCHO GET HERE?

I'M A BIT MORE CONCERNED WITH OUR GETTING OUT OF HERE.

THAT WAS PRINCESS LEIA. BUT I THOUGHT SHE WAS A PRISONER?

ARRORRORONK!

WHICH LEAVES THE QUESTION OF WHO IS IN THE Y-WING WITH TYCHO. YOU KNOW, WORKING FOR THE EMPIRE WAS NEVER THIS CONFUSING.

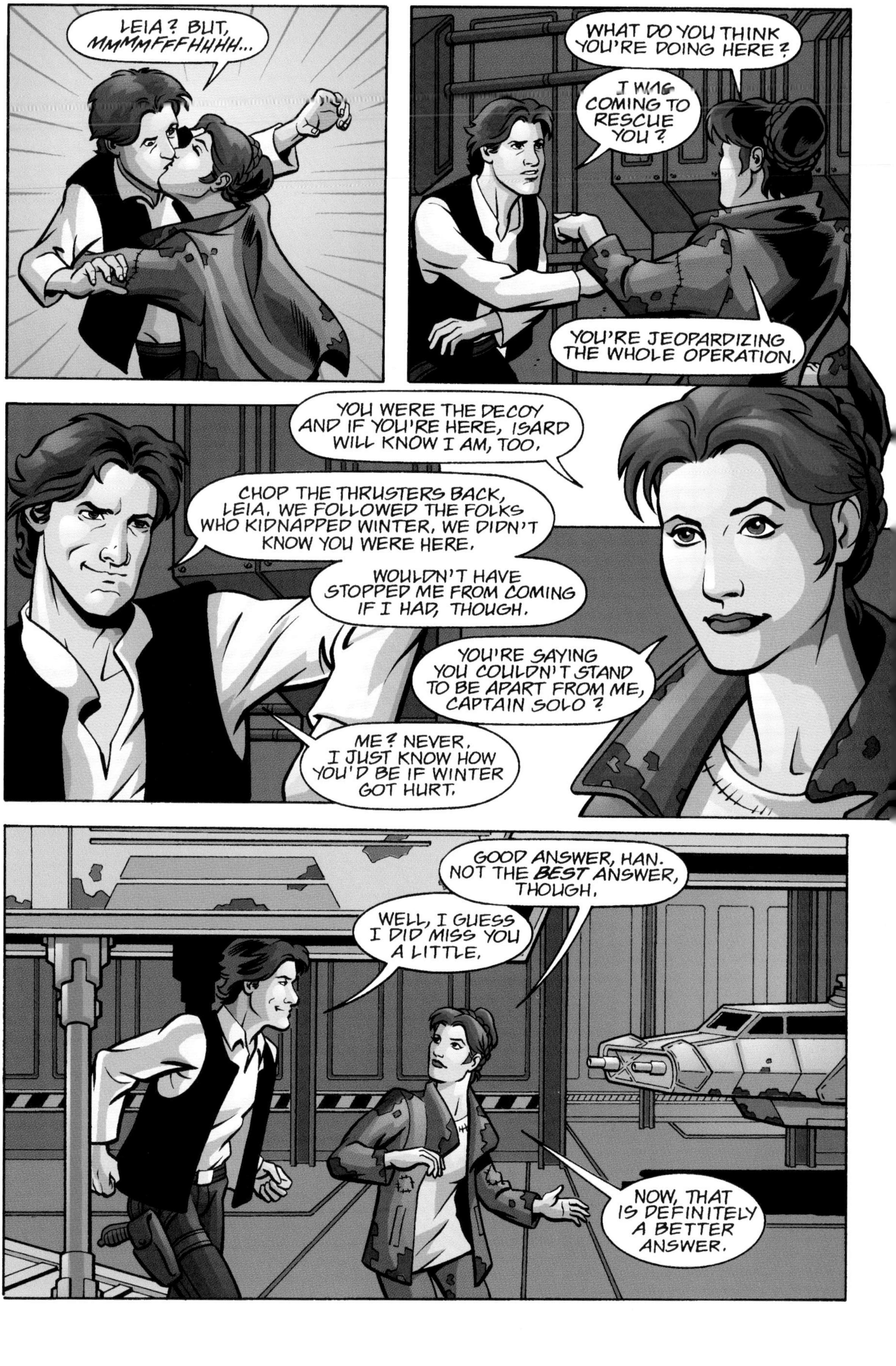
LEIA? BUT, MMMMFFFHHHH...
WHAT DO YOU THINK YOU'RE DOING HERE?
I WAS COMING TO RESCUE YOU?
YOU'RE JEOPARDIZING THE WHOLE OPERATION.
YOU WERE THE DECOY AND IF YOU'RE HERE, ISARD WILL KNOW I AM, TOO.
CHOP THE THRUSTERS BACK, LEIA. WE FOLLOWED THE FOLKS WHO KIDNAPPED WINTER. WE DIDN'T KNOW YOU WERE HERE.
WOULDN'T HAVE STOPPED ME FROM COMING IF I HAD, THOUGH.
YOU'RE SAYING YOU COULDN'T STAND TO BE APART FROM ME, CAPTAIN SOLO?
ME? NEVER. I JUST KNOW HOW YOU'D BE IF WINTER GOT HURT.
GOOD ANSWER, HAN. NOT THE *BEST* ANSWER, THOUGH.
WELL, I GUESS I DID MISS YOU A LITTLE.
NOW, THAT IS DEFINITELY A BETTER ANSWER.

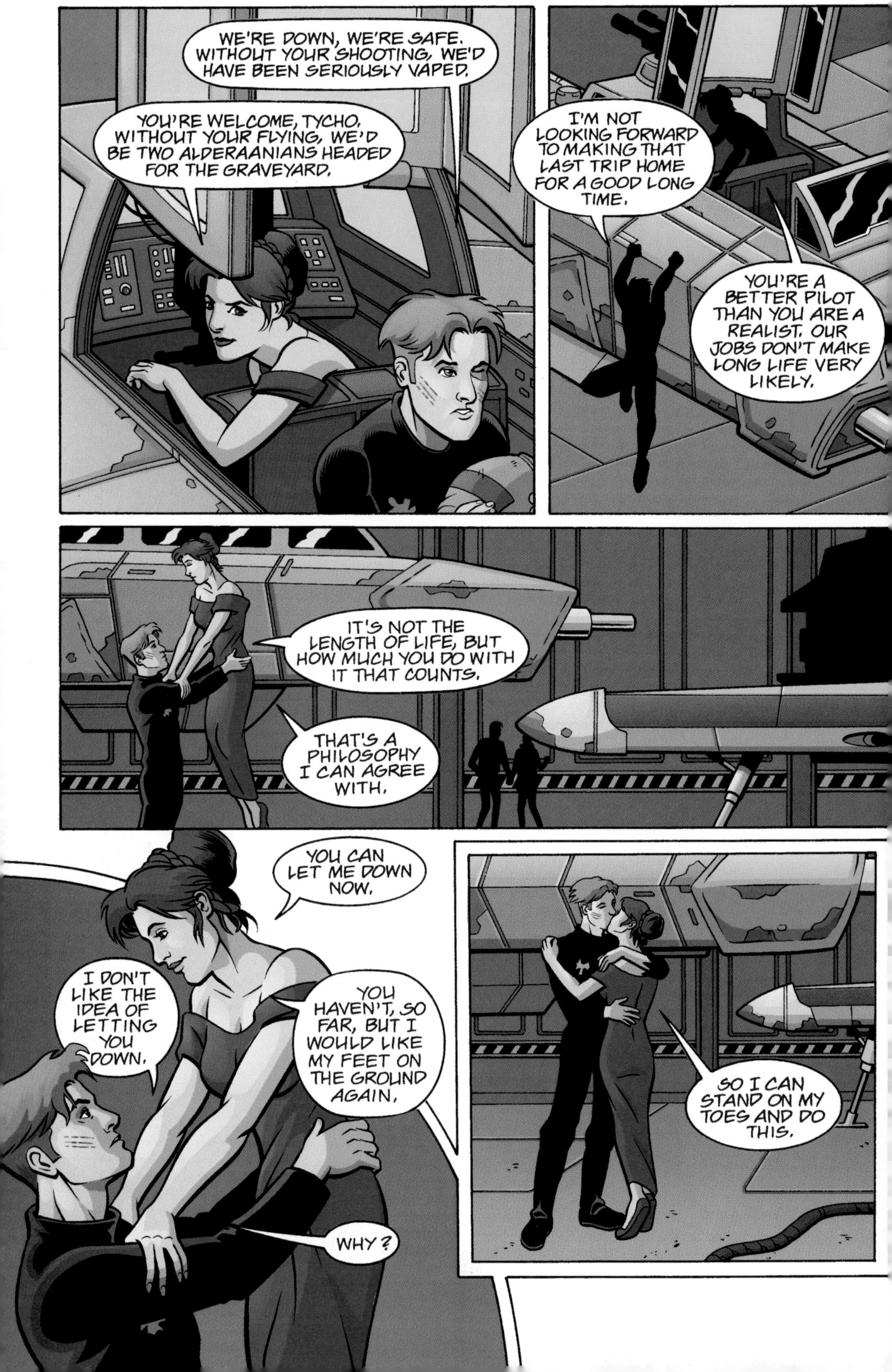
WE'RE DOWN, WE'RE SAFE. WITHOUT YOUR SHOOTING, WE'D HAVE BEEN SERIOUSLY VAPED.
YOU'RE WELCOME, TYCHO. WITHOUT YOUR FLYING, WE'D BE TWO ALDERAANIANS HEADED FOR THE GRAVEYARD.
I'M NOT LOOKING FORWARD TO MAKING THAT LAST TRIP HOME FOR A GOOD LONG TIME.
YOU'RE A BETTER PILOT THAN YOU ARE A REALIST. OUR JOBS DON'T MAKE LONG LIFE VERY LIKELY.
IT'S NOT THE LENGTH OF LIFE, BUT HOW MUCH YOU DO WITH IT THAT COUNTS.
THAT'S A PHILOSOPHY I CAN AGREE WITH.
YOU CAN LET ME DOWN NOW.
I DON'T LIKE THE IDEA OF LETTING YOU DOWN.
YOU HAVEN'T, SO FAR, BUT I WOULD LIKE MY FEET ON THE GROUND AGAIN.
WHY?
SO I CAN STAND ON MY TOES AND DO THIS.

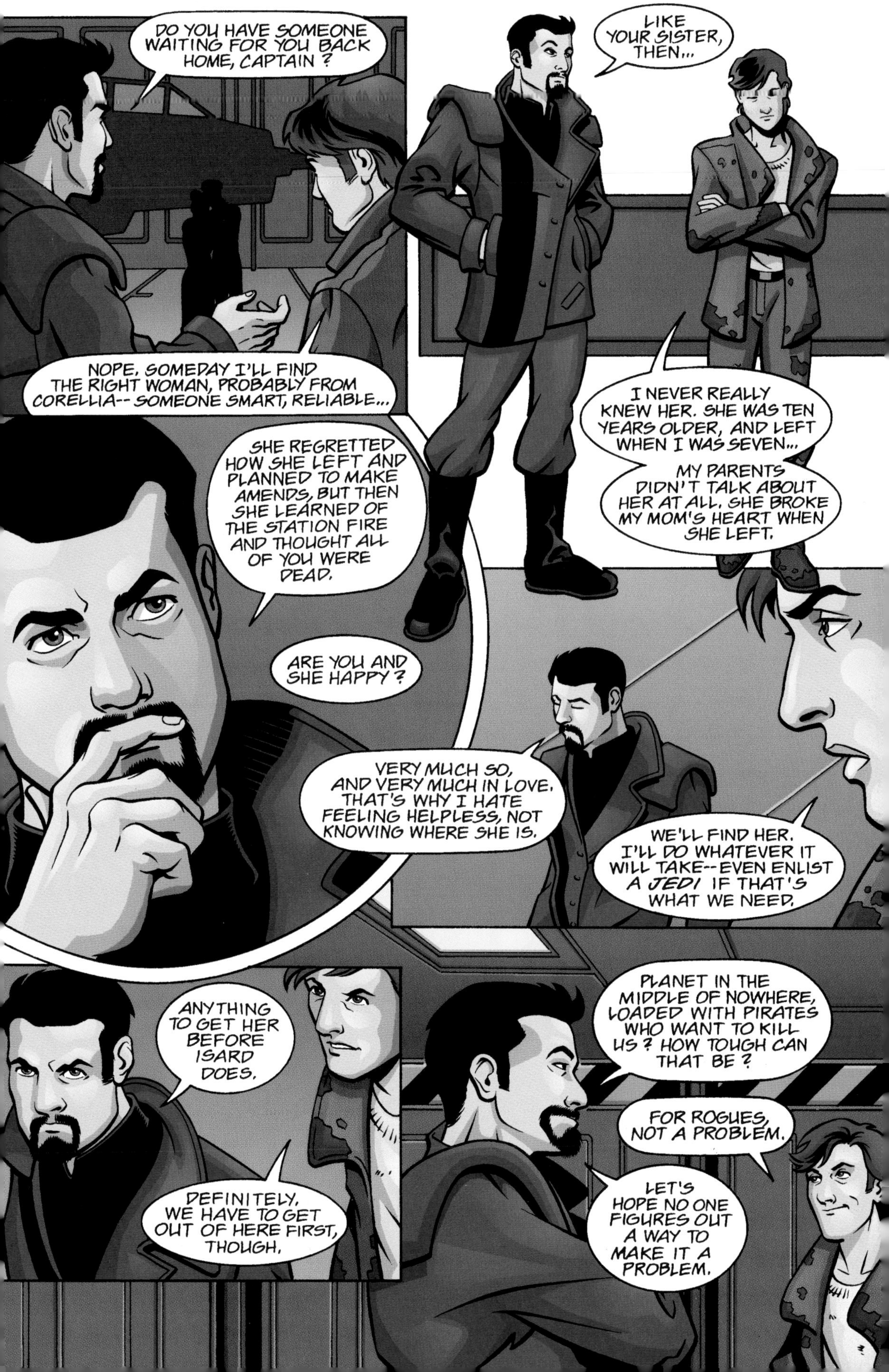
DO YOU HAVE SOMEONE WAITING FOR YOU BACK HOME, CAPTAIN ?
NOPE, SOMEDAY I'LL FIND THE RIGHT WOMAN, PROBABLY FROM CORELLIA-- SOMEONE SMART, RELIABLE...
LIKE YOUR SISTER, THEN...
I NEVER REALLY KNEW HER. SHE WAS TEN YEARS OLDER, AND LEFT WHEN I WAS SEVEN...
MY PARENTS DIDN'T TALK ABOUT HER AT ALL. SHE BROKE MY MOM'S HEART WHEN SHE LEFT.
SHE REGRETTED HOW SHE LEFT AND PLANNED TO MAKE AMENDS, BUT THEN SHE LEARNED OF THE STATION FIRE AND THOUGHT ALL OF YOU WERE DEAD.
ARE YOU AND SHE HAPPY ?
VERY MUCH SO, AND VERY MUCH IN LOVE. THAT'S WHY I HATE FEELING HELPLESS, NOT KNOWING WHERE SHE IS.
WE'LL FIND HER. I'LL DO WHATEVER IT WILL TAKE--EVEN ENLIST A *JEDI* IF THAT'S WHAT WE NEED.
ANYTHING TO GET HER BEFORE ISARD DOES.
DEFINITELY. WE HAVE TO GET OUT OF HERE FIRST, THOUGH.
PLANET IN THE MIDDLE OF NOWHERE, LOADED WITH PIRATES WHO WANT TO KILL US ? HOW TOUGH CAN THAT BE ?
FOR ROGUES, NOT A PROBLEM.
LET'S HOPE NO ONE FIGURES OUT A WAY TO MAKE IT A PROBLEM.

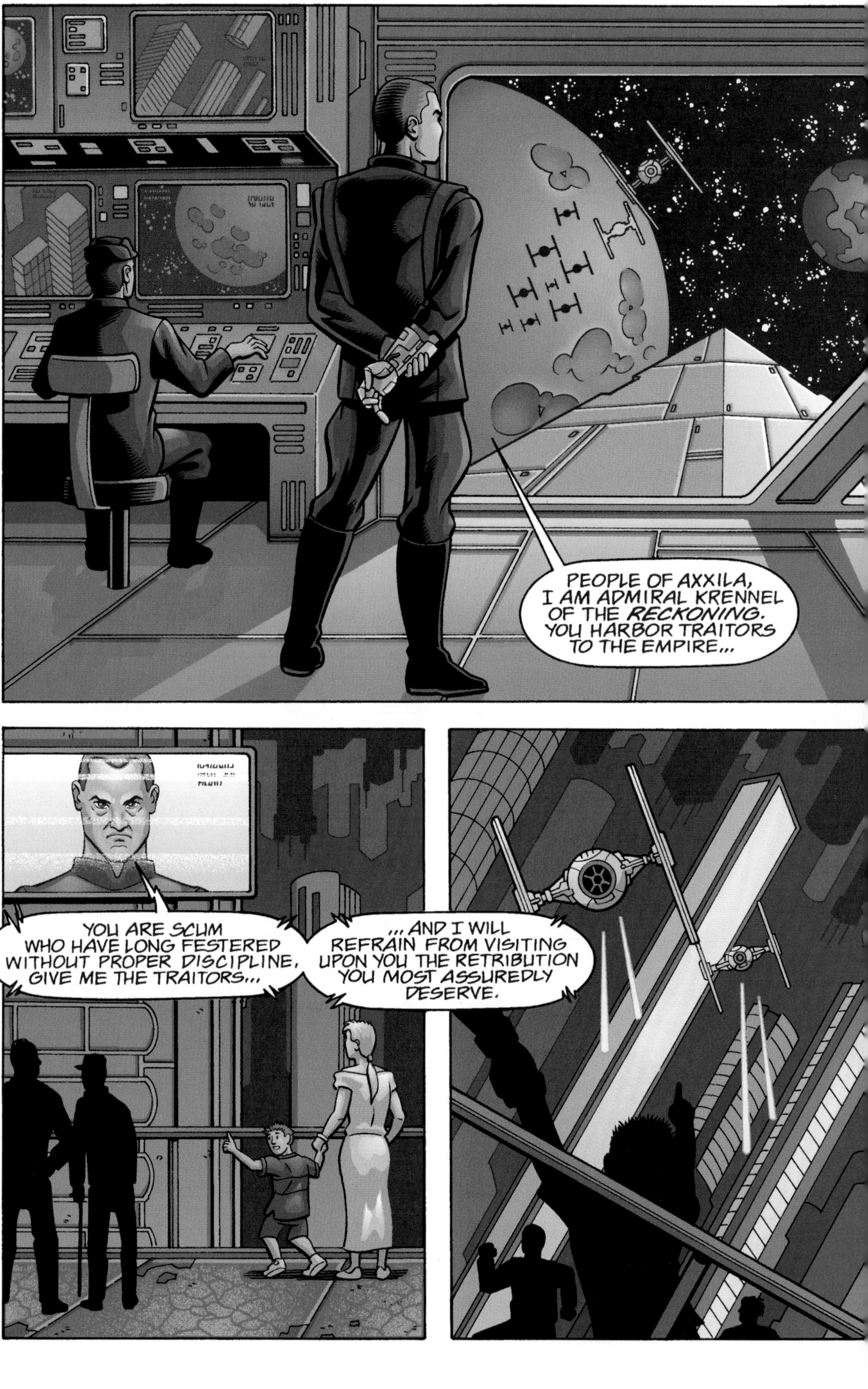
PEOPLE OF AXXILA, I AM ADMIRAL KRENNEL OF THE *RECKONING*. YOU HARBOR TRAITORS TO THE EMPIRE...
YOU ARE SCUM WHO HAVE LONG FESTERED WITHOUT PROPER DISCIPLINE. GIVE ME THE TRAITORS...
...AND I WILL REFRAIN FROM VISITING UPON YOU THE RETRIBUTION YOU MOST ASSUREDLY DESERVE.

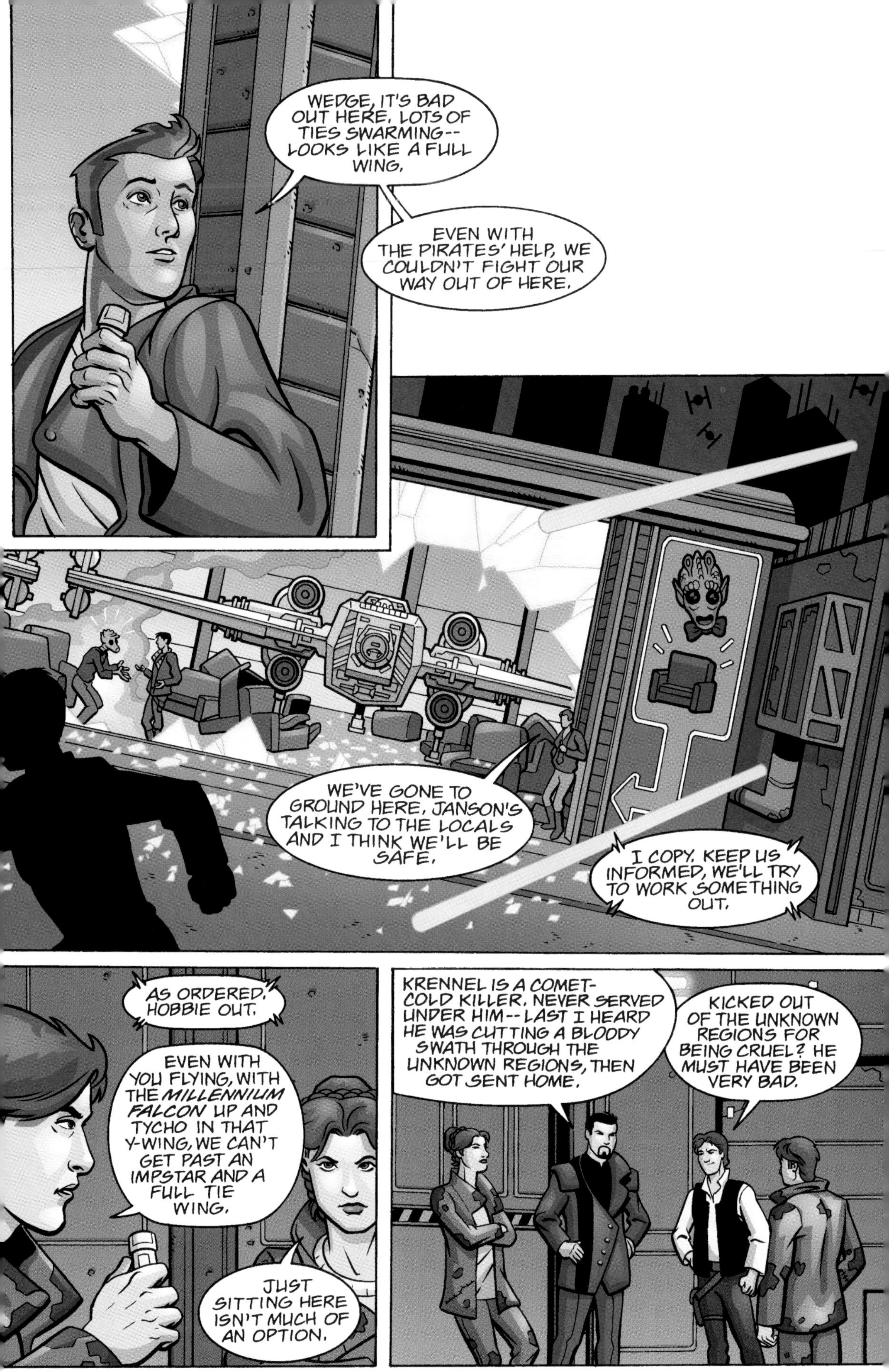
WEDGE, IT'S BAD OUT HERE. LOTS OF TIES SWARMING-- LOOKS LIKE A FULL WING.
EVEN WITH THE PIRATES' HELP, WE COULDN'T FIGHT OUR WAY OUT OF HERE.
WE'VE GONE TO GROUND HERE. JANSON'S TALKING TO THE LOCALS AND I THINK WE'LL BE SAFE.
I COPY. KEEP US INFORMED. WE'LL TRY TO WORK SOMETHING OUT.
AS ORDERED. HOBBIE OUT.
EVEN WITH YOU FLYING, WITH THE *MILLENNIUM FALCON* UP AND TYCHO IN THAT Y-WING, WE CAN'T GET PAST AN IMPSTAR AND A FULL TIE WING.
JUST SITTING HERE ISN'T MUCH OF AN OPTION.
KRENNEL IS A COMET-COLD KILLER. NEVER SERVED UNDER HIM-- LAST I HEARD HE WAS CUTTING A BLOODY SWATH THROUGH THE UNKNOWN REGIONS, THEN GOT SENT HOME.
KICKED OUT OF THE UNKNOWN REGIONS FOR BEING CRUEL? HE MUST HAVE BEEN VERY BAD.

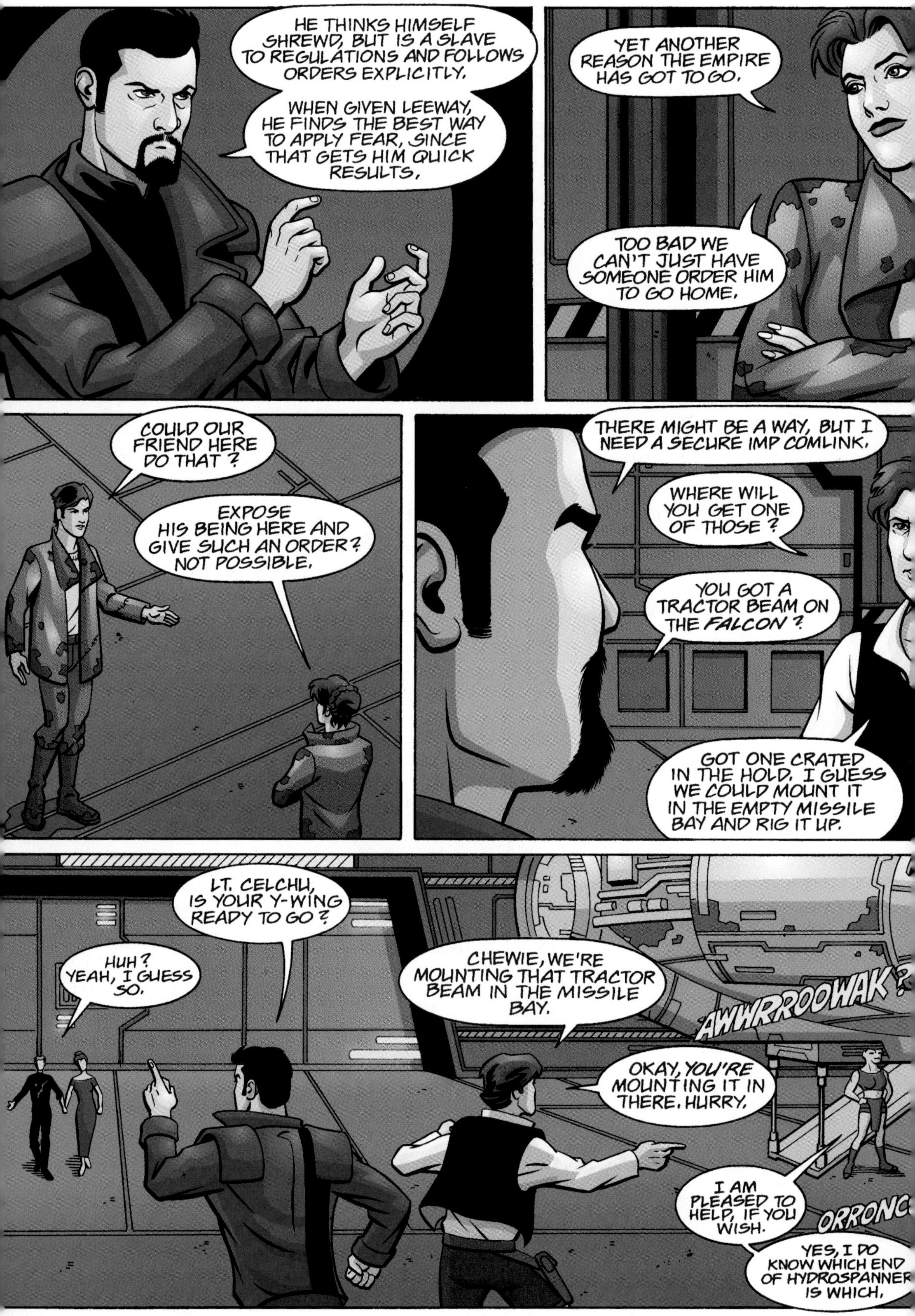
HE THINKS HIMSELF SHREWD, BUT IS A SLAVE TO REGULATIONS AND FOLLOWS ORDERS EXPLICITLY.
WHEN GIVEN LEEWAY, HE FINDS THE BEST WAY TO APPLY FEAR, SINCE THAT GETS HIM QUICK RESULTS.
YET ANOTHER REASON THE EMPIRE HAS GOT TO GO.
TOO BAD WE CAN'T JUST HAVE SOMEONE ORDER HIM TO GO HOME.
COULD OUR FRIEND HERE DO THAT?
EXPOSE HIS BEING HERE AND GIVE SUCH AN ORDER? NOT POSSIBLE.
THERE MIGHT BE A WAY, BUT I NEED A SECURE IMP COMLINK.
WHERE WILL YOU GET ONE OF THOSE?
YOU GOT A TRACTOR BEAM ON THE *FALCON*?
GOT ONE CRATED IN THE HOLD. I GUESS WE COULD MOUNT IT IN THE EMPTY MISSILE BAY AND RIG IT UP.
LT. CELCHU, IS YOUR Y-WING READY TO GO?
HUH? YEAH, I GUESS SO.
CHEWIE, WE'RE MOUNTING THAT TRACTOR BEAM IN THE MISSILE BAY.
AWWRROOWAK?
OKAY, *YOU'RE* MOUNTING IT IN THERE. HURRY.
I AM PLEASED TO HELP, IF YOU WISH.
ORRONC
YES, I DO KNOW WHICH END OF HYDROSPANNER IS WHICH.

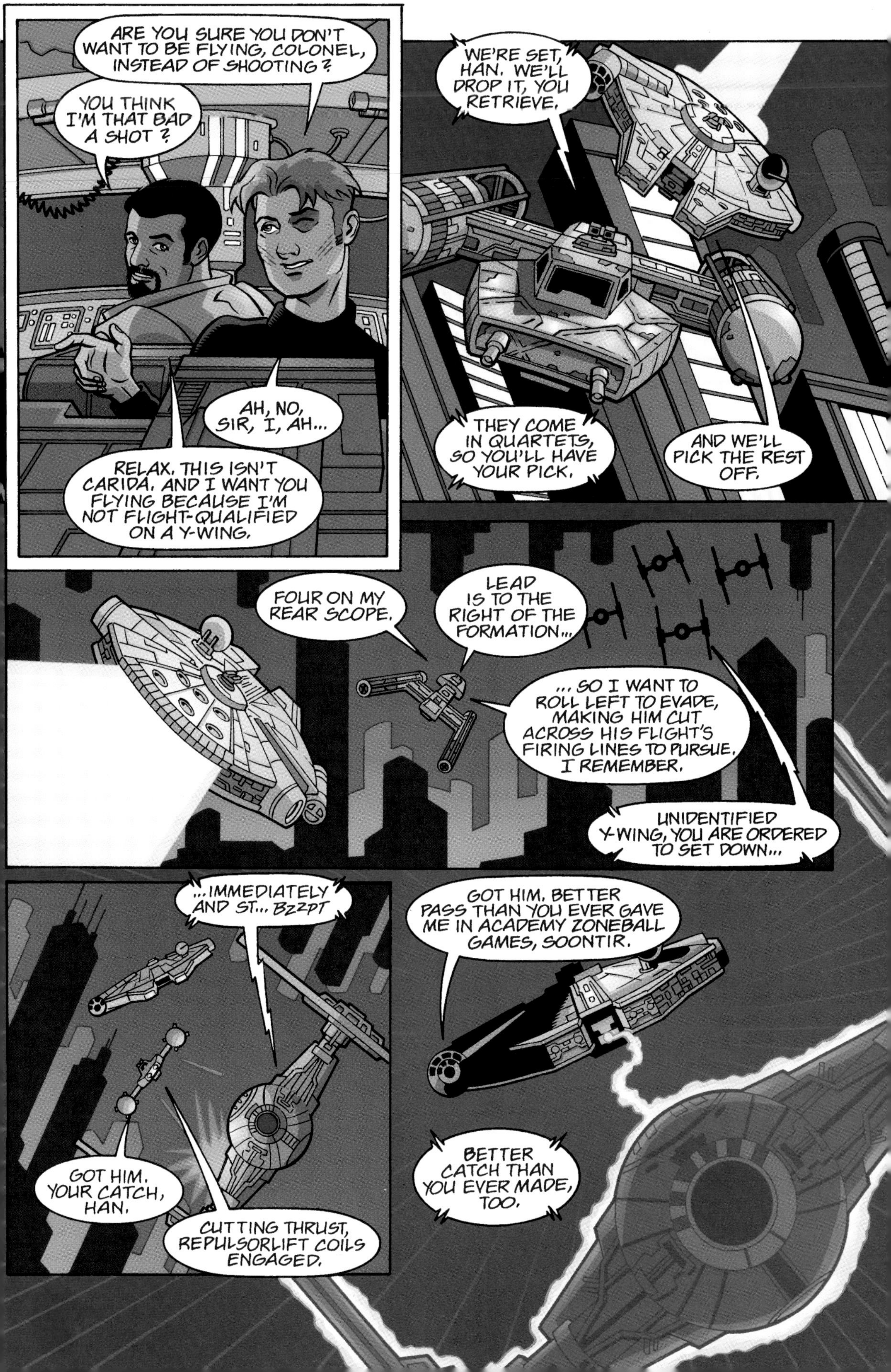
ARE YOU SURE YOU DON'T WANT TO BE FLYING, COLONEL, INSTEAD OF SHOOTING?
YOU THINK I'M THAT BAD A SHOT?
AH, NO, SIR, I, AH...
RELAX. THIS ISN'T CARIDA. AND I WANT YOU FLYING BECAUSE I'M NOT FLIGHT-QUALIFIED ON A Y-WING.
WE'RE SET, HAN. WE'LL DROP IT, YOU RETRIEVE.
THEY COME IN QUARTETS, SO YOU'LL HAVE YOUR PICK.
AND WE'LL PICK THE REST OFF.
FOUR ON MY REAR SCOPE.
LEAD IS TO THE RIGHT OF THE FORMATION...
... SO I WANT TO ROLL LEFT TO EVADE, MAKING HIM CUT ACROSS HIS FLIGHT'S FIRING LINES TO PURSUE. I REMEMBER.
UNIDENTIFIED Y-WING, YOU ARE ORDERED TO SET DOWN...
...IMMEDIATELY AND ST... BZZPT
GOT HIM. YOUR CATCH, HAN.
CUTTING THRUST, REPULSORLIFT COILS ENGAGED.
GOT HIM. BETTER PASS THAN YOU EVER GAVE ME IN ACADEMY ZONEBALL GAMES, SOONTIR.
BETTER CATCH THAN YOU EVER MADE, TOO.

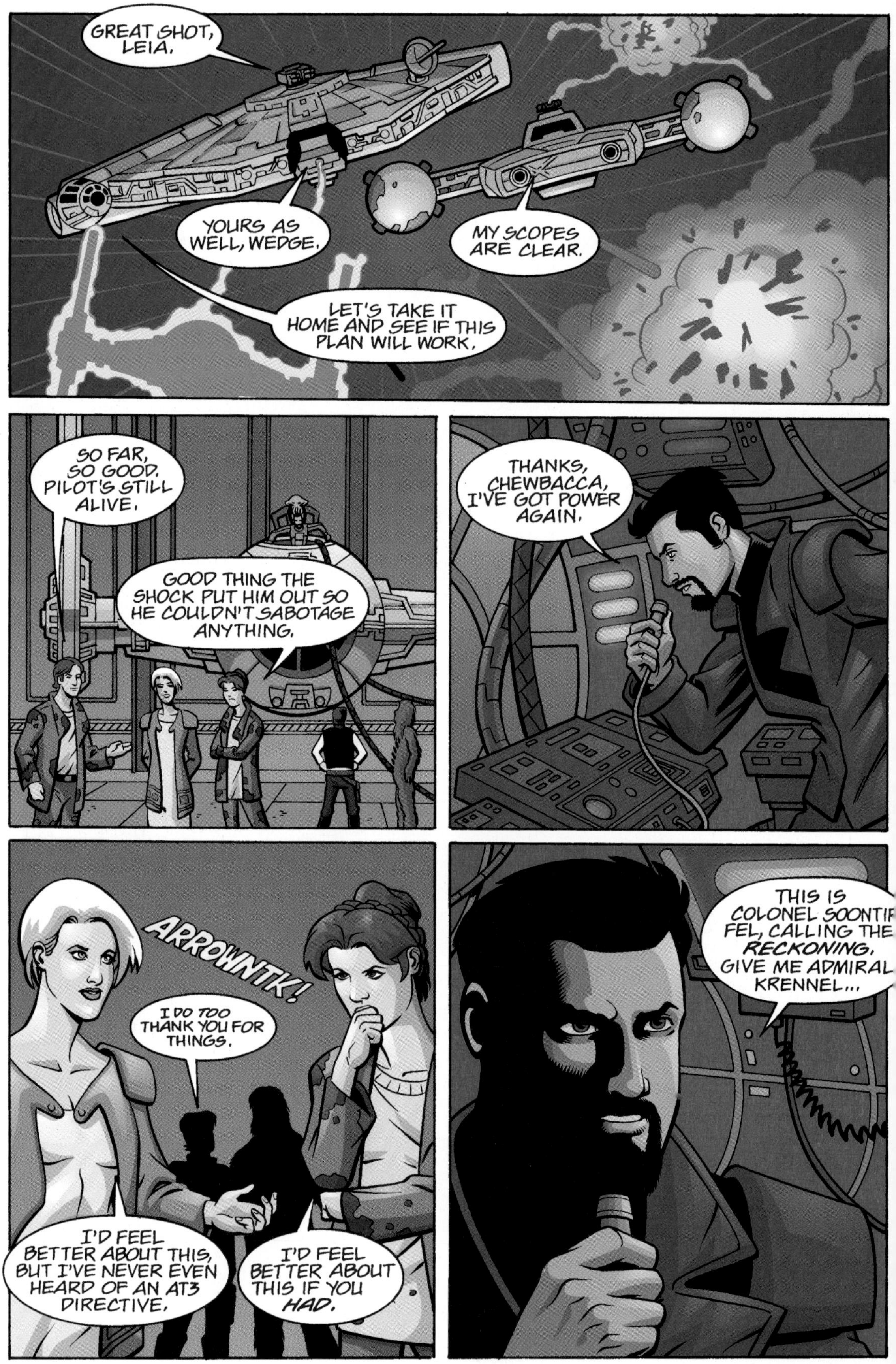
GREAT SHOT, LEIA.
YOURS AS WELL, WEDGE.
MY SCOPES ARE CLEAR.
LET'S TAKE IT HOME AND SEE IF THIS PLAN WILL WORK.
SO FAR, SO GOOD. PILOT'S STILL ALIVE.
GOOD THING THE SHOCK PUT HIM OUT SO HE COULDN'T SABOTAGE ANYTHING.
THANKS, CHEWBACCA, I'VE GOT POWER AGAIN.
ARROWNTK!
I DO TOO THANK YOU FOR THINGS.
I'D FEEL BETTER ABOUT THIS, BUT I'VE NEVER EVEN HEARD OF AN AT3 DIRECTIVE.
I'D FEEL BETTER ABOUT THIS IF YOU *HAD*.
THIS IS COLONEL SOONTIF FEL, CALLING THE *RECKONING*. GIVE ME ADMIRAL KRENNEL...

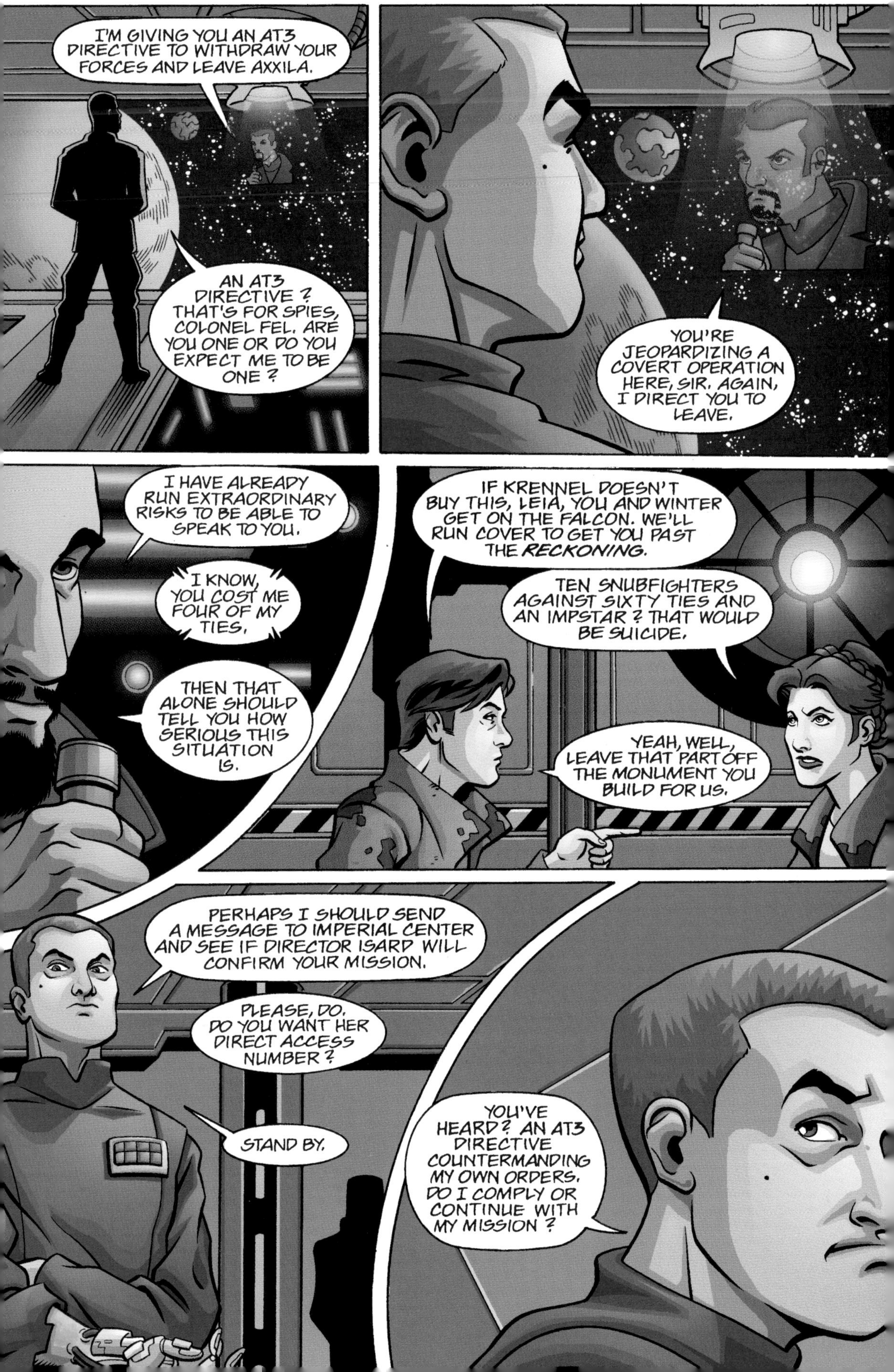
I'M GIVING YOU AN AT3 DIRECTIVE TO WITHDRAW YOUR FORCES AND LEAVE AXXILA.
AN AT3 DIRECTIVE? THAT'S FOR SPIES, COLONEL FEL. ARE YOU ONE OR DO YOU EXPECT ME TO BE ONE?
YOU'RE JEOPARDIZING A COVERT OPERATION HERE, SIR. AGAIN, I DIRECT YOU TO LEAVE.
I HAVE ALREADY RUN EXTRAORDINARY RISKS TO BE ABLE TO SPEAK TO YOU.
I KNOW, YOU COST ME FOUR OF MY TIES.
THEN THAT ALONE SHOULD TELL YOU HOW SERIOUS THIS SITUATION IS.
IF KRENNEL DOESN'T BUY THIS, LEIA, YOU AND WINTER GET ON THE FALCON. WE'LL RUN COVER TO GET YOU PAST THE *RECKONING*.
TEN SNUBFIGHTERS AGAINST SIXTY TIES AND AN IMPSTAR? THAT WOULD BE SUICIDE.
YEAH, WELL, LEAVE THAT PART OFF THE MONUMENT YOU BUILD FOR US.
PERHAPS I SHOULD SEND A MESSAGE TO IMPERIAL CENTER AND SEE IF DIRECTOR ISARD WILL CONFIRM YOUR MISSION.
PLEASE, DO. DO YOU WANT HER DIRECT ACCESS NUMBER?
STAND BY.
YOU'VE HEARD? AN AT3 DIRECTIVE COUNTERMANDING MY OWN ORDERS. DO I COMPLY OR CONTINUE WITH MY MISSION?

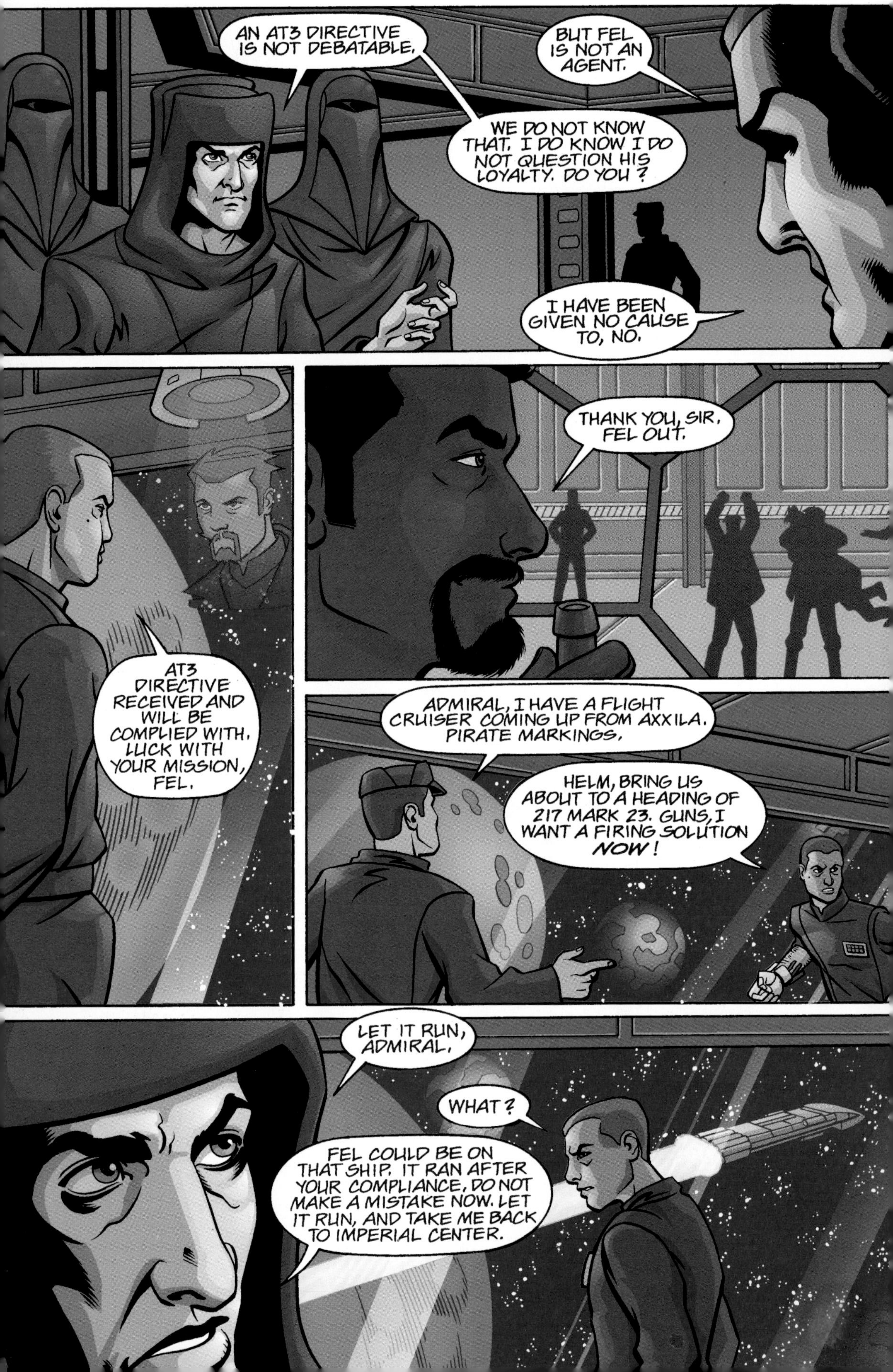
AN AT3 DIRECTIVE IS NOT DEBATABLE.
BUT FEL IS NOT AN AGENT.
WE DO NOT KNOW THAT. I DO KNOW I DO NOT QUESTION HIS LOYALTY. DO YOU ?
I HAVE BEEN GIVEN NO CAUSE TO, NO.
AT3 DIRECTIVE RECEIVED AND WILL BE COMPLIED WITH. LUCK WITH YOUR MISSION, FEL.
THANK YOU, SIR. FEL OUT.
ADMIRAL, I HAVE A FLIGHT CRUISER COMING UP FROM AXXILA. PIRATE MARKINGS.
HELM, BRING US ABOUT TO A HEADING OF 217 MARK 23. GUNS, I WANT A FIRING SOLUTION NOW !
LET IT RUN, ADMIRAL.
WHAT ?
FEL COULD BE ON THAT SHIP. IT RAN AFTER YOUR COMPLIANCE. DO NOT MAKE A MISTAKE NOW. LET IT RUN, AND TAKE ME BACK TO IMPERIAL CENTER.

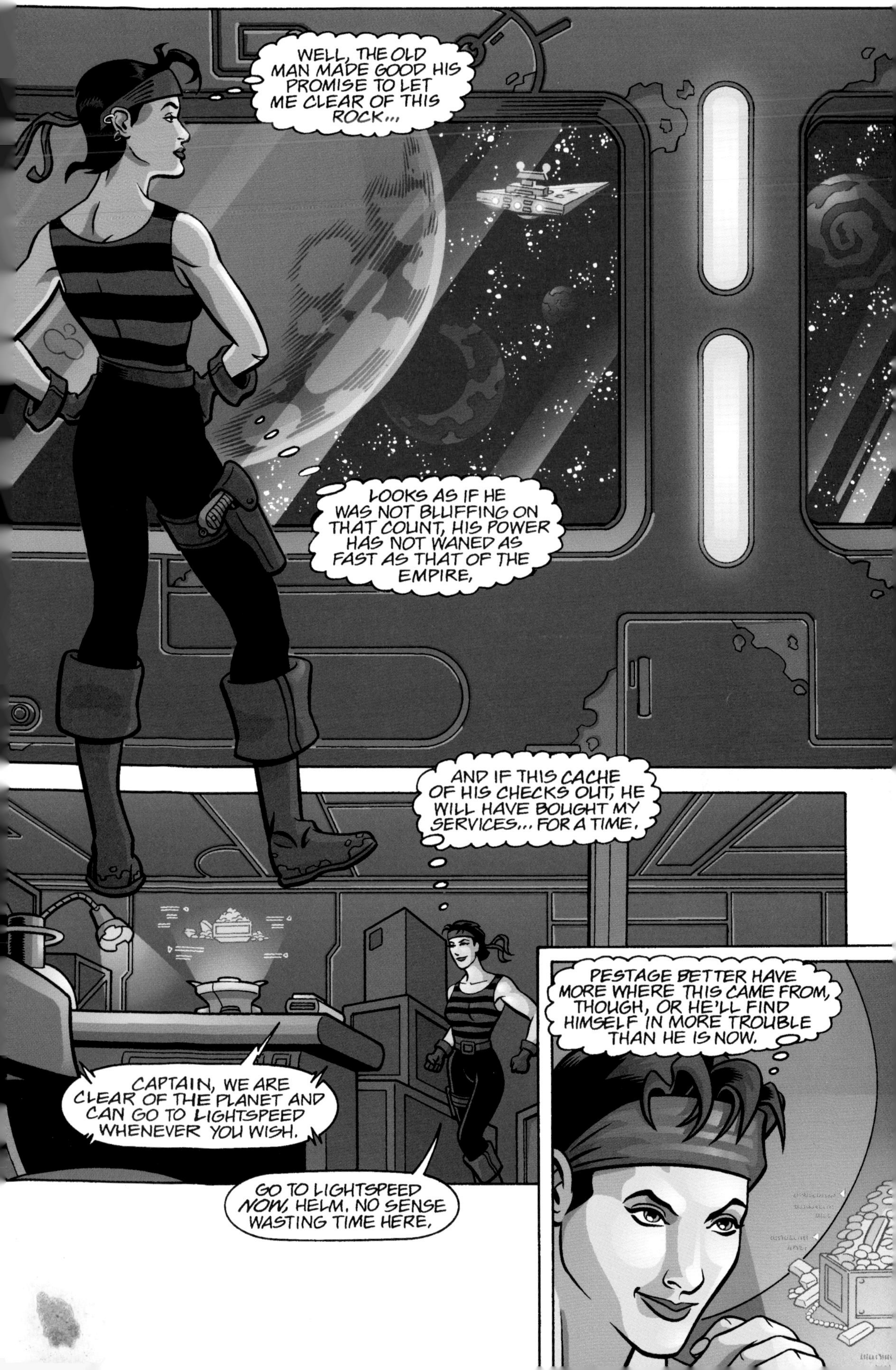

WELL, THE OLD MAN MADE GOOD HIS PROMISE TO LET ME CLEAR OF THIS ROCK...
LOOKS AS IF HE WAS NOT BLUFFING ON THAT COUNT, HIS POWER HAS NOT WANED AS FAST AS THAT OF THE EMPIRE,
AND IF THIS CACHE OF HIS CHECKS OUT, HE WILL HAVE BOUGHT MY SERVICES... FOR A TIME.
CAPTAIN, WE ARE CLEAR OF THE PLANET AND CAN GO TO LIGHTSPEED WHENEVER YOU WISH.
GO TO LIGHTSPEED NOW, HELM. NO SENSE WASTING TIME HERE,
PESTAGE BETTER HAVE MORE WHERE THIS CAME FROM, THOUGH, OR HE'LL FIND HIMSELF IN MORE TROUBLE THAN HE IS NOW.

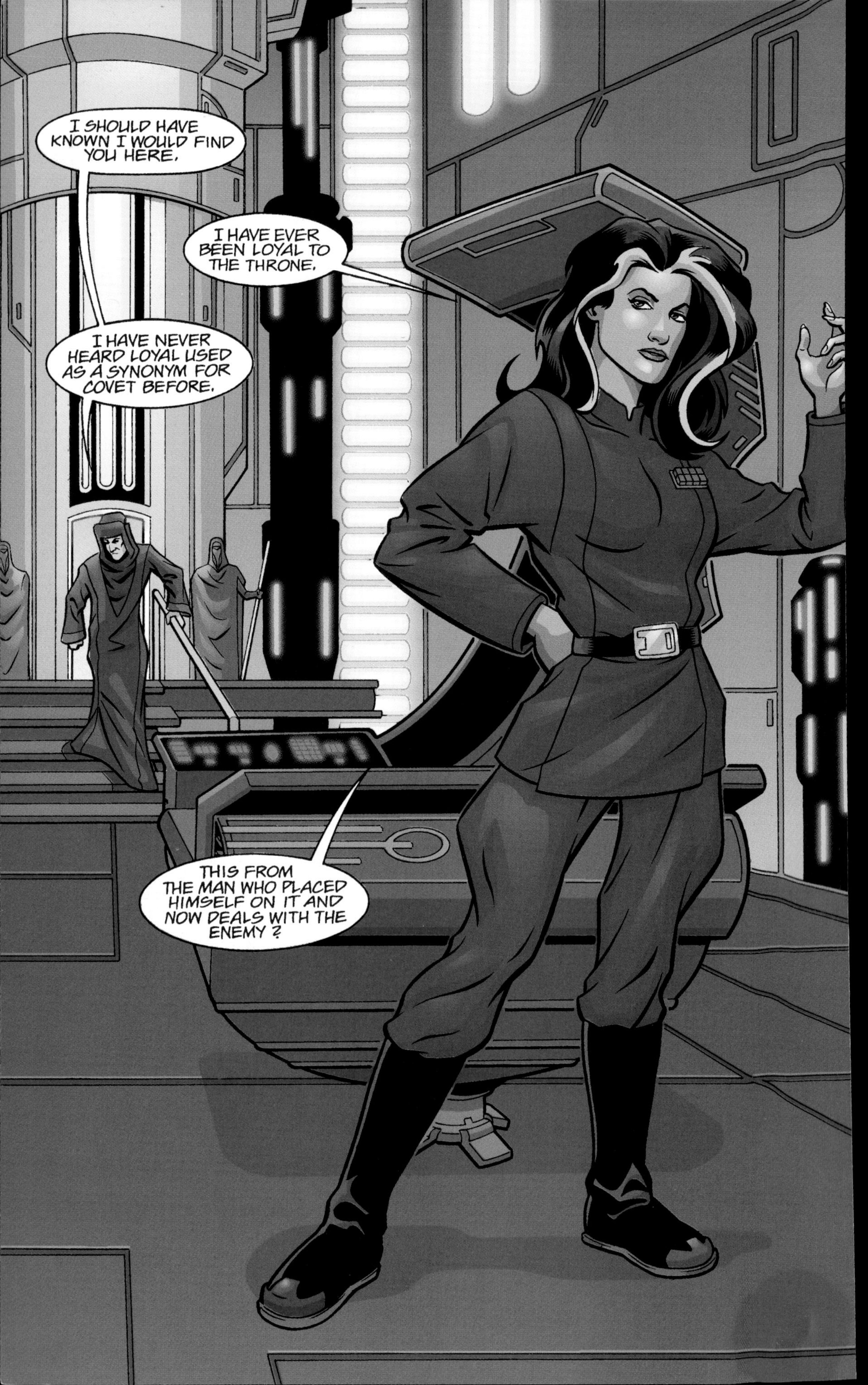
I SHOULD HAVE KNOWN I WOULD FIND YOU HERE.
I HAVE EVER BEEN LOYAL TO THE THRONE.
I HAVE NEVER HEARD LOYAL USED AS A SYNONYM FOR COVET BEFORE.
THIS FROM THE MAN WHO PLACED HIMSELF ON IT AND NOW DEALS WITH THE ENEMY ?

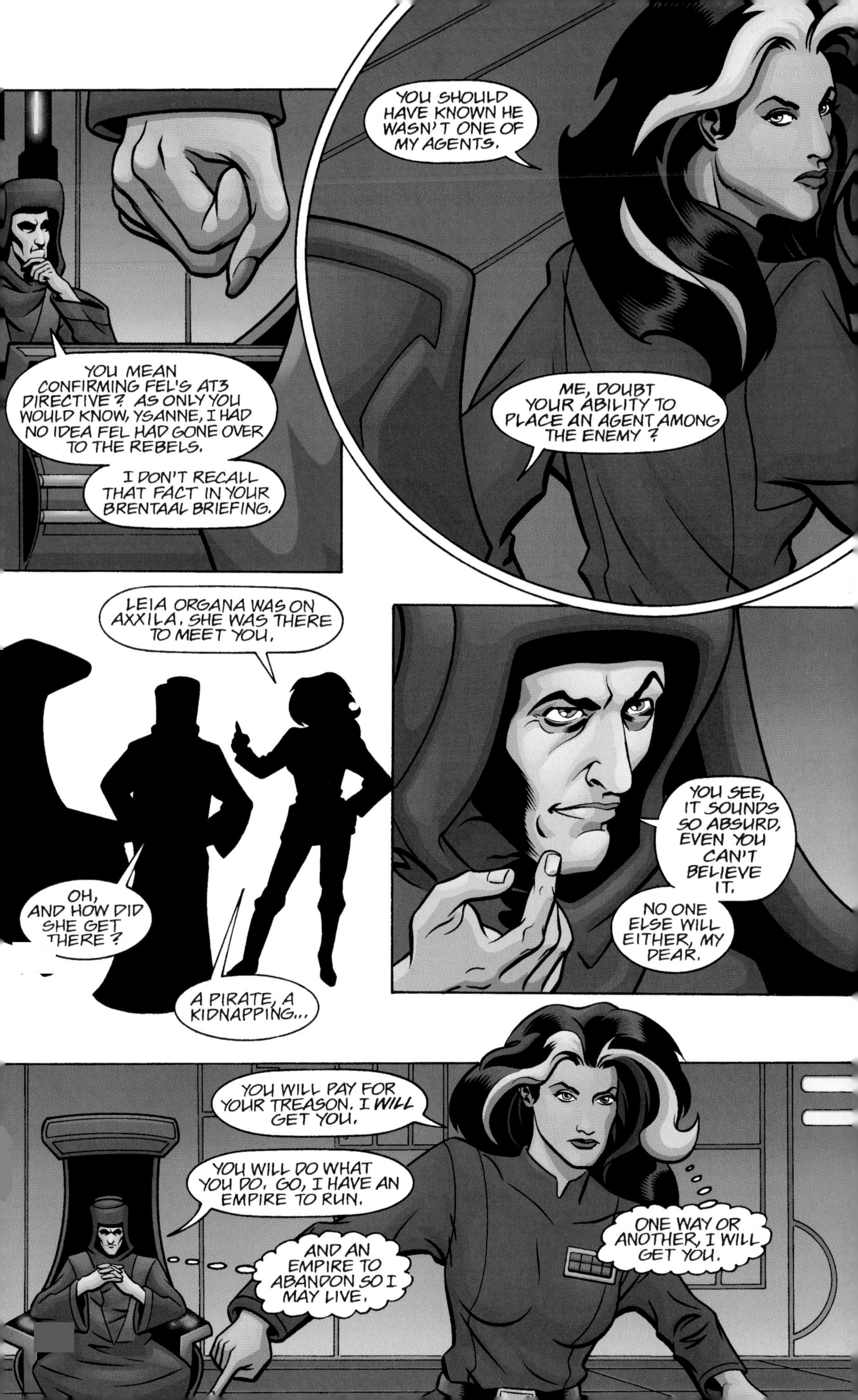
YOU MEAN CONFIRMING FEL'S AT3 DIRECTIVE? AS ONLY YOU WOULD KNOW, YSANNE, I HAD NO IDEA FEL HAD GONE OVER TO THE REBELS.
I DON'T RECALL THAT FACT IN YOUR BRENTAAL BRIEFING.
YOU SHOULD HAVE KNOWN HE WASN'T ONE OF MY AGENTS.
ME, DOUBT YOUR ABILITY TO PLACE AN AGENT AMONG THE ENEMY?
LEIA ORGANA WAS ON AXXILA. SHE WAS THERE TO MEET YOU.
OH, AND HOW DID SHE GET THERE?
A PIRATE, A KIDNAPPING...
YOU SEE, IT SOUNDS SO ABSURD, EVEN YOU CAN'T BELIEVE IT.
NO ONE ELSE WILL EITHER, MY DEAR.
YOU WILL PAY FOR YOUR TREASON. I WILL GET YOU.
YOU WILL DO WHAT YOU DO. GO, I HAVE AN EMPIRE TO RUN.
AND AN EMPIRE TO ABANDON SO I MAY LIVE.
ONE WAY OR ANOTHER, I WILL GET YOU.

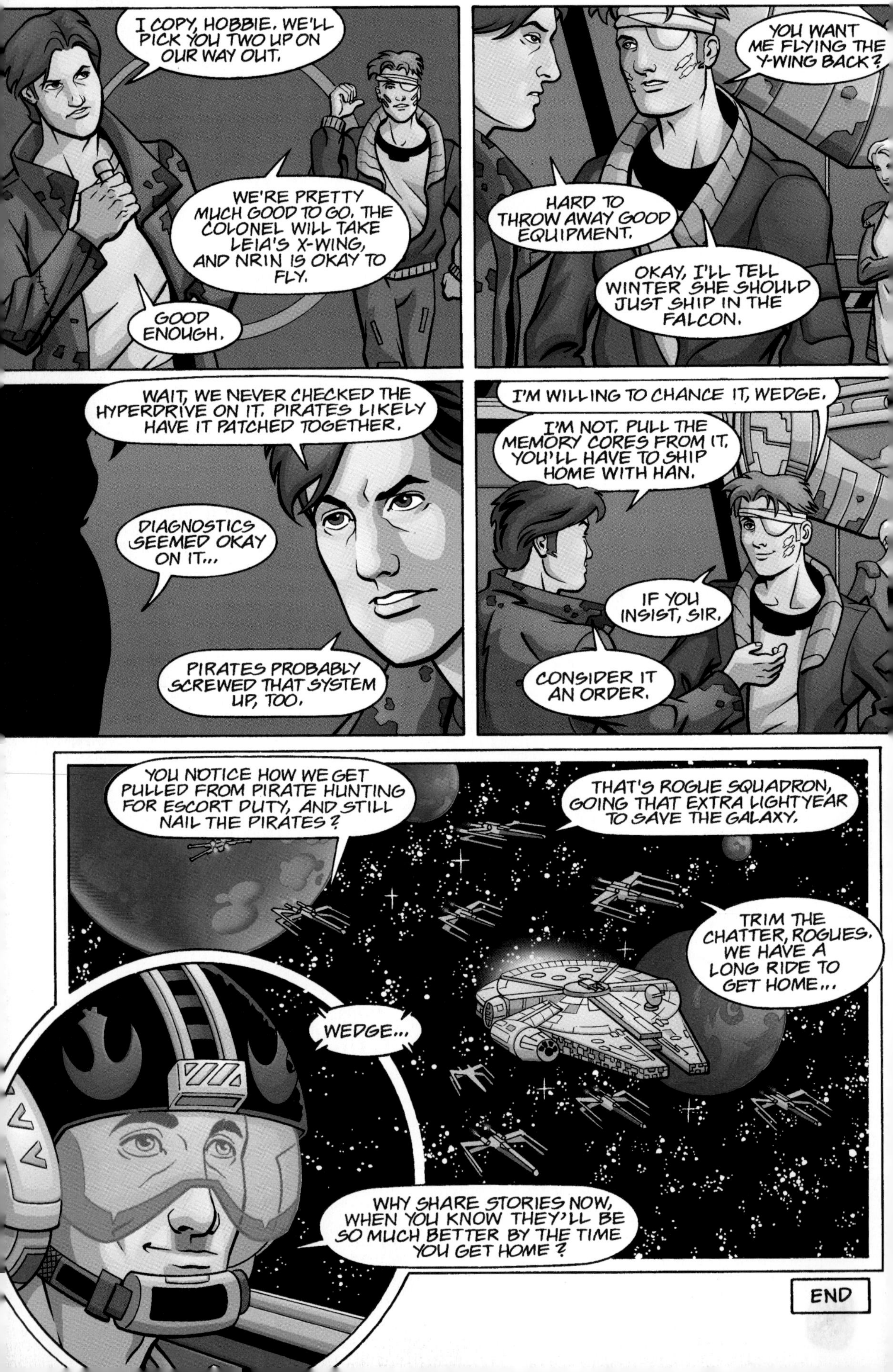
I COPY, HOBBIE. WE'LL PICK YOU TWO UP ON OUR WAY OUT.
WE'RE PRETTY MUCH GOOD TO GO. THE COLONEL WILL TAKE LEIA'S X-WING, AND NRIN IS OKAY TO FLY.
GOOD ENOUGH.
YOU WANT ME FLYING THE Y-WING BACK?
HARD TO THROW AWAY GOOD EQUIPMENT.
OKAY, I'LL TELL WINTER SHE SHOULD JUST SHIP IN THE FALCON.
WAIT, WE NEVER CHECKED THE HYPERDRIVE ON IT. PIRATES LIKELY HAVE IT PATCHED TOGETHER.
DIAGNOSTICS SEEMED OKAY ON IT...
PIRATES PROBABLY SCREWED THAT SYSTEM UP, TOO.
I'M WILLING TO CHANCE IT, WEDGE.
I'M NOT. PULL THE MEMORY CORES FROM IT. YOU'LL HAVE TO SHIP HOME WITH HAN.
IF YOU INSIST, SIR.
CONSIDER IT AN ORDER.
YOU NOTICE HOW WE GET PULLED FROM PIRATE HUNTING FOR ESCORT DUTY, AND STILL NAIL THE PIRATES?
THAT'S ROGUE SQUADRON, GOING THAT EXTRA LIGHTYEAR TO SAVE THE GALAXY.
TRIM THE CHATTER, ROGUES. WE HAVE A LONG RIDE TO GET HOME...
WEDGE...
WHY SHARE STORIES NOW, WHEN YOU KNOW THEY'LL BE SO MUCH BETTER BY THE TIME YOU GET HOME?
END

STAR WARS X-WING ROGUE SQUADRON MASQUERADE

BIOGRAPHIES

Michael A. Stackpole

Michael A. Stackpole is an award-winning game designer and novelist who has seven *Star Wars* novels to his credit. The most recent, *Onslaught*, was published by Del Rey in February 2000 and will be followed by *Ruin* in June 2000. His most recent fantasy novel, *The Dark Glory War*, was released in March 2000. *Masquerade* was, for him, a great challenge since he had to script for Han, Leia, and Chewbacca — and he knew there would be no forgiveness for screwing up with them.

Drew Johnson

Much as Dark Horse Comics had its humble beginnings in the back room of a comics shop, artist Drew Johnson stepped into the role of comics penciller from behind the counter of a comics shop in Eugene, Oregon, just down I-5 from Dark Horse. And Drew's first step was a big one — *Star Wars: X-Wing Rogue Squadron*. Joining the Rebels to help finish an issue of *Family Ties* (collected in *Blood and Honor*), Drew re-upped for a tour as pencilling point-man on *Masquerade*. Drew's most recent work can be found in the pages of *Starwoman and the JSA* and in *Challengers of the Unknown*, both from DC Comics. Drew lives in Eugene at his drawing table, surrounded by posters and toys.

Gary Martin

Gary Martin has been working in comics since 1980; his credits including *Blue Devil*, *Doom Patrol*, *Ghost*, *Wonder Woman*, *Marvel Comics Presents*, and *Nexus*, where Gary's inks over Steve Rude earned Gary a Harvey Award nomination in 1998. Aside from being one of the most respected and sought-after inkers in comics, Gary is also the author of *The Art of Comic Book Inking*, the definitive "how-to" for one of the industry's most important, but least understood, professions. Gary's first contributions to the *Star Wars* universe came on the X-Wing Rogue Squadron one-shot *The Making of Baron Fel* (collected in *Blood and Honor*) before taking the assignment for *Masquerade*. Gary is currently writing and drawing a daily comic strip he created entitled *Captain Stupendous*, which can be viewed at *eHero.com*.

STAR WARS®
X-WING
ROGUE SQUADRON
MASQUERADE
G A L L E R Y

Featuring the original
comic-book series
cover paintings by
John Nadeau.

NADEAU 97

NADEAU 98

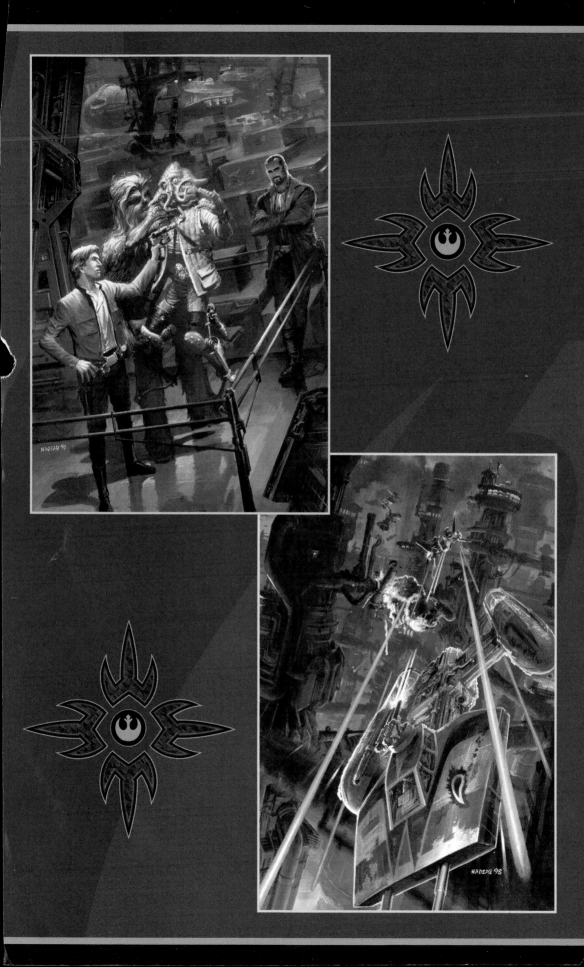